umour, solid research, and lots of examples, the authors cut through prevailing myths about happiness to show what actually creates a fulfilling, contributing life. Brave, bold, and brilliant.'

Rick Hanson, author of *Buddha's Brain*

'At long last, here's a book on why happiness can make us sad and mindfulness might be overrated. If you haven't read it yet, you should feel guilty – and it turns out that will be good for you.'

Adam Grant, author of *Give and Take*

'Full of scientific research yet laugh-out-loud funny, this book is a must read. The authors turn everything on its head – questioning the wisdom of positive psychology and the pursuit of happiness – all in order to help us flourish and be happy!'

Kristin Neff, author of *Self-Compassion*

'I feel like I have five new superpowers after reading this book. The dark side does indeed have an upside – and this book teaches us how to harness it, so we can truly lead more heroic and purposeful lives.'

Jane McGonigal, author of *Reality Is Broken*

ABOUT THE AUTHORS

Todd Kashdan is a recognized authority on personality, well-being and social relationships. He has published more than 150 scholarly articles and trains professionals to become emotionally and socially agile. He has been honored with the Faculty Member of the Year at George Mason University and the 2013 Distinguished Scientific Early Career Award from the American Psychological Association. His work has been featured in several media outlets, including the *New York Times* and the *Washington Post.*

Robert Biswas-Diener is a world expert on positive psychology. He has published more than 40 scholarly articles, has trained thousands of professionals on six continents, and sits on the editorial boards of the *Journal of Happiness Studies* and the *Journal of Positive Psychology.*

The Power of Negative Emotion

How Anger, Guilt and Self Doubt are Essential to Success and Fulfillment

Todd Kashdan
Robert Biswas-Diener

ONEWORLD

A Oneworld book

First published in Great Britain and the Commonwealth by
Oneworld Publications, 2015

First published in the US by Hudson Street Press, a member of
Penguin Group (USA) LLC, 2014

A CIP record for this title is available from the British Library

ISBN 978-1-78074-660-9
eISBN 978-1-78074-661-6

Designed by Eve L. Kirch
Printed and bound in Great Britain by Clays Ltd, St Ives plc

Oneworld Publications
10 Bloomsbury Street
London WC1B 3SR
England

CONTENTS

INTRODUCTION
THE PROMISE OF WHOLENESS

PERHAPS THE MOST difficult test commonly used for recruiting elite special forces soldiers has nothing to do with marksmanship or proficiency in hand-to-hand combat. It's a simple jog down a remote road. Young men are instructed to don full gear and report to the starting point early in the morning, often sleep deprived and hungry. What makes this particular run unusually challenging is that none of the candidates are told the length of the course. Is it three hundred yards? Three miles? Thirty miles?

The stakes are high as the recruits begin their jog into the unknown. Some sprint forward in hopes of being first if the run is short. Others pace themselves, carefully conserving energy in the thought that the run could turn out to be a marathon. Some keep to themselves, trusting in their resolve and determination. Others jog together as a group, shouting words of encouragement. Running with sixty-pound packs is tiring, but the physical exertion is less demanding than the mental strain. The pressure of not knowing the distance to the finish line pushes many to the breaking point.

Ambiguous tasks are a good place to observe how personality traits bubble to the surface. Although few of us are elite soldiers, we've all experienced the kind of psychological distress these trainees encounter on their training run: managing unclear expectations, struggling with self-motivation, and balancing the use of social support with private reflection. These issues are endemic not only to the workplace, but also to relationships, health, and every aspect of life in which we seek to thrive and succeed. Not surprisingly, the leading predictor of success in elite military training programs is the same quality that distinguishes those best equipped to resolve marital conflict, to achieve favorable deal terms in business negotiations, and to bestow the gifts of good parenting on their children: the ability to tolerate psychological discomfort.

This is what psychologists refer to as *distress tolerance*, a quality found in people who can handle the emotional equivalent of camping (no shampoo, flush toilets, or walls to keep out creepy crawlers), who don't shy away from anger, guilt, or boredom just because they feel bad. Instead, they withstand the discomfort of those feelings and—when appropriate—even draw from this darker palette of emotions. You might be asking, why would I want to do that? Pain hurts. I'd rather be happy. If this question occurs to you, we're nodding our heads in full agreement. We want you to be happy too. Distress tolerance is important not just because it makes you a better camper or soldier, but also because it allows you to become stronger, wiser, mentally agile, and, most important, happier in a more resilient, and therefore durable, way. After more than a decade of working with patients, clients, students, small companies, and organizations as large as the military and the Fortune 100, we, the authors, are putting forward a new way to pursue what is desirable in life; it's not happiness, exactly, although it does have the side effect of making us happier. We call this state *wholeness*.

Beyond Happiness, Becoming Whole

There will always be experts—especially in psychology—who argue that one particular way of being (happy, hardy, optimistic) is a cure-all. In this book, we take a different approach. Instead of suggesting that one state is best, we suggest that they all are. We believe—and new research supports—the idea that every emotion is useful. Even the ones we think of as negative, including the painful ones. Anger is a good example. Research shows that only rarely does anger turn into the kind of overwhelming rage that leads to violence. Instead, it tends to bubble up when you perceive an encroachment on your rights as a person. Anger stirs you to defend yourself and those you care about, and to maintain healthy boundaries. Similarly, embarrassment is sometimes an early warning sign of humiliation. More often it's a signal that we've made a small mistake and that a small correction is required. Even guilt is not as awful as you might guess. It's a signal that you're violating your own moral code and therefore need to adjust either your actions or your code.

All psychological states have some adaptive advantage. Rather than steering you toward a single feeling state, then, we urge you to consider the usefulness of many—especially the ones we turn away from—and to develop the ability to navigate every one. For some people, seeing the bright side of life is an uphill battle; for others, feeling sad is an unusual event. We don't suggest an extra helping of happiness or a dash of negativity; we suggest both. It is by appropriately flipping back and forth between these two states that you can achieve a balanced, stabilizing sense of wholeness. Simply put, people who are able to use the whole range of their natural psychological gifts—those folks who are comfortable with being both positive and negative, and can therefore draw from the full range of human emotions—are the healthiest and, often, the most successful.

Wholeness does not come easily, however. We get comfortable with pursuing a certain set of emotions. They make us feel good. Riding high in the moment is hard to pass up—think of a perfect kiss when your lips meld into the moistness of your partner's, or of hearing the cheers of fellow employees when your name is announced for having won an award. Other emotions, like anger and guilt, are so painful that we avoid or suppress them. It turns out that the uncertainty, frustration, and occasional dash of guilt that stem from broken hearts, missed goals in the penalty shootout, and botched interviews are the seeds of growth in knowledge and maturity. These often unwanted, negative experiences end up shaping some of the most memorable and inspiring experiences of our lives. By learning to embrace and use negative emotions as well as positive ones, we position ourselves for success.

Two Authors, One Quest

So who are we, the authors in whom you have chosen to invest your time and entrust your confidence? Both of us entered the field of positive psychology more than a decade ago, when this new scientific movement was just finding its legs. We were drawn to the promise of a fresh discipline with a new way of tackling old issues. In a discipline dominated by anxiety and depression research, we found the focus of positive psychology refreshing.

We'll give you just a single example: sex. In the years since Sigmund Freud made it the main event, human sexuality has been a bit sidelined from psychology. Scientists, like many people, can be prudes. Given the amount of time we think about sex, crave sex, have sex, or, more easily, purchase *50 Shades of Gray* novels, you'd think that human sexuality would be the most researched topic in history: we should know more about sex than we do about the speed of light or genetic engineering. But when we recently entered the keyword terms *sex* and *depression* into the leading professional psychological database, we found just over two thousand hits for the former and two hundred thousand hits for the latter. Now *that's* depressing!

The two of us went about investigating whether sex can serve as a free, fun form of therapy for anxiety. We were particularly interested in socially anxious folks who avoid making social connections for fear of rejection. In our study, we had more than a hundred participants report on hundreds of sexual episodes across a two-week period. We had people rate the degree to which they felt intimacy, experienced pleasure, and reached an orgasmic climax during sexual episodes. It turns out that people who suffer with social anxiety problems benefit from sexual contact, even as much as twenty-four hours after an anxiety attack. Sex that left people feeling intimately tied to another person lowered anxiety the following day by 10 percent. Even better, hot sex—escapades that were downright lusty—lowered anxiety by 25 percent!

We concluded that there is a place, even a curative place, for talking about positive experiences in conjunction with so-called negative experiences like anxiety and depression. But even as we tilled the fields of positive psychology, both of us were also increasingly put off by the gung-ho happiology we often witnessed. Over the past fifteen years, positive psychology has been transformed from a reminder that "positive experiences are important" to a kind of smiling fascism.

Nowhere is cultural shift toward the positive more obvious than in the world of business. It was only three decades ago that Jack Welch took the helm of General Electric and introduced the world to "stretch goals." His idea was that placing people in uncomfortable and demanding positions could accelerate personal growth and, ultimately, performance. Fast forward to the present moment, when the latest business management fad is the idea that a good mood translates to business success. The so-called happiness advantage. Some data even back this up: happy employees get better customer evaluations, are more likely to help a colleague, and make more money. There are enough data that positivity evangelists feel comfortable touting an upbeat approach as a workplace panacea. Discussed less frequently, however, are the research findings that the most satisfied people of all actually make less money and are less conscientious in their work habits.

Some companies that surfed the happiness wave to success have been wondering how to deal with legitimate discontent within the ranks. At Ruby Receptionists, for instance—a business that *Fortune* magazine rated the "#1 best small business place to work in America"—employees are rightly proud of their positive work culture. They are supportive of one another. Their office is fun and playful. Receptionists receive paid sabbaticals, on-site fitness classes, bonus trips to Hawaii, and a host of other upbeat perks. People can walk around 90 percent of the time with authentic smiles on their faces. But the company has wrestled with the other 10 percent. Management and employees are uncertain what to do about the gripes, frustrations, cattiness, and other negative experiences that are an inevitable part of professional life.

We began to wonder too, and in our research we became more and more interested in the intersection of positive and negative.

Drawing on the Power of Negative Emotion

In 1972, as the world's attention turned to the Olympic Games in Munich, Germany, American athlete Frank Shorter was mentally preparing for the greatest challenge of his career: appearances in both the marathon and the 10,000 meter event. It would turn out to be one of the weirder moments in Olympic history. On the morning of September 10, there were a number of reasons why Shorter had a difficult time finding that all-important inner focus. He had earlier finished a disappointing fifth place in the 10,000 meter race; his teammate, legendary runner Steve Prefontaine, petered out in the last lap of the 5,000 meter race to take fourth, failing to medal; and, of course, the games themselves were eclipsed in emotional significance by the shocking massacre of Israeli athletes by Palestinian militants.

For Shorter, the marathon must have been a roller coaster of doubt and confidence: confidence as he glanced over his shoulder to assess the size of his lead, and doubt when he finally entered the stadium for the last part of the race and inexplicably found himself in second place. Unbeknownst to him, while Shorter was running toward the stadium, a German student named Norbert Sudhaus slipped past security, jumped onto the racetrack, and impersonated an athlete running in the lead position. To further complicate matters, just before Shorter entered the stadium, the crowd had erupted in cheers for the impostor in first place, and Shorter had to redouble his efforts amid a chorus of boos as the audience realized it had been duped. Despite the many mental, emotional, and physical obstacles, Shorter ended up with the gold medal.

Frank Shorter's unusual case is proof that in running, as in so many other aspects of life, two experiences are taking place at the same time. Although a long-distance race seems to be a physical feat, mostly a matter of putting one foot in front of the other, it is, actually, a largely mental affair. We have interviewed dozens of athletes—especially runners—and the same themes emerge. Time and again, we were told that there was "more than one race" on the track that day. Many athletes distinguish between the beginning, the middle, and the end of the race. Intense focus marks the beginning of the race, the middle is characterized by deep self-reflection, and the end is an all-out burst of primal energy. It is this last portion, in particular, that bears so directly on our thesis. This is the part of the race where athletes are most likely to use anger, self-castigation, an aggressive desire to crush the competition, and other so-called negative states to spur their own performance to new highs. If positivity and optimism account for 80 percent of success, more or less, then tapping the whole range of experience offers that remaining 20 percent edge.

We are no different from you, dear reader. We prematurely discard our painful feelings, thoughts, and urges without giving them a fair chance. Seduced by the obvious benefits of kindness, compassion, mindfulness, optimism, and positivity on our health, social relationships, and work, we often forget the value of uncomfortable states. Our minds were changed on this issue, however, when we considered results from a number of studies showing the counterintuitive truth: happiness sometimes backfires, and bad states are sometimes good.

What's more, we are attracted to the notion of wholeness because it fits with all that we know about science and life. Wholeness has an ancient place of honor in myths across all cultures and, therefore, in the archetypal landscape of the human psyche. Wouldn't it be great to possess full access to the endless energies of creation instead of shackling ourselves to just being positive, cheerful, kind, loving, and selfless? We'll never free ourselves to soar in that infinite potential if we're busy trying to avoid the darker parts of our selves, the aspects we fail to appreciate.

What we're offering you here is an anti-happiness book that, paradoxically, opens you up to a far greater degree of joy than you could ever experience with a more direct approach. In fact, the latest studies show that *there is no direct path to happiness*. We are not opposed to happiness, positivity, kindness, or mindfulness. In fact, we embrace them. We also wish to ask you, the reader, one further question: are you ready for more? Will you join us in taking happiness to the next level? To go there you'll need access to everything in the human psychological rucksack, which means unpacking and integrating previously ignored and underappreciated parts of who you are. In the pages that follow, you will learn how to become more emotionally, socially, and mentally agile. By accepting the challenge of drawing on the power of negative emotion when it's most helpful, you bring wholeness within reach, perhaps for the first time.

CHAPTER 1

The False Nose of Happiness

IN SIXTEENTH-CENTURY DENMARK, Tycho Brahe was as renowned for his flamboyant lifestyle as he was for his scientific genius. Brahe's nose was cut off in a duel (he replaced it with a metal one), and he attended parties with his pet moose (who drank copious amounts of alcohol), but Brahe's lasting claim to fame is his contribution to astronomy. Instead of accepting ancient philosophical or religious notions about the nature of the heavens, Brahe carefully observed and charted all the stars he could see in the night skies. His notes led to a number of astounding discoveries, including the birth and death of stars, a phenomenon that contradicted ancient notions that all things celestial were fixed. False nose and inebriated moose aside, Brahe's work earned him a place in history as the father of modern astronomy who formed the foundation on which his assistant, Johannes Kepler, and all modern astronomers, would build their science.

Today psychology is having a "Brahe moment." Until this point, people have been pretty good about creating intuitive approaches to improving their quality of life. You've probably come across some of these theories, such as the Abraham Maslow hierarchy of needs—the idea that people have to satisfy basic requirements like food and safety before they can address their need for self-esteem and fulfillment. There's also no shortage of commonsense advice on how to become happier: be kind, count your blessings, commute less, spend more time with friends and family, be frugal, and everything in moderation. Great suggestions, but is there reason to believe that these chestnuts are either universally applicable or always true?

Fortunately, we are living in a remarkable time in psychology, thanks to the introduction of sophisticated neuroscience, advanced statistics, handheld computers that allow for better sampling of daily experiences, and other methodological and technical breakthroughs. This is our Brahe moment, when the fundamental understanding of quality of life changes. In the field of psychology in general, and on the subject of happiness specifically, these new tools have yielded two transformative findings: first, we tend to go about the business of happiness all wrong; second, we can do something to fix this.

Why the Way We've Been Pursuing Happiness Is Not Going to Make Us Happy

Humans have come a long way since we lived in hunter-gatherer societies. As we spend less time worrying about shelter, drought, or our next kill, it makes sense that we would turn our collective attention to the pursuit of happiness. In fact, in a study of more than ten thousand participants from forty-eight countries, psychologists Ed Diener of the University of Illinois and Shigehiro Oishi of the University of Virginia discovered that people from every corner of the globe rated happiness as being more important than other highly desirable personal outcomes, such as a meaningful life, becoming rich, and getting into heaven.

The rush to happiness is spurred on, at least in part, by a growing body of research suggesting that happiness doesn't just feel good: it's good for you. Happiness researchers have linked positive feelings to a host of benefits, ranging from higher incomes to better immune system functioning to boosts in kindness. Not only are these desirable outcomes related to happiness, but science also points to positive emotions as their cause. Some researchers, like Barbara Fredrickson from the University of North Carolina, even argue that happiness is humanity's evolutionary birthright. It is happiness, the argument goes, that helps people to build personal and social resources that are vital to success in life and—from an evolutionary point of view—survival itself.

But one question keeps raising its not so happy head: if happiness provides an evolutionary advantage, and if we value it so highly and possess thousands of years of good advice about how to achieve it, why isn't it more widespread? Why aren't we talking about the current happiness epidemic instead of skyrocketing rates of depression and anxiety? Examining data from the European Social Survey, University of Cambridge researchers Felicia Huppert and Timothy So calculated that only 20 percent of adults in the UK were psychologically flourishing. The figure for the US is even lower.

The Flourishing Scale

Eight statements with which you may agree or disagree follow. Using the following 1–7 scale, please provide a response for each statement.

7—Strongly agree

6—Agree

5—Slightly agree

4—Neither agree nor disagree

3—Slightly disagree

2—Disagree

1—Strongly disagree

____ I lead a purposeful and meaningful life.

____ My social relationships are supportive and rewarding.

____ I am engaged and interested in my daily activities.

____ I actively contribute to the happiness and well-being of others.

____ I am competent and capable in the activities that are important to me.

____ I am a good person and live a good life.

____ I am optimistic about my future.

____ People respect me.

Scoring:

Add the responses, varying from 1 to 7, for all eight items. The possible range of scores is from 8 (lowest possible) to 56 (highest possible). A high score indicates a person with many psychological resources and strengths.

How could this possibly be the case? It turns out that, despite all the attention being paid to the topic, people are not very good at making choices that lead to happiness. We don't mean to criticize your gym workouts, Mediterranean vacations, meditation practice, or decision to put your kids in four different after-school enrichment activities. We're as guilty as you when it comes to missing the mark where happiness is concerned. In fact, a range of brand-new research shows that, more or less, everyone is off the mark.

Let's begin with the research of Barbara Mellers at the University of Pennsylvania and her colleagues Tim Wilson and Daniel Gilbert—author of the bestselling book *Stumbling on Happiness*. This trio conducted a series of studies on what can be called emotional time travel errors. Just as trained meteorologists make small mistakes that can have a big impact on forecasting the week's weather, it turns out that people do much the same thing when predicting how an event will make them feel in the future. We overestimate, for instance, how happy we will be if our favored political candidate wins the election or our home team wins the game. We also tend to underestimate how difficult things will be, like moving to a new city.

Take, for example, the study in which Mellers and her colleagues investigated women who took a pregnancy test at Planned Parenthood. (It's important that none of the women in this study were trying to get pregnant.) Roughly speaking, the women fell into two groups: those who dreaded having a baby and hoped for a negative result, and those who hoped the pregnancy test turned out positive. The researchers asked women to make predictions about how happy they would be if their hoped-for outcome came to pass. Women who were hoping for a negative result expected to feel a sense of elation if they ended up with an empty womb. Women who wanted to be pregnant also expected to feel joyful if they got the positive result they were hoping for.

After the test was over, the researchers found—to their surprise—neither agony nor ecstasy. In fact, they found nothing more than a tiny blip in the women's emotional equilibrium. Women who wanted a baby were not crestfallen when told it didn't work out; instead, they were mildly disappointed and then bounced back to their regular mood (we might expect different results if these women had been unsuccessfully trying for months or years). As for women who didn't want a baby but ended up with an unplanned, living embryo inside them, their anticipated dread never materialized; instead, they had a softer reaction (and a small minority found an unexpected burst of pleasure). It turns out that one reason we wrongly predict what will make us happy in the future is that we overlook our capacity to tolerate, and even adapt to, discomfort. Sure, that new job—to take a different example—is intimidating the first week, but before long you're cruising along as if you had worked there for years.

The big reason you should care about emotional time travel errors is that nearly every decision you make now is based on an assumption of how you expect to feel in the future. You purchase a dream suburban house with five bedrooms and a sprawling lawn, picturing yourself having coffee on the sweeping veranda while mentally minimizing the added thirty-minute drive to visit friends and to get to work. You give up being with your family for long stretches of time to have a better shot at that big promotion. You choose a mate, decide when (or whether) to have a baby, or select the part of the country where you'll live, but these big decisions are often compromised by lack of insight into your emotional world. You're not alone in this. It turns out that we all tend to exaggerate how positively we'll feel in response to positive events and underestimate our capacity to tolerate distress. When it comes to how we're going to feel in the future, we most often guess wrong.

Most damning of all when your pursuit of happiness is concerned is information gathered in a recent series of studies by Iris Mauss from the University of California, Berkeley. Mauss is a bit like Tycho Brahe;

instead of accepting commonly held assumptions like "we can achieve happiness," she prefers to chart the metaphorical skies to see what actually hangs in the emotional heavens. She even asks unpopular questions such as "Should people be pursuing happiness?" In one study, Mauss and her colleagues found that people who value the pursuit of happiness actually feel lonelier than other folks. Researchers manipulated the importance placed on happiness by having half the participants read a fake newspaper article extolling the many benefits of happiness. Those who read the article reported feeling lonelier than those who did not, and even produced lower rates of progesterone (a hormone that gets a boost when we feel connected to other people). It turns out that putting too much stock in happiness has health implications too!

To put it succinctly, we humans are horrible at guessing how happy we will feel in the future, and yet we base important life decisions on these flawed predictions. We purchase TVs, plan retirement, and say yes to dinner dates all because of an imperfect guess about how happy they will make us. No wonder we fare poorly in the happiness department, and business is booming for happiness authors, coaches, and consultants. The universal heavy-lifting approach to happiness—when someone follows a prescribed set of commonsense steps that are held out as helpful for everyone—doesn't work. It's a bit like Brahe's false nose: a reasonably close approximation, but it won't really help you smell any better. So what we—all of us—need with regard to happiness is a new set of strategies. We need a more relevant and complete understanding of what's involved.

In a world where rejection, failure, self-doubt, hypocrisy, loss, boredom, and annoying and obnoxious people are inevitable, we, the authors, reject the notion that positivity is the only place to search for answers. We reject the belief that being healthy is marked by a life with as little pain as possible. In fact, it's only when we are unwilling to take on the inevitable pain in life—whether it's the death of a parent, a divorce, or not getting that big promotion at work—that pain turns into something we experience as suffering. Suffering arises when we turn our backs on an escalation in emotional, physical, or social discomfort.

Rather than working to promote more happiness, we endorse the ability to access the full range of psychological states, both the positive and the negative, to respond effectively to what life offers. In a word, wholeness. When faced with the inevitable challenges life brings, we fare best when we stop making ineffective or unnecessary attempts at controlling negative thoughts and feelings. A whole person acts in the service of what he or she defines as important, and sometimes that requires us to draw on the darker range of our emotions.

Scientific research supports the idea that what we usually see as negative feelings can be more beneficial than positive ones. Studies have shown the following, for example:

- Students who are confused but work through the confusion perform better on subsequent tests than their peers who "get it" right away.
- Centenarians—people who are a hundred years old or older—find that negative feelings, not positive ones, are associated with better health and more physical activity.
- Police detectives who have themselves been victims of crime show more grit and work engagement when working with civilian victims of crime.
- Spouses who forgave physical or verbal aggression were likely to receive more of it, whereas those who were unforgiving enjoyed a precipitous decline in spousal aggression.

- Workers who are in a bad mood in the morning but shift to a good mood in the afternoon are more engrossed in their work than their counterparts who were happy all day.

With regard to creativity, researchers have found that the ideas suggested by folks who experience both negative and positive moods are judged as 9 percent more creative than ideas put forward by happy people; at work, the stress associated with challenges appears to promote motivation. Ronald Bedlow and his colleagues, who conducted this last study on worker involvement, described their discovery this way:

> We argue that it is the balance of being able to endure phases of negative affect and then engage in a shift to positive affect that is adaptive. Minimization of negative experiences and suppression of negative affect are functional neither for work motivation nor for personal development.

The Bedlow research team also emphasizes a vital and often overlooked point regarding psychological states: they're temporary. When people speak of happiness, or depression for that matter, they make the assumption that these experiences are relatively stable. In the modern positive psychology movement it has become vogue to talk about *sustainable happiness*, as if once the switch is flipped on the smile is permanent. The truth is, we shift between states, positive and negative. People who are whole, those of us who are willing and able to shift to the upside or the downside to get the best possible outcomes in a given situation, are the healthiest, most successful, best learners, and enjoy the deepest well-being. We think of this as the *20 percent edge* because wholeness describes those who experience positivity roughly 80 percent of the time but who can also avail themselves of the benefits of negative states the other 20 percent. We do not mean to suggest, of course, that these percentiles are exact figures that should be used as definitive cut-offs. Rather, we argue that the 80:20 ratio is a useful rule-of-thumb approach to understanding wholeness.

The Rising Tide of Anxiety

Anxiety is one of the top news stories of the last decade. Wars, terrorism, housing market crises, childhood obesity—all of these are important geopolitical and economic events. But the insidious rise in anxiety is every bit as noteworthy. Stress is epidemic and, like any virus, does not discriminate based on social class, IQ, or occupation. According to the Mental Health Foundation anxiety is the most prevalent mental health problem in the UK. More than one in ten people are likely to have a 'disabling anxiety disorder' at some state in their life. This statistic only highlights the suffering of people who wrestle with diagnosable anxieties. According to a YouGov survey a whopping one in five people report feeling anxious all of the time or a lot of the time. Anxiety in the US is even more widespread.

Paradoxically, we are increasingly stressed because we put such an emphasis on comfort. We have air purifiers, heated car seats, polarized sunglasses, bubble baths, waterproof jackets, electric blankets, and beds that conform to the unique shape of our spines. It's difficult to emphasize this point strongly enough: while people have historically chosen pleasure over pain—and who wouldn't?—the modern era is an outlier in human history. We don't just enjoy our creature comforts; we are addicted to them.

Why is comfort indicative of a problem? Our current high levels mirror the trend in using antibacterial soaps. These soaps mean we are exposed to fewer bacteria and are therefore less able to resist them. Yes, life in ye olde days was more rough and tumble, but it had the positive side effect of mentally toughening up our forebears. Evidence for this can be seen in the sentiment expressed in the classic 1939 British wartime public service announcement "Keep calm and carry on." In other words, bombs may be falling, but don't panic: go on about your business. Today we're moving in the opposite direction. Consider the popular contemporary American public service announcement "Give a hoot, don't pollute." At the heart of this message is the idea that modern people have so many luxury and convenience items that—hey!—can't we just quit throwing them on the ground and throw them in the garbage bin instead? When citizen waste is a pressing issue, you know society has reached an elevated state of creature comfort.

Given so many amenities available to us today, we've developed a tendency to avoid discomfort. We whip out our smartphones the moment we're left alone—boredom vanquished! We jockey for the fastest line on the motorway—no frustrating waits! We flip on the television when we get home from work—no other unwinding and de-stressing needed! What most folks don't realize is that this seemingly natural attraction to an easier life is rooted in avoidance of discomfort. People who fear rejection avoid meeting others; people who fear failure don't take risks; and people who fear intimacy turn to television and e-mail when they get home from work. Avoidance is the tectonic issue of our time.

Two types of avoidance cause problems for people: avoiding pleasure and avoiding pain. At first glance, it might be hard to believe that we sometimes want to steer clear of pleasure, but we all know people who can't enjoy fun because they believe there are better ways to spend time. (You may even be one of them.) In this same vein, we can also be afraid that by celebrating happiness we will jinx it, or fear that celebrating something good—a birthday, a promotion, the perfect cardio kickboxing class—will focus too much attention on us, thereby turning other people off. Psychologists call this disqualifying the positive. Unfortunately, by disqualifying positives we lose out on those amazing golden moments that are part of a life well lived. By depriving others of the opportunity to share in our positive emotions, our social relationships become less intimate. When we fail to savor the details of positive events, it becomes more difficult for us to access these memories for a mood boost on a rainy day.

The other form of avoidance, by far the more common, is turning away from so-called negative psychological states, such as anger and anxiety. This sentiment reflects the philosophy of the Hedonists of ancient Greece—the intellectual crosstown rivals of the Stoics—who held the view that the best life is to be found in pleasure. The problem with the hedonistic philosophy is that people can become overly skeptical of anything negative. This is especially true in modern times, when we advise friends to "find the silver lining," "turn that frown upside down," and "buck up." Not to mention Fritz Strack's famous study showing that research participants who held a pencil between their teeth (unknowingly activating smile muscles) wrote clearer, more positive statements about themselves than other participants. In a cringeworthy move, happiness consultants have been using this study as evidence that people should "fake it until they make it." Essentially, all of these strategies try to talk people out of their negative states. Unfortunately, avoiding problems also means avoiding finding the solutions to those problems.

Can you imagine the historic fights for racial equality or gender rights without a touch of anger? Can you imagine living in a world in which no one felt remorse? Can you imagine a trip to an exotic country in which everything proceeded according to plan? Or a life in which you never wrestled with the tough decision to give up on a goal but, rather, just continued to plug away despite the low chance of success? There is a not so hidden prejudice against negative states, and the consequence of avoiding these states is that you inadvertently stunt your growth, maturity, adventure, and meaning and purpose in life.

What Wholeness Looks Like

This might be an opportune time to illustrate what wholeness looks like in real life. Here we turn for support to scientists who believe that personal stories are as meaningful as the artificial happiness scales that dominate so much research. If there is anything close to a true blood test or X-ray for quality of life, it's the rich stories of our daily experiences. The stories we tell about the events of our day—I had a flat tire, I was late for a meeting, I met a really interesting person, I saw an amazing sunset—reveal accomplishments, failings, attitudes, desires, and yearnings; they flesh out our identities and what we aspire to be and to do. In this spirit, we briefly describe three people we've come across who embody aspects of this quality we call wholeness.

Beyond the Impostor Syndrome

Although Jennifer was in her third year of graduate school in clinical psychology at Pacific University, she still checked her mailbox expecting to receive a letter printed on university stationary. In her imagination, the letter would say, "Jennifer, we're sorry but we made a terrible mistake when we accepted you to our graduate program. Your application should have been turned down." Jennifer, like many people, was feeling the sense of personal inadequacy known as impostor syndrome, which is especially common when people jump up to a new level: a promotion at work, a change of career, or advanced schooling. Often these feelings of self-doubt are uncomfortable, even painful. In the most extreme cases, they are upsetting enough to cause the person to reject the new opportunity.

What many people fail to realize is the fact that doubt, in moderation, performs a healthy function. Doubt is a psychological state that prompts us to take stock of our skills and to work to improve in areas where they might be deficient. Karl Wheatley, a researcher at Cleveland State University, argues that doubt can be beneficial—at least in the case of schoolteachers. He points to the fact that when teachers experience uncertainty about their performance, these feelings spur collaboration with others, foster personal reflection, motivate personal development, and prepare the person to accept change.

In Jennifer's case as an inexperienced therapist, she used doubt to help her make good decisions about which clinical patients to refer to more experienced therapists and which ones to treat herself. When she became more skilled, she used doubt as motivation to continue to refine her abilities and to monitor her psychotherapy patients for progress. By embracing doubt as one tool among many (rather than suppressing or rejecting it), Jennifer became a first-rate therapist and continues to improve to this day.

The Virtues of Throwing in the Towel

In 1995, a Swedish adventurer named Göran Kropp set a new standard for extreme among an already superfluous group of Mount Everest climbers. Unlike his high-altitude peers, Kropp wanted to ascend the mountain without the aid of supplemental oxygen, fixed ropes and ladders, Sherpa climbing support, porters for gear, or motorized transportation of any sort. To do this, he embarked on a bicycle journey of more than eight thousand miles between his home in Sweden and Kathmandu. From there, he ferried multiple loads to Everest base camp on his back. From base camp, he blazed a trail through steep rock, ice, and snow before any other expedition. On the day of his summit bid, however, Kropp made the difficult decision to turn around just three hundred feet shy of the highest point on earth. His choice was based on the late-afternoon conditions and the likelihood that he would have to descend cold, fatigued, and in the dark.

Kropp's amazing feat of self-control, the decision to turn around so close to his goal after having invested so much, turned out to be a prescient choice. A week later, members of several expeditions were afflicted with what can only be called summit fever and were stranded high on Everest's flanks by severe weather after failing to turn back at the agreed-upon time. The days that followed became known as the 1996 Everest Disaster, a period that claimed eight lives in the deadliest season on the mountain in history. In this context, Kropp's decision to turn back was, perhaps, lifesaving. It also throws new light on the commonly held assumption that perseverance is good and that quitting is bad.

Goals are an easy sell. People with specific goals have a yardstick by which to measure success, guidelines for adhering to their values, a clear target to motivate them, and a compass for making decisions. Businesses use goals to improve performance, and sports teams use goals—often literally—to tally success. To many people, having a goal is synonymous with commitment, and commitment to a goal—in turn—is nearly synonymous with success. Legendary boxer Muhammad Ali once quipped, "I hated every minute of training but I said, 'Don't quit. Suffer now and live the rest of your life as a champion.'" And there you have it—the clear sentiment that doubling down on goals is more likely to lead to success. Quitting, on the other hand, is reserved for the morally and physically weak.

As you might guess, we challenge the notion that giving up (an indisputable psychological discomfort, by the way) is so awful. Blind allegiance to goals has led to, among other things, "gold fever," most often associated with the California Gold Rush of 1859, when miners expended enormous physical, emotional, and financial capital in their fruitless pursuit of riches. In fact, researcher Eva Pomerantz of the University of Illinois argues that heavy investment in a goal can erode a person's psychological quality of life by creating a spike in their anxiety. This is especially true when people push themselves by focusing on the potential negative impact of not achieving their goals.

One of the major benefits of low moods—those that we would argue are typically uncomfortable for people and which they often try to avoid—is that when we feel them we tend to pull back from our goals. Sadness, frustration, doubt, confusion, and even guilt all serve a similar purpose: they signal you to apply the brakes, to retreat within yourself in order to reflect, and to conserve energy and resources. This is especially important in our human tendency to continue investing in impossible causes, or to act based on sunk costs, instead of making the decision to cut one's losses when the desired outcome looks less and less likely. Whole people have the ability to approach goals flexibly by continuing to invest when progress occurs at an acceptable pace, and by swapping old goals out for new ones when failure is almost certain.

The Benefits of Fantasy

From the time she was a schoolgirl, Melanie Baumgartner dreamed of being a judge. While at university, however, she fell in love and her life took an unexpected turn. Rather than go on to law school, Melanie found new meaning in being a stay-at-home mother. Ferrying her children home from school, she sometimes caught herself daydreaming about that other life, the one in which she holds a gavel and calls for order in the court.

In a psychological phenomenon known as *sehnsucht* [pronounced ZAYN zookt], it's not unusual to find that yearning for a missed opportunity or unfulfilled goal can inspire a rich fantasy in which we imagine ourselves successful in those aims. *Sehnsucht* is important as a psychological balm against the sting of opportunity lost: participants in an international research study who felt *sehnsucht* were able to embrace the fantasy, plumbing it for emotional reward. The one noteworthy exception was Americans. Unlike their European counterparts, they are far more likely to see their dreams as achievable, so they're often reluctant to relegate them to the realm of fantasy, which they tend to see as a negative. But fantasy can be a valuable resource.

Today Melanie's children are grown and she may return to law school. She feels less of a burning need to be a judge, however, in part because she has reaped the emotional rewards of her fantasies. *Sehnsucht* is one of many strategies that whole people employ to help them manage the psychological fallout from the road not taken, to make quitting palatable when it makes sense and to handle disappointment.

Our Approach in This Book

We know that pain sucks. So we want to clarify that we don't want your heart to be torn apart by frustrated goals, or by a romantic partner who sleeps with your sibling. Nor are we pushing you to hold your breath in ice-cold water without flinching. We're just arguing that accumulating emotions that feel good right now and avoiding emotions that feel unpleasant right now is not the best strategy for living well. In this book, we offer wholeness as an alternative to only trying to profit from the positive. The central feature of a person who is whole is that they show great skill in negotiating all that life serves up. They possess what we call emotional agility. Why? Because they can get the best possible outcome in a situation by matching their behavior—from the positive side or the negative side—to the challenge being faced. They can draw both sides of nearly every personality trait: serious and playful, passionate and objective, extraverted and introverted, selfless and selfish. They are kind but selective about who their time and energy goes to. Finally, people who are whole benefit from their unwillingness to discard qualities just because society deems them less valuable. In the following section, we flesh out what it means to be emotionally, socially, and mentally agile so that you can understand the breadth, beauty, and benefits of being whole.

Emotional Agility

The trick when wholeness is concerned is not to avoid negative emotions, but to take the negative out of them. This can be seen in the science behind successful psychotherapy. Psychologists Jonathan Adler from the Franklin W. Olin College of Engineering and Hal Hershfield from New York University tested the prevailing wisdom suggesting that therapy works by getting rid of people's problems, such as depression, and then helping them enact new strategies that boost their positivity. These researchers carefully observed forty-seven adults being treated by a therapist for anxiety and depression, and getting help coping with stressful events such as the transition to parenthood. Adler and Hershfield wanted to know what happens before a client's problems resolve, before their quality of life improves, and before they begin to truly like themselves.

You might be surprised, as the researchers were, to find that people in therapy don't simply experience fewer negatives and more positives and then, lo and behold, describe themselves as happier. What actually happens is that success in therapy begins when people start to become comfortable experiencing mixed emotions (both happy and sad) about their work, their relationships, and any situation they enter. Consider this description from a client after a few sessions:

> This has been a difficult couple of weeks. My wife and I celebrated the good news of a healthy pregnancy report at nine weeks (the time when we lost our pregnancy last January). But I also feel the sadness of still looking for a job and for my wife, whose grandmother is dying. It feels like "what more can I take?" But at the same time I also feel reasonably confident and happy. Not that I don't feel down, but I'm also grateful for the good things in my life, especially my marriage.

The crucial point here is that this person, and others like him who show the capacity to experience both positive and negative emotions about their lives, showed the greatest subsequent gains in well-being. However, the opposite did not prove to be the case: feeling positive did not improve people's ability to be emotionally agile. This study suggests that instead of happiness providing the biggest advantage, the greatest advantage stems from being at full capacity, being whole, tolerating both the good and the bad as they come into play.

Social Agility

Humans are primates and, therefore, social creatures. Like our chimpanzee cousins, we have brains highly developed for social interaction; we can, for example, easily interpret subtle facial expressions in a way that dogs, and pigs, and hawks, cannot. We also have highly evolved language centers to help us express vast quantities of complex information, including the full range of intentions and desires. We are so social, in fact, that researchers frequently argue that we can only survive through interdependence. Dacher Keltner, a psychologist at Berkeley, claims that generosity, hospitality, and benevolence are our natural states. Although you can easily point to instances of selfishness, deception, greed, and other social ills, you likely think people are capable of incredible good. In fact, you teach your children that kindness is the supreme virtue.

The beneficial side effects of kindness are numerous: kind people live longer, earn more, and are better citizens, and the warm intimate relationships they cultivate can ameliorate much of the damage from a problematic childhood. But if we take a closer look at the social world, we have to share an uncomfortable fact: whether we're involved in love, work, or play, we need to be kind, but we also need to be selective. We simply do not have the luxury of giving ourselves fully to everyone. Time and energy are limited resources that we must spend wisely.

Sometimes we even need to turn to the opposite of kindness in a given situation. Those of us who are willing to access our disagreeable side are at an advantage, whether as parents, athletes, soldiers, teachers, or entrepreneurs. And here's the part that might be difficult to grasp: it's better this way, for everyone. Even the best parents have periods of time when they are unwilling to extend themselves to their kids; parenting, like any job, requires an occasional lunch break. It's when parents don't take care of themselves that kids suffer in needless, unexpected ways.

Before you toss this book out the window or sell it on Ebay, we'd like to introduce you to one of our scientific heroes, Esther Kim, a sociologist from Yale University. Kim is unusual among academics in that she gets out of the laboratory and into the world. In fact, to observe how strangers interact with one another, she rode public buses thousands of miles. In particular, she was fascinated by the way that people would subtly warn off new passengers from sitting in the empty seat beside them.

We can all relate to the experience of watching a passenger walk down the center aisle of a bus, train, or plane while we silently chant the mantra "not next to me, not next to me." Kim observed a dazzling display of creative avoidance tactics: people sat in the aisle seat and donned headphones so that they could pretend not to hear the stranger ask about the empty window seat; they placed a bag on the empty seat; they scowled, stretched across both seats, and pretended to sleep; the list goes on. These travelers aren't rude; they're human. They're concerned about personal safety, about the energy it takes to interact with a stranger, and about their own comfort on a long journey. Kim's study illustrates one way in which we all have the propensity to deviate from the "be nice" norm.

Social agility is the ability to recognize how one situation differs from another, and to adjust our behavior to match these changing demands. Socially agile people are proactive, selecting, and influencing the situations they encounter. Depending on the specifics of the situation, socially agile people can be warm, tell white lies, or apply pressure; they can name-drop, flirt, compliment, and offer support. They can even casually mention that the refrigerator was recently cleaned in order to get full credit from a spouse or housemate. Socially agile people are not Machiavellian, but they do operate by a more inclusive and flexible set of social rules than the basic "play nice." Interestingly, in many instances when we bend the rules, it's not with personal gain in mind but to help others feel good, to strengthen relationships, and to achieve meaningful goals.

Mental Agility

The psychological concept of mindfulness has a smoking-hot reputation. Rooted in Buddhist practices, it is the Scarlett Johansson of mental strategies. A mindful person is someone who is focused on living in the present moment, and on "gently observing" what is happening in the present moment, as opposed to judging it. Mindful people, supposedly, pay better attention and are more likely to appreciate life than the rest of us. Head to the local bookstore and you will find a full shelf devoted to tomes on mindful eating, mindful parenting, mindful leadership, and even mindful poker. Pundits argue that this hyperaware state is, perhaps, the optimal state of human functioning, a place we want to enter and remain in perpetuity. In keeping with the bubble-busting theme of this book, let us be the first to tell you that it is impossible to remain in a constant mindful state. Whether you're brushing your teeth or driving to your kids' school on autopilot, it's a blessing to have a brain that allows you to find shortcuts that free mental energy for more meaningful, passionate endeavors. It's essential to have a subconscious system that can automatically process information without intentional effort or self-awareness.

One of the most fascinating areas of psychology deals specifically with how susceptible we all are to the influences of subtle cues that exist below our conscious awareness. In one study, for instance, Dutch psychologist Ap Dijksterhuis had students engage in a writing assignment before taking a test. A portion of the students were required to write about what it would be like to be a professor. Students randomly assigned to the "professor condition" were able to answer 60 percent of the trivia questions correctly, as opposed to the 50 percent accuracy of those in the control condition.

Engaging the subconscious mind is a unique way in which people can actually change their behavior, often toward the better, without the effort normally required. For example, researchers in one study subtly primed some participants—but not others—with the smell of cleaning products (hidden in a bucket in a corner of the laboratory). When the participants were later asked to eat a crumbly cookie, it was those who had smelled the cleaners who ate more carefully and wiped away their mess. The subconscious also works by helping people to process complex information. In the so-called "sleep on it" phenomenon, people who are distracted—and therefore not mindful—are better able to arrive at good purchasing decisions than those who muscle it through conscious effort.

Although the "be here now" mentality of mindfulness certainly has its perks, it's a mistake to think that it's the only desirable state. When we draw on the complete self, the whole of who we are, we can switch between mindfulness and mindlessness as circumstances demand. This helps us conserve mental resources and focus on the issues we deem most important.

CHAPTER 2

The Rise of the Comfortable Class

TO SOCIAL SCIENTISTS, Google is more than a search engine. It is, in many ways, a thermometer that takes the temperature of society. Google can be used to track collective attitudes and to chart popular trends. Take the example of a simple image search for the words *discomfort* and *comfort.* Hitting the enter key on *discomfort* yields images of people furrowing their brows, massaging their temples, favoring an achy joint, or cradling their stomachs. By contrast, a search for *comfort* returns images such as soft beds, plush armchairs, and luxury jets. The implication, we believe, is clear: discomfort is internal; it is a subjective phenomenon experienced by the individual, whereas its antidote, comfort, is to be found externally, in the material world around us.

This popular view of discomfort as an internal, unpleasant, and often unmanageable state lies at the heart of this book. If wholeness refers to the ability to experience and use the full range of psychological states—emotional, cognitive, and social—then our widespread uneasiness with discomfort must be implicated in narrowing our experience. Avoiding uncomfortable yet useful states keeps us from reaching our full potential. Interestingly, this arm's-length relationship we have with discomfort is a largely Western—and specifically American—phenomenon. Despite its pockets of desperate poverty and breathtaking disparities in income, the United States is a remarkably orderly, convenient, and comfortable place to live. The traffic lights work, the cinemas are temperature controlled, bathtubs are as common as garden hoses, everyone has access to shampoo, and people choose mattresses based on size, material, and softness.

As the world slowly grows wealthier, it is not only Americans who are becoming more comfortable. The closer your society is to that of America—Australia, Canada, and the United Kingdom jump to mind—the more likely it is that you hold similar (but not identical) attitudes regarding comfort. The further removed your culture is—think Zimbabwe, China, and Pakistan—the more likely you are to be comfortable with being uncomfortable. However, even in many parts of the economically developing world, we see an emerging middle class distinguished by comfort every bit as much as they are set apart by income.

If you want to get a sense of just how deeply ingrained our tilt toward comfort and a positive attitude really is, ask yourself the following question: "Was Jesus happy?" This is exactly the question posed by psychologist Shigehiro Oishi and his colleagues at the University of Virginia. These scientists were less concerned with finding a factual answer to this question than they were in using it to take the pulse of people's attitudes. The researchers figured that because there is only one Jesus, and one common narrative of his life (the biblical one), then any large-scale differences in opinion about his happiness should provide us with a cultural Rorschach test, in which people project their biases. To investigate this premise, they asked dozens of people in the United States and South Korea to write down their open-ended thoughts about Jesus. (The number of Christians was roughly the same—about 60 percent—in both groups.)

It turns out that Americans were far more likely than their South Korean counterparts to believe that Jesus was happy. Furthermore, they were significantly more likely than the Koreans to describe Jesus as being extraverted, open, and agreeable. More interesting still, the Koreans were far more likely to mention discomfort in relation to Jesus. They were more likely—in many cases five times more likely—to mention suffering, sacrifice, crucifixion, and blood. Even though uncomfortable events such as persecution and crucifixion are central to the Jesus narrative, the Americans were significantly more likely to say that Jesus was awesome, nice, and good.

Just because Americans tend toward the positive doesn't necessarily mean that they veer away from hardship. Or does it? Christie Napa Scollon, a researcher at Singapore Management University, and her colleague Laura King, a University of Missouri researcher, conducted an unusual series of studies. Instead of taking the usual approach, in which experts create sophisticated statistical models of happiness and determine where people fall on the scale, these researchers simply reached out to everyday people and asked them to consider the extent to which wealth, happiness, and hard work factored into their opinions of "the good life," which included both well-being and meaning. Americans, it turned out, placed a premium on feeling happy and preferred an easy life to a hardworking life, especially when hard work was quantified as a number of hours on the job. Researchers also found that Americans tended to see satisfying relationships as more important to the good life than satisfying work. In fact, they found that participants passed harsh judgments on hypothetical people who did not have good relationships but found their work highly rewarding; participants found them immoral, and in some cases even hell-bound.

Our appetite for the happy, comfortable life is not just a matter of abstract academic interest. We see it clearly in our behavior, specifically as consumers. Since World War II, we have enjoyed a period of unprecedented wealth. Even in the current economic context, in which we live in the shadow of a housing market crash, high levels of unemployment, and large-scale bankruptcies, the vast majority of us are faring better—materially speaking—than ever before. Home ownership is staggeringly high, as is ownership of consumer electronics, automobiles, and air-conditioning. We are stampeding toward comfort and convenience. According to sociologist Juliet Schor, modern people fantasize about luxury vacations, nicer homes, and more comfort. She cites a longitudinal study from the University of Connecticut in which people were asked to indicate which basic items they felt were necessities. In the 1970s, 13 percent endorsed air-conditioning in an automobile, and 25 percent needed AC at home. By the mid-1990s, however, attitudes had changed to include more creature comforts. For example, 41 percent of respondents now felt that they needed air-conditioning while driving, and 50 percent needed it at home.

This sudden desire for air-conditioning is particularly interesting when you consider it in the context of Maslow's hierarchy of needs. Way back in 1954 Maslow suggested that people first satisfy their basic needs, such as food and shelter, before going on to social needs, and only when these are satisfied does the work begin on self-esteem and creativity. Most people make the mistake of thinking that

Maslow was writing a prescription for the good life. What Maslow intended, however, was to describe the basic workings of human motivation.

What is interesting, in light of our modern addiction to comfort, is to consider what the word *basic* in the phrase *basic needs* actually means. It's easy to see that access to clean water is a basic survival need. In the abstract, it is even easy to see that thermoregulation—keeping yourself warm or cool as circumstances demand—is a basic need. But while we humans obviously need clothing to stay warm and dry and to help protect us from the dangers of hypothermia, it is harder to justify air-conditioning in the car as a basic need, especially considering that an automobile itself is a luxury of almost miraculous proportion.

If people's appetites continue on this trajectory, then pretty soon having air-conditioning in your car won't be enough. Before long, you will need heated seats or separate heating and cooling zones for the driver and each passenger. Oh, wait, that's what's emerging right now as a standard feature in new cars! It would be interesting to see the numbers of people who now view having a video screen in their car as a necessity.

Here we arrive at the thesis of this chapter. As people become better able to satisfy their desire for comfort, they narrow their range of experiences and fall out of practice navigating life's hardships. To put this in a linear way: (1) material comforts and convenience items lead to (2) an urge to use external goods to be at ease, which leads to (3) lower psychological immunity to circumstances that are less comfortable and more inconvenient. Make no mistake; material comforts affect our ability to psychologically adjust to our surrounding and to deal with difficulties. The comfort associated with air-conditioning translates, over time, to a situation in which internal states such as anger, doubt, giving up, uncertainty, and mindlessness quickly become overwhelming, or are seen as immoral. It is our comfort addiction that splinters us as individuals and prevents us from enjoying the full range of psychological well-being.

Whereas our grandfathers and grandmothers could handle a bit of dust, sunshine, and rain, modern people seem less able to. In the last twenty years hospital admissions for food allergies among children have risen by 500 percent, and studies have shown that children from more affluent backgrounds have a higher likelihood of developing a peanut allergy. Similarly, asthma now affects one in 11 children in the UK and the UK has among the highest prevalence rates of asthma symptoms in children worldwide. One possibility is the so-called "hygiene hypothesis," in which modern living conditions among the middle class are too clean and provide too few opportunities to be exposed to and build resistance to infectious agents.

What happened to us? How did Western societies change so dramatically? What happened between the time we were cave people scratching out a tenuous daily existence and today, when television commercials or a five-minute traffic delay seem intolerable? When did we lose our immunity to discomfort?

The Origins of Comfort Addiction

Questions of comfort and discomfort have been around as long as people have. It is easy to imagine the first caveman who picked up the rock he was using as a pillow and saying "Ugh! Want softer!" and then laying his head down on a pile of pine needles. The same impulse toward keeping warm (or cool), toward letting aching muscles relax, and toward feeling soft textures has been a universal motivation throughout the ages.

In fact, Hamlet's famous "To be, or not to be" speech from Shakespeare's play is primarily about whether to try to overcome adversity. Observe:

> *To be, or not to be, that is the question:*
> *Whether 'tis Nobler in the mind to suffer*
> *The Slings and Arrows of outrageous Fortune,*
> *Or to take Arms against a Sea of troubles.*

The fictional young prince of Denmark is asking a question similar to one that concerns depressed modern people living in Pensacola, Toronto, or Manchester: should I choose life or death? His answer was based on degrees of comfort. He concluded that he would stick with life, despite its curveballs, not because he was adventurous or hardy, but because the alternative—the unknown realm of the hereafter—was even more anxiety-provoking than the trials of everyday life. Again, check out the prince in action:

> *But that the dread of something after death,*
> *The undiscovered Country, from whose bourn*
> *No Traveller returns, Puzzles the will,*
> *And makes us rather bear those ills we have.*

In 1930, Sigmund Freud, the most prominent figure in the history of psychology, wrote about the perils of the siren song of comfort. He said, "It means putting enjoyment before caution and soon brings its own punishment." Freud was skeptical not of enjoying a plush pillow or a cool evening breeze but of enjoyment as a primary motivator for action. His instinct told him that the pursuit of comfort, rather than comfort itself, could lead to selfish decisions and, ultimately, have negative social consequences.

More critical still was the German philosopher Hegel. "What the English call 'comfort,'" Hegel wrote, "is something inexhaustible and illimitable." Hegel concluded that "the need for greater comfort does not exactly arise within you directly; it is suggested to you by those who hope to make a profit from its creation." It is noteworthy that Hegel, like Freud, focused not on the achievement of comfort but on the dangers associated with the "need for comfort." Hegel suggests that a person's need for comfort is an illusion, of the kind fostered today by advertising gurus. Hegel argues that this urge, like an addiction to coffee, may feel right, but it is neither natural nor healthy.

In the more modern age, industrialization has led to comfort and convenience in unprecedented proportion. In a study of pace of life, psychologist Robert Levine and his colleagues found a consistent relationship between GDP and faster living. By measuring how quickly people walk, how quickly postal employees complete a basic task, and how accurate public clocks are, Levine was able to estimate the relative pace of life of societies. Not only is national wealth associated with a faster pace of life, but a faster pace of life is also associated with a higher rate of energy consumption; think cars, kitchen appliances, and water heaters—all items related to convenience and comfort. Here comes the kicker: a faster pace of life is also related to lower rates of achievement and money saving. The more convenient everything is, the less likely people are to engage in troublesome self-control. Just look at the example of frustration. In places where things get done quickly, people find waiting in lines or in traffic almost intolerable. To put it another way, the more comfortable your life is, the less patient you are likely to be with perceived problems.

Although this book is primarily about psychological comfort, we should linger a moment to mention that there is a direct relationship between basic physical comfort (in psychology we call these *comfortable sensations*) and more complex psychological comforts (which we might think of as *emotional states*). We are all, after all, shackled to this physical existence—Shakespeare's "mortal coil"—by our bodies. Our bodies are the membrane, so to speak, between the events of the world and that person we see as the self. Our bodies serve as a sort of thermostat—often literally—by which we experience the comforts and discomforts of the world. Researchers have noted that everyone has a specific range within which they can adjust to ambient environmental conditions, which include odors, noises, and temperature. This is why you don't notice how cool your office is until you walk into the blast of August heat outside. Seeking physical comfort is normal, and your natural ability to adapt is part of that impulse.

You may be surprised to learn that feelings of disgust provide a perfect example of how physical and psychological sensations sometimes intertwine. Disgust is an emotion that helps us avoid things that might be toxic, like rotten food. Researchers measure *disgust sensitivity* in all sorts of creative ways. They have research participants blow their nose using a roll of toilet paper. They have them drink apple juice out of a bedpan. They see how close they will stand to a severed pig's head. There is also a more psychological brand of disgust, known as *moral disgust*. People, it turns out, are just as likely to want to avoid a bed that a murderer slept in as they are to steer clear of vomit. They are as reluctant to try on a sweater that once belonged to Hitler as they are to eat chocolate molded to look like dog poop. It turns out that disgust sensitivity relates directly to people's sense of comfort, especially when it comes to the natural world.

Researchers Robert Bixler and Myron Floyd were curious to explore their hypothesis that people's comfort range has become more constricted over the years. When they asked hundreds of US middle school students how they felt about nature, researchers found that fearful and disgusted children were likely to opt for indoor social recreation or—if some awful adult actually pushed them out-of-doors—they were more likely to favor manicured park paths. The kids were also asked how much they would miss modern comforts if they went on a week-long outdoor "re-creation" of the settling of Texas: 0 was "I would not miss this at all" and 4 was "I could not live without it." The average response for a bath or shower was a 3. Flush toilets rated a 2.63, hot water a 2.69, and air-conditioning a 2.66. Of course, all of these are things that the actual settlers of Texas readily lived without. Americans have steadily grown softer between the time they crossed the country in covered wagons and the advent of the La-Z-Boy and the Sony Playstation. What is considered comfort has become more and more limited.

It is noteworthy that this study of the attitudes of children toward comfort was published in 1997 because, as it turns out, the 1990s are when comfort addiction began in earnest. It is here that we started seeing the dramatic rise of the comfortable class, and even heard the phrase *comfort food* for the first time, a sure indication that our relationship with basic needs was shifting.

Now, decades later, in the context of the Arab Spring and wars in Iraq and Afghanistan, it is difficult to remember what a special time the 1990s were. For people who lived through the protest movements of the 1960s and the gasoline shortages of the 1970s, the 1980s and—especially—the 1990s were a different era. There was a sense that the world was getting better. After decades of institutionalized injustice, the apartheid system in South Africa crumbled. Decades of cold war came abruptly to an end. Stock markets were heading toward the stratosphere, and the Internet was becoming a new global engine for creativity and finance. In short, everything seemed comfortable in a way that we'd never seen before in all of human history.

As these political and economic tides rose, so did expectations. We began seeing happiness not as a desirable goal but as a moral imperative. In fact, researcher Shigehiro Oishi—of the Jesus study mentioned earlier—and his colleagues used Google to track instances of the phrase *happy person* in American books from 1800 to 2008. As you might guess, authors in the 1800s and early 1900s ignored this phrase. Then, during the Roaring Twenties, books began to feature the happy person, a phenomenon that swelled to a huge crescendo in 1990, when you'd be hard-pressed to walk into a bookstore without purchasing something that included the phrase. In the years that followed, the use didn't recede much from its peak. From 1990 to 2008, the number of references equaled that of the preceding fifty years. Clearly social norms were on the move.

It was in the early 1990s too, that the first "death with dignity" laws were passed in the United States. In essence, these laws provide for a planned death for people who find life too physically uncomfortable or undignified—itself a form of mental discomfort. These laws, regardless of what you think about them personally, reflect a society that has moved so far beyond fulfilling basic needs that we can begin shaping the time and nature of a person's death. It was also in the early 1990s that we saw the first use of the term *comfort zone*, the range of experience that feels familiar and generates a sense of ease, in the context of business. One early piece of business writing explicitly cautioned managers to steer workers out of the comfort zone.

The icing on the comfort cake is, perhaps, the single greatest comfort-related invention of all time. It was NASA scientists who, in the 1960s, first created a technology to help relieve astronauts of discomfort during liftoffs and in space. But it was not until 1991 that this technology was placed on the open market for civilians to enjoy: memory foam was introduced as the most comfortable, body-conforming mattress pads and pillows on the planet. Marketers determined that during the 1990s people were finally willing to pay exorbitant prices to own a bed that perfectly adapted to their exact dimensions for the ultimate in sleep comfort. As if spring-coil mattresses and waterbeds were not comfortable enough, we finally had a material that could make every minor contour of our bodies feel rested. After two hundred thousand years of sleeping, humans could finally sleep in the fashion to which we are—apparently—entitled.

As we became more comfortable, researchers observed a related drop in our psychological health. Anxiety, in particular, seemed to be on the rise. The year 1996 was the first time in history that students at college health clinics began complaining of anxiety more frequently than they sought help for depression or relationship problems, a trend that continues to this day. Similarly, the 1990s saw an uptick in aggression on American roads. In statistics gathered for the AAA Foundation for Traffic Safety, the number of aggressive incidents on the road grew from 1,129 in 1990 to 1,708 in 1995, a 50 percent increase. The

American ability to tolerate the small frustrations of rush hour and the perceived personal slight of being cut off while driving was diminishing. The 1990s saw more than ten thousand road-rage incidents recorded in which more than two hundred people died and another twelve thousand were injured. In the 1990s, life was so good that people were sometimes at a loss about what to do when it went off the rails.

Most important, in the mid-1990s an ominous term related to psychological comfort first cropped up. While people were getting better sleep, enjoying more convenience, and expecting greater happiness, they were also adjusting to a life without too many trials or hardships, and the term *experiential avoidance* entered the psychological lexicon. Experiential avoidance can be defined as attempts to bury unwanted thoughts or feelings, to hide from them so actively that we have little energy left over for being present as life unfolds. Yep, this was the first time that people experienced enough choice, enough freedom, and enough personal empowerment that they could avoid things—lots of things. And they did. Especially emotions. Our growing discomfort with uncertainty, doubt, boredom, and negative emotions led to measurable changes. One common escape strategy, for instance, is watching television. Although television is inarguably entertaining, it also serves the function of taking us away from the cares of our daily lives. Between the 1950s and the 1970s, the average number of hours of household television viewing was between five and six a day. In the 1980s and 1990s, however, that number spiked to seven and a half hours a day.

How Can You Avoid What Is Inside You?

The primary resource for US mental health professionals wanting to diagnose and treat mental illnesses is the *Diagnostic and Statistical Manual of Mental Disorders*, more widely known as the DSM. In 1980, the DSM was an imposing book: it weighed in at 494 pages and listed a dizzying 265 mental illnesses. But by 1994, it had become a behemoth, doubling in size to 886 pages and adding thirty-two mental illnesses. Mental health professionals seemed to agree that feeling too sad, feeling too anxious, feeling angry too often or too intensely, and confronting difficult thoughts were signs of illness. The DSM catalogs many legitimate problems, such as schizophrenia, but it is more difficult to accept the notion that feeling blue for two weeks or longer to a degree that interferes with work or relationships is a clinically significant problem. The general population got the message, though: pain is bad, and it's something health professionals can help you to avoid. But how can you avoid what is inside you?

With good reason, leaders of the American Psychological Association named Dr. Albert Ellis the "second most prominent psychologist in the 20th century" (he was one place ahead of Sigmund Freud in the rankings, and behind only Carl Rogers). Ellis became the founder of cognitive behavioral therapy (CBT). He argued that three major dysfunctional beliefs directly ramp up distress and destructive behavior:

1. *"I must do well and win the approval of others to be accepted."*
2. *"Other people must do 'the right thing' or else they are no good."*

3. *"Life must be easy, without discomfort or inconvenience."*

In the 1950s and 1960s, these ideas were revolutionary. Instead of implicating unresolved childhood conflicts or traumatic events as the causes of psychological difficulties, Ellis proposed that problems spring from the beliefs that people adopt about themselves, other people, and the world around them. Ellis didn't just articulate the problem, he created a system of therapy by which counselors could help their clients to identify personally troubling beliefs and dispute them. His methods were effective, and reproducible, and quickly became the centerpiece of psychotherapy for decades. Rebranded in 1990 as *learned optimism* by Dr. Martin Seligman—the founder of *positive psychology*—Ellis's ideas teach people how to reduce the emotional pain that sabotages happiness. For all its merit, this is the logical extension of our addiction to physical comfort. If physical conditions are not to our liking, then we work to modify them until they are; similarly, if our moods and memories make us unhappy, we should modify them until they are less distressing.

This idea faced few challenges for thirty years. Then some of the hippies exposed to the human potential movement and Eastern philosophy in the 1960s grew up, became psychologists, and pioneered a new form of therapy known as *acceptance and commitment therapy*, or ACT. Doctors Steven Hayes, Kelly Wilson, Elizabeth Gifford, Victoria Follette, and Kirk Strosahl asked provocative new questions. What if professional therapists are using the wrong criteria to determine what is normal and abnormal? What if paying attention to the intensity and negativity of thoughts, feelings, and behaviors is not the best gauge of mental health? What if, instead, we looked at what people do with these thoughts, feelings, and behaviors? This group of researcher-clinicians noticed that when people are psychologically hurt they act in much the same way as people who are physically injured. When you twist your ankle, for instance, you tend to restrict your use of that leg. The same holds true for mental hardships. When a friend or lover hurts your feelings, you restrict the friendship by interacting less. When emotions boil over, you avoid them by watching TV, sleeping, or having a beer.

The alternative to changing or avoiding painful thoughts, feelings, sensations, and memories is to learn that you can withstand psychological discomfort just as you can withstand the physical discomfort of going for a walk on a rainy afternoon. It may not be your preference, but you can without question do it. Step back and imagine how liberating it would be to enjoy a life where unwanted thoughts and feelings are not an enemy we must battle against and ultimately defeat. Instead, imagine that these thoughts and feelings are like music on the radio playing in the background; they are always there, but we can choose how much attention is warranted. The central premise of ACT is that you carry your difficult thoughts and feelings inside; you observe them, but you and they are not the same.

That idea bears repeating: you are not your psychological experiences, even though they can affect you. It may sound strange—radical even—to suggest that somehow you are not the same thing as your thoughts and feelings. You are not just the uncomfortable thoughts in your mind—and the feelings they trigger—precisely because you can observe those thoughts and feelings. Whatever or whoever this observer is—the self, the personality, the soul, call it what you will—it is, by definition, set apart from those feelings and the fact that you can observe them is proof of this. When you recognize this observer as being separate from the pain, you can become better at tolerating that pain.

Most of our problems arise not from distressing thoughts or feelings, as Ellis was suggesting, but from the unwillingness to approach them. It might be fair to say that, when anxiety is concerned, there is really only one underlying problem: avoidance. A quick look through the most recent DSM shows that there are all sorts of anxiety disorders, ranging from social anxiety to post-traumatic stress disorder to panic disorder. Although each of these is a legitimate form of pain, they all have a common denominator. When you think people are rejecting you, or when you're worried that your character flaws will be exposed, it makes sense to try to get rid of those anxious feelings. Unfortunately, instead of making us feel calmer, avoiding our anxiety has the opposite effect of intensifying it over time.

Many therapists are familiar with the way their clients often have secondary emotional problems. A person might feel guilty, for instance, and then feel guilty about feeling guilty. Or a patient might feel depressed, and then feel angry at himself for feeling depressed. It is largely the same with anxiety. People feel anxious about certain situations, and then this stress is compounded by a fear of feeling anxious. Imagine how much easier life would be if you could remove this second layer of mental trouble by simply feeling robust enough to withstand anxiety.

This notion of having a hardier attitude in regard to your internal states is not a trivial point. Not only would developing a tolerance of more challenging psychological states help you, as an individual, it would also be good for society in the long term. This is because comfort addiction is not just a plague that is relevant to you; it is also—collectively speaking—the legacy to our children.

Comfort Addiction Harms Our Children

In modern society, there is much hand wringing over the many ills that beset our children. Obesity. Bullying. Video games. Sexting. Drug use. Unwanted pregnancy. Sexually transmitted disease. Violence. Failing grades. Skateboarding. The list of perceived dangers falls on parental ears like an avalanche, and in a fit of well-intentioned protectionism we come rushing to the rescue as never before. Beginning in the mid-1980s, people began sporting Baby on Board signs in their automobiles as a caution to other drivers and a way of invoking a safer world. We no longer live in an adult-centric era when children should be seen and not heard. Nowadays, children are the focal point, and parents act as a sort of private security force to ensure their safety and well-being.

Indeed, over the last thirty years, parents have become more and more preoccupied with safety. We now routinely go trick-or-treating with our children, for instance, when that was almost never the case in the 1950s, 1960s, and 1970s. In fact, researchers tracking parental attitudes have noted that parents are far more likely these days to organize children's play activities and to drive their children to those activities. Australian researchers Trine Fotel and Thyra Thomsen were curious to see whether these higher rates of driving might be due to other factors, such as longer distances to schools. They discovered that approximately 55 to 60 percent of the increase in being chauffeured to school is due directly to perceptions of risk. Despite statistics showing that accidents involving bicycling children are declining, parents are more afraid than ever to have their sons and daughters sharing the road with drivers. After complaining about dangerous traffic conditions, one mother concluded:

> It was a problem for him that I didn't teach him how to behave [while cycling] in traffic. Only when I saw how much he was teased by other children for always being taken to school by car, did I realize how it affected him. I had to do something about it, and it turned out he was pretty good at cycling.

One of the most obvious changes in children's culture has taken place on the playground. Only a few decades ago, school playgrounds were worlds made of wood, but rotting planks and abundant splinters induced parents and officials alike to replace their jungle gyms with metal and plastic versions. In a recent study on playground safety, Anita Bundy and her colleagues arranged to put a number of loose, purposeless objects around a play area, including large cardboard boxes, plastic barrels, hay bales, car tires, and lengths of tubing. After carefully collecting data from the playing children and their adult teacher-supervisors, the researchers discovered that this more unstructured playground equipment led to a number of changes. First, the children showed a significant increase in vigorous physical activity. Second, the supervisors worried more. Supervising teachers widely praised what they saw as substantial increases in creative play, social play, and less aggressive play, so if the old-school playground materials led to such tangible benefits what were the teachers worried about? Researchers reported that they were primarily worried about the risk of physical injury and felt personally responsible for preventing it.

So terrifying is the school setting, it would seem, that parents are swooping into the classroom to help protect their children from potential psychological dangers such as bullying, self-esteem issues, acceptance, and falling behind academically. This is what sociologist Catharine Warner calls *emotional safeguarding*, or what we refer to as *helicopter parenting*. Interestingly, these intrusions are most common among middle-class parents; that is, they are more frequent among those who are most comfortable. In an analysis of this parenting trend, Warner concludes that well-intentioned parents have competing desires for their children. On the one hand, they want their children to be challenged intellectually, but on the other, they want their kids to be happy, popular, understood, and otherwise psychologically comfortable. It is as if we parents, collectively, cannot see that the very same challenge, frustration, and failure we believe will encourage our beloved children's academic growth would also serve their psychological needs.

Here is the comfort attitude summed up nicely in a comment made by a parent of a first grader who participated in Warner's study:

> We want her to be in a place where she feels safe, where her self-esteem is really promoted as opposed to being stomped on. I think that is our foremost concern. And then of course we want her to be in a place where she is nurtured, but at the same time she is challenged appropriately.

If you are thirty years old or older, we are fairly certain your parents never said anything like this at your parent-teacher conference. Instead, they probably looked your teacher in the eye and asked, "How's the reading going?" It's not that the old ways were harsh, or that only now have we opened our eyes to our children's well-being. It is, at least in no small part, that modern parents have it wrong. We see danger everywhere. Here is the other side of the story from a first-grade teacher—a teacher highly praised by parents—who participated in the Warner study.

> Parents are always saying, "Oh my child is anxious about coming to school, and they don't want to come to school." But the reality is they get here and they're totally fine. I always feel like maybe it's the parent that is feeling anxious about something, and then the child just adopts that feeling.

There it is in a nutshell. The world feels dangerous. Legitimate dangers are, without doubt, all around us, but we have adopted a collective worldview that magnifies these looming threats. Where our children are concerned, if we insist on too antiseptic an upbringing, they will be ill prepared for the storms of their teens and of adulthood. In many ways, modern parents are blind to the widespread benefits of challenge. Don't worry, we aren't pointing our fingers at you; we are ready to accept our fair share of the blame as well. It can be so easy to recognize the idea that intellectual challenge is a vital part of education, yet at the same time so difficult to appreciate the fact that challenge is equally beneficial to social and emotional development.

What's the Alternative?

To get a better look at an alternate reality of sorts—a world where negative states are tolerated—you have to fly across the ocean to Asia. People from Asian cultures are often referred to as collectivists, because their basic social unit is the group rather than the individual. Collectivists are more likely to put their desires on hold if that contributes to the larger good of the group. Collectivists are more likely to want to fit in than to be unique. Collectivists are more likely to see themselves as having fluid identities rather than stable traits that carry over from one situation to the next. Legendary social psychologist Robert Wyer once summed it up this way:

> Individualists believe that if someone invites you over to their house for dinner you must reciprocate by inviting them over to your house at a later date. Collectivists, on the other hand, might believe that if a specific person invites you for dinner you ought to later invite someone, anyone, to dinner.

At the risk of painting with too broad a brush, it turns out that Asians relate to their emotional experiences quite differently than Westerners do. By way of example, if you ask a Caucasian American or Canadian "Are you happy?" both will conduct a quick internal calculation. Chances are that they have been tracking their moment-to-moment moods and a quick peek inside will yield a fairly accurate answer. However, when the same question is posed to a South Korean woman, for example, she will be far more likely to place weight equally on her actual internal experience and on cultural norms for how she ought to feel in that particular situation.

Researchers have discovered interesting cultural differences in how people think they ought to feel. Asians, for example, are more likely to shoot for low-arousal positive emotions such as peace, harmony, contentedness, and calm. By contrast, Westerners are more likely to aspire to high-arousal positive emotions such as enthusiasm, joy, and pride. That is, they liked to get pumped up, and this emotional leaning might be self-reinforcing. In one study we conducted, we examined the emotional experiences of people from various cultures. We found that the intensity of pleasant emotional experience affected how Americans remembered their emotional experiences; they remembered having more good feelings if they had intense good feelings. This recall bias was not true for Japanese people.

The differences between Easterners and Westerners are particularly pronounced when negative psychological experiences are concerned, and the biggest difference in East-West emotional relations is in suppression. Psychologically speaking, suppression has its roots in Freudian defense mechanisms, which are mental tricks that people employ to keep emotional pain at bay. Repressing (forgetting) bad experiences is one example. Using humor to laugh off hardship is another. Suppression simply means dampening or pushing down experience. Many Westerners cling to a stereotype of people from Asian cultures as being suppressed because they are typically difficult to read. This is because most collectivist cultures promote use of a poker face to help navigate the social world. But if Asians are more prone to suppressing the expression of emotion, they are not when it comes to the actual experience of emotion. In fact, Asians tend to be quite tolerant of unpleasant emotional experiences. Studies show that when they experience bouts of sadness or irritation, they do not rush to distraction or humor in the way that their Western counterparts do.

This trend can be seen in the ways that Americans and people from Asian cultures differ when they become depressed. You, like virtually everyone else you know, have an intuitive sense of what depression is. Perhaps you've been depressed yourself. Either way, you know that it involves feeling blue, loss of energy, an inability to enjoy life, and perhaps difficulties with sleep, self-care, or concentration. At the extreme end, it can include feelings of hopelessness and suicidal thoughts. Many Western people deal with such overwhelming feelings by using some kind of numbing strategy to avoid them, which might include substance abuse or sleep. Asians tend not to do so.

In one study, researchers showed a funny film clip to both European Americans and Asian Americans, all of whom were clinically depressed. The Asian Americans laughed and smiled at the comedic scenes, whereas the European Americans did not. In another study, depressed European Americans showed only muted reactions to sad film clips. Their Asian American counterparts, on the other hand, were more likely to weep. The European Americans, it seems, had flipped off a switch, whereas the Asian Americans were still very much experiencing their emotions. In short, Asians appear to be more comfortable with unpleasant feelings. It is here, perhaps, that we can benefit from looking at this phenomenon more closely.

It turns out that these cultural leanings toward or away from negative psychological states have been learned. It's surprising to think that your feelings have been taught to you in the same way you learned your mother tongue, but that is exactly what happens. This point has been brilliantly illustrated in a series of studies by Jeanne Tsai of Stanford University and her colleagues. In one study, researchers identified the best-selling children's books published in the United States and in Taiwan in 2005. A detailed analysis of the pictures in these storybooks yielded the insight that American books portrayed significantly wider smiles, more excited facial expressions, and more exuberant movement. In a follow-up study, Tsai and her colleagues read individually to Taiwanese and American children, after which the children were randomly assigned to hear either an excited, American version of a story about swimming in a pool (cannonball!) or a calm, Taiwanese version of the same story (pleasantly floating).

Afterward, each child was presented with a series of playground activities, each of which had an excited version and a calmer form. "Would you rather," one such question asked, "play with a drum that you play fast BOOM-BOOM-BOOM, or a drum that you play slow and soft, tap-tap-tap?" Regardless of their cultural origin, children who had been exposed to the exciting story tended to choose the more exciting activities. How many stories have you read to your children regarding a character's ability to tolerate negative emotions? To be fair, Dr. Seuss turned to this theme in several books, including *I Had Trouble in Getting to Solla Sallew*, but he seems to be an exception. Books about tolerating negativity are far more likely in Asia. We Americans, by contrast, expose our kids to happy birthdays and happy meals and happy endings, but not a lot of sadness or grief in between. Concerned parents and educators may see an opportunity here to use educational materials and everyday social interactions to help our kids tolerate discomfort.

We do not mean to romanticize Asian culture. In fact, a wide range of research suggests that Asians also have a tendency to avoid savoring positive emotional experiences. It may be that they are more likely to see conditions as continually in flux, and are therefore more leery of hanging on to positive moments in the way that Americans seem so keen to do. Regardless of the psychological dynamics involved, Asians seem to sacrifice a bit of happiness at the top of the scale even as they better tolerate the anxious emotions at the bottom. Our point here is simply to emphasize the very real possibility that Americans and other Westerners can learn their way out of comfort addiction, and the psychological intolerance that goes with it.

If Western societies can open themselves to a little more danger, a bit more risk, a touch more hardship, and even a little more failure, then we stand to regain some of the mental toughness that goes hand in glove with such experiences. Of course, we are not recommending that you immediately jettison your air-conditioning, smartphones, or flush toilets. Nor are we encouraging anyone to let their kids play in dangerously run-down playgrounds, or dash out and purchase Taiwanese storybooks for their children in the hopes of boosting their tolerance of negative moods. Even so, some change is necessary if we want to be hardier, more psychologically well-rounded people. It's always daunting to consider making a major shift, so we're going to encourage you to take baby steps as we explore the benefits of emotional discomfort, the positive consequences of difficult cognitive states, and the ways we expand our horizons by tolerating tough social situations.

Psychology's Holy Grail

It's tempting to think of modern psychology as being synonymous with psychotherapy. Movies portraying psychologists almost always cast these professionals as counselors, and rarely, if ever, as researchers. This stereotype has some truth to it: there are about 175,000 psychologists in the United States and well over half of them are therapists at the master's or doctoral level. The rest of us are, more or less, researchers, professors, or consultants. Because so much of psychology today is devoted to addressing depression, anxiety, and other prevalent mental health problems, it can be easy to overlook the simple fact that the science of psychology has long been principally focused on optimal human functioning.

Psychology is a relatively young science. In its earliest days as a legitimate empirical endeavor, physicians such as Hermann von Helmholtz labored to understand basic human functions in a reliable way.

He was able, for example, to compute the speed at which electrical nerve impulses travel through the body (ninety feet per second). At the turn of the last century, in 1900, psychologists shifted from trying to understand what makes people tick to understanding what makes people tick well. The greatest minds of the twentieth century were largely focused on how humans flourish. The works of William James and Sigmund Freud, just to take two prominent examples, were chock-full of words like *congruent*, *growth*, and *whole*. They believed that humans are different from other animals in that we, collectively, can transcend our nature and mentally envision futures, which we can then work toward (or in the case of hellish scenarios, move away from).

After World War II, psychology veered away from a focus on psychological health and emphasized psychological illness. Words like *potential* were replaced with words like *symptom* and *disorder*. Given the legions of soldiers returning home from the front with depression and trauma, it made sense for the psychological establishment to create more effective treatments for these maladies. This trend continues—more or less—through modern times. Even so, there have been torchbearers for the positive aspects of psychology, scholars too enamored with positive topics such as generosity, resilience, trust, and forgiveness to focus only on mental disorder. In the 1950s, 1960s, and 1970s, Abraham Maslow, Carl Rogers, and other humanists rekindled interest in human potential. More recently, positive psychologists—ourselves included—have returned to attend to the shiniest aspects of human nature.

The timing of these topics dovetailed with a new wave of prosperity. As the global economy improved from the 1970s through the 1980s and 1990s, as we have mentioned earlier, our collective focus shifted toward comfort and success. Too much comfort has undermined our hardiness, but the attention to becoming successful has bolstered growing research in positive psychology. What we suggest is that these two interests, in human potential and in how to manage the dark sides of humanity, do not need to be in conflict with each other. By merging these two themes, we gain full access to the complexity of what it means to be human.

THE TAKEAWAYS

1. Modern people are less accustomed to hardship than our forebears, who had to contend with world wars, economic depressions, influenza epidemics, and other pervasive hardships.
2. Relative wealth and advances in technology mean that, nowadays, we enjoy unprecedented comfort. They also mean that we increasingly view discomfort as toxic, unmanageable, and intolerable.
3. Attitudes toward comfort are more than just personal opinions, they are embedded in culture. The social and economic climate of the 1980s and 1990s helped shape our modern views of comfort and discomfort.
4. Perhaps the group most directly affected by modern leanings toward comfort is children. Parents are increasingly involved in school, social life, and recreation in an attempt to create an environment that is safe, hygienic, and psychologically supportive. Ironically, this trend might be making the lives of our children more difficult rather than less.
5. Asians, by virtue of their unique socialization, have a different relationship with so-called negative emotions than Westerners do. Asians are better able to tolerate

unpleasant emotions. Because they do not attempt to avoid or suppress these feelings, they are also more open to positive moods, even if they do not try to artificially savor them for long periods.

CHAPTER 3

What's So Good About Feeling Bad?

During the first half of a professional basketball game when Pat Riley was coach of the Los Angeles Lakers, the team was completely unfocused. They were watching the cheerleaders, telling each other jokes, and generally ignoring what was happening on the basketball court. The only one who had his head in the game was star player Kareem Abdul-Jabbar. At halftime, Riley threw a calculated fit that began with yelling and climaxed with his upending a tray full of paper cups filled with water. The only casualty, Kareem, was soaked. Seeing this, his teammates felt guilty that their bad behavior had led to Kareem's unfairly suffering from the coach's anger, so they pulled themselves together and overcame a twenty-point deficit to win the game. It turns out that Riley had always intended for the water to land on Kareem, and his strategy worked.

Does anyone think the team would have played better if Riley had gone into the locker room at halftime intending to create an atmosphere of joy, love, or contentment? Expressing anger—in this instance—was exactly what the problem called for. As we see from the reactions of the players, negative emotions can be highly motivational. Unless you open yourself to unwelcome negative feelings, you will miss out on important opportunities to wield some of life's most useful tools. If you fall prey to the temptation to constantly search for something positive to grab on to in hopes of eliminating, hiding, or concealing negative emotions, you will lose in the game of life. You cannot get rid of the negative emotions without unintentionally squelching happiness, meaning, grit, curiosity, maturity, wisdom, and personal growth. Choose to numb the negatives and you numb the positives too. Remember the depressed Americans who didn't laugh at the comic film?

Why Bad Can Be More Powerful Than Good

Roy Baumeister and his colleagues at Florida State University published an article titled "Bad is stronger than good." This bold heading suggests that psychologists went out and somehow measured good and evil in the world and found metrics favoring the negative side. Actually, the article is about the way we have a stronger reaction to negative life events than we do to positive ones. To take just one example, in a survey of random American adults, having a very pleasant day did not influence the quality of the following day. Having a crappy day, on the other hand, did spill over into how people felt when they woke up (groggy), ate breakfast (porridge is prison food), and went to work (tailgating and cutting off cars to shave off two minutes on the motorway). This same pattern emerges time and again in psychological research.

- When sex works well in a marriage, it accounts for about 20 percent of the difference in marital satisfaction between spouses.

When sex goes poorly, on the other hand, it accounts for a whopping 50 to 75 percent of the variation.

- Schoolchildren were asked whether anybody in their class was an "undesirable friend." If they put someone on the undesirable list, they also described that person as being bad at sports and homework, as well as having a host of other failings. Yet, when they listed someone as a "desirable friend," the positive judgment had no influence on whether the person was also viewed as athletic, studious, or attractive.
- People react more strongly to unpleasant smells—wrinkling their noses longer—than they do to pleasant odors that briefly put a smile on their faces.

The Baumeister team has compiled a comprehensive and compelling case that negative events, experiences, relationships, and psychological states take an extra toll on our sensitivities, compared with their positive counterparts. You might wonder at this seemingly pessimistic conclusion, but we remind you that—in the abstract—negativity is our evolutionary birthright. Negative evaluations are essential to survival (that bitter leaf is also poisonous), and nowhere is this more true than in negative emotions. Emotions serve as a tracking system for experience, and provide a quick mental thumbs-up or -down that signals you to approach or avoid any given situation.

It is easy to see that having a brief spat with your spouse might be more memorable than a pleasant good-bye kiss in the morning, but what about unpleasant states such as frustration and disappointment? Are they felt more keenly than their upbeat cousins, enthusiasm and contentment? Try this as an entry point for thinking about negative emotions: take a moment and write down all the words for negative emotions you can think of, and then do the same for positive emotions. Most likely your first list is longer than the second. This may be because negative words carry more specific meaning than positive ones do (simply contrast *love* and *anger* or *happy* and *fear*). In another study, researchers interested in how people remember the emotional events of their lives tracked the actual day-to-day moods of adults and then had them recall the frequency and intensity of their emotions throughout the two-week study. As you might imagine, people were more prone to remember the intense events—both positive and negative. Interestingly, they underestimated the frequency of their past positive emotions but had no difficulty accurately recalling their negative events. We also have far more techniques for reducing, terminating, and tolerating negative emotions than we have skills for enhancing positive feelings.

Think back to the last time you had to navigate a customer service situation. Perhaps you were trying to make a doctor's appointment when few convenient times were available, or you may have been speaking with a credit card rep in an effort to get a onetime waiver on a late payment charge. Maybe you were speaking with an airline representative in hopes of finagling priority seating. Can you remember your approach? Did you adopt a warm tone and play nice? Or did you raise your voice and speak aggressively? You are a nice person, we're guessing, so you probably chose the kind route. The tough pill for most of us to swallow is that those overbearing screamers often get their way.

Feisty personalities, although unpleasant, can be tremendously effective. The psychological agility we're advocating here would expand your repertoire to give you access to the tougher, more direct, and sometimes more effective approach. You're probably avoiding this strategy because you think that being negative is, well, negative. You may think that aggressive, hostile, or downright mean people are generally jerks and that you don't want to run with that crowd. The good news is that a whole range of negativity—of beneficial negativity, mind you—has nothing to do with being a jerk.

Negative emotions can also help you focus on the situation at hand. When you are about to drill a hole in the wall, chances are that you pay close attention to the measurements involved as well as to the position of your hand. The anxiety associated with the downside risk encourages you to drill in exactly the right spot. (Cutting pieces of birthday cake with a plastic knife is a very different experience, in which a good-enough approach is, in fact, good enough.) Research by Kate Harkness from Queen's University shows that people prone to depressed moods also tend to notice more details. This is particularly true when it comes to facial expressions. Happy-go-lucky individuals take in the broad strokes—okay, you have a nose and some eyes and it looks like your eyebrows are raised. The less upbeat folks in the Harkness studies, by contrast, were eagle-eyed when it came to facial expression, attuned to the smallest quiver of a lip or the slightest narrowing of the eyes. This is why—and you've probably noticed this—when you are in a fight with your romantic partner (a negative event), you read even the tiniest changes in their demeanor, things you'd never notice when you were in a good mood. The point is this: if happy people gloss over the fine print and if that leads to more comfortable interactions, then shouldn't we all be satisfied with their close-enough approach? Well, no. Would you really prefer a happy, easy-going solicitor to a somewhat grumpier one who would be sure to catch every little problem in that new contract? We wouldn't either.

The culture of air traffic control (ATC) tends to the negative. This is, in part, because ATC is a safety-conscious industry in which the downside risk of mistakes can be high. At the minor end of the spectrum, errors lead to delays and logistical complications; at the other end, costs can run into tens of millions of dollars and hundreds of people dead. Pushing tin, as ATC work is sometimes irreverently called, requires an eye for detail; those little blips on the radar screen are actually airplanes, each with its own call number, altitude, speed, and flight plan. Negative emotions like anxiety and suspiciousness can act like an attentional funnel that narrows the mind's eye to important details. There is no room in ATC for good enough. In keeping with what we've seen, when all goes right in the control tower, no one notices; people only pay special attention when things go wrong.

Greg Petto, an air traffic controller in Louisville, Kentucky, told us that his tower is responsible for fifty square miles of air traffic between the ground and an altitude of ten thousand feet. This is a high-stress job in which planes that come within three miles of one another are cutting it dangerously close. Petto describes the radar room as a *dojo*, the Japanese word for a martial arts training room. The controllers manage seven hundred flights every day and their busiest time is in the middle of the night, when local Federal Express jets take to the skies in record numbers. We asked him whether knowing that FedEx is transporting packages, and not human cargo, makes ATC seem like less of a high-stakes game at night.

"To be honest," he replied, "I have to think of all planes as dots on a screen. If I stopped to actually think about the real deal up in the sky, I'd go crazy." And then he added, "It feels good though, to line up all the planes at just the right distance and at just the right time. It feels really good." Despite his pride in his work, Petto is the first to admit that there is a little negativity built into the controllers themselves. They can be a bit bratty or competitive when they get wound tight. "We deal with it by poking fun at one another, or by going home and praying, or drinking, depending on your cultural leanings."

It's important to linger here for a moment and point out that most people make a huge mistake where negative emotions are concerned. They typically separate the experience of negative feelings from the expression of negative feelings. Most people we chat with are quick to accept that feeling bad is a valid, and even inevitable, psychological experience. On the other hand, expressing frustration, or even too much sadness, is anathema to most folks. It's as if we expect ourselves to be computers, whose inner processes are largely hidden and divorced from what appears on the screen. This attitude exists in varying degrees across cultures; it's part of the idea that it's easier to live in a society where people are smiling than it is to coexist with people who are shouting. It misses the point that emotional expressions exist for a reason. Emotional expressions are an important way in which we communicate with others. A furrowed brow or a frown warns people off when you aren't in the mood (and sometimes you're not in the mood). A gasp of fear has a contagious effect such that bystanders also feel a jolt of adrenaline and look around nervously. Expressing feelings, including negative ones, is a big part of the human emotional experience.

If Negative Emotions Are So Helpful, Why Don't We Like Them More?

Take a moment to consider this: how much would you pay to avoid a repeat of that public speaking performance when the crowd refused to smile or stop fidgeting? Think of a time that you bullied an innocent person because of your insecurities: how much would it be worth to you to avoid replaying that cringeworthy experience? On the flip side, how much would you spend to relive the excitement of the first date with your now husband/wife/romantic partner? Think of the best massage in your life: how much would you spend for one just as relaxing, if you could have it right now?

Dr. Hi Po Bobo Lau from the University of Hong Kong and his team posed these very questions in their research. Enter the dreamlike scenario of participants in the study. Think of a specific time in your life when you felt very happy. Now, how much (assign a price tag between $2 and $200) would you be willing to spend to re-create this feeling? Once you come up with an exact dollar amount let's move on to other positive emotions. A sense of calm? Excitement? Now let's focus on negative emotions. Think of a specific memory when you felt intense regret. How much would you pay to avoid that feeling again? What about fear? Embarrassment? What we're asking you to do is put an exact dollar amount on each of these emotions. You might guess by now that avoiding pain was worth more money to participants than buying happiness. But let's be precise, down to the penny. This is what Dr. Lau's subjects were willing to pay:

$44.30 for calm tranquility,
$62.80 for excitement,
$79.06 for happiness,
$83.27 to avoid fear,
$92.80 to avoid sadness,
$99.81 to avoid embarrassment, and
$106.26 to avoid regret.

Only one emotion was more valuable than avoiding regret, and that was love. Sure, happiness, excitement, and feeling calm are good, but as social creatures we want someone who will accept, value, and care for our innermost self. Love was worth $113.55. If you, the reader, are not from Hong Kong, you might be skeptical about these dollar figures. So let it be known that when posed the same questions, adults from the United Kingdom had the same shopping experience: while tranquility ($53.47) and excitement ($60.90) were worth purchasing, they were no match for the need to escape embarrassment ($71.83) and regret ($64.40), and nothing was worth more than love ($115.16).

These dollar amounts offer a window into how motivated we human beings are to alter our inner and outer worlds. Of utmost importance is the desire to be accepted. This is a problem because we have zero control over what other people will say and do to us; we only control how we think and act. This lack of control, this feeling of uncertainty, might be the ultimate uncomfortable psychological state. Not far behind are fears of feeling regret and embarrassment. So the three most valuable emotional states center on how we are viewed by other people; unfortunately, concerns about negative emotions often get in the way of winning approval in the immediate moment. But this is only one reason for our hate-hate affair with negative emotions.

We avoid negative emotions not because we're too dumb to know better, but for four basic—and very intuitive—reasons:

1. They are unpleasant.
2. They represent getting stuck in a rut.
3. They are associated with a loss of personal control.
4. They are perceived (correctly!) as having social costs.

Let's take a closer look at these four fundamental motives. First, we avoid feeling crappy because feeling crappy feels crappy. That is, negative emotions are unpleasant. The idea of spending the afternoon experiencing stress or disappointment is about as enticing as spending the day getting a Brazilian wax treatment. People make a mistake not in their desire to avoid the unpleasant but, rather, in underestimating their ability to adequately tolerate the distress of negative emotions. As we saw in the example of the women waiting to learn whether they were pregnant, negative emotions actually feel a little less bad than most of us might anticipate. You have been both angry and fearful and—chances are—you are feeling neither in this particular moment; those feelings passed, and you're none the worse for living through them. You're more capable of handling unpleasant emotions than you give yourself credit for.

Consider the last time you were bored, for instance. Peter Toohey of the University of Calgary argues that boredom is a functional tool; it lets you know when social interactions or routines are leaving you with cravings that you're not satisfying. There may be little you can do about feeling bored when you're listening to a lengthy speech, or sitting in an airplane on a long flight, but often you can extract yourself from boring situations. Boredom is often an important indicator that you are making poor choices, or entering new situations with a limiting attitude (perhaps you're being closed-minded, or overly judgmental). More interesting still, while you likely loathe being bored, you deal with the feeling just fine in every single instance, and it passes before long. When you think about being bored, you naturally focus on how uncomfortable it is; what you gloss over is that you have effectively dealt with boredom hundreds (if not thousands) of times over the course of your life.

A second common reason people steer clear of negative emotions is the belief that these feelings are like quicksand—we can get bogged down in them and see no hope of escape. It is a common notion that depression, for instance, is a difficult state to change, and the more chronic the negative emotion the higher the risk that it might somehow become permanent. So let's take a look at Exhibit A, people who wrestle with depression for years. Here, in fact, some evidence supports the popular belief. Up to 60 percent of adults who have one clinically significant major depressive episode have a second, and those who have two have about a 70 percent chance of having a third, which then skyrockets to a 90 percent chance of having a fourth. Yes, these statistics are alarming, especially if you forget to do the maths. If a hundred people struggle with a bout of depression, then sixty of them go on to a second episode, forty-two suffer a third episode, and thirty-eight have a fourth. For those thirty-eight people, this is a serious problem, no doubt. But a large majority of the people who wrestle with depression will not be confined to an emotional prison from which there is no escape. Most will be freed after a small handful of—admittedly unpleasant—episodes. The same is true of other emotions: while there is a tendency to worry that anger will flip some internal switch turning us into violent thugs, or that panic will imprison us to a life of cowering under tables, you have to look no further than your personal experience to know this isn't true.

A third reason we avoid unpleasant feelings is that we fear that, like a psychological tsunami, they'll crash over us and sweep us away to some random—and perhaps unwanted—destination of thoughts and behavior. That is, people are typically afraid, even if they do not often articulate this concern, that their moods may lead them to lose control and do things they otherwise wouldn't. The most obvious case of this is anger. There is, of course, an element of truth to this, which has led to the US justice system's stance that second-degree murder in the heat of the moment is less serious than planned first-degree murder. It's as if the legal community got together and agreed, "Yes, there is a tendency for hotheaded people to get a bit out of control." But how many people do you know who've committed murder in the first or the second degree? It's extremely unusual, which is why it makes the news.

Anger is unlikely to make you a criminal, but it can affect you in surprising ways. Researchers were interested in the term *hotheaded* and wondered whether anger is somehow associated in people's minds with heat. In one study, they presented some (but not all) participants with words related to anger, such as *scornful*, *hostile*, and *irritated* and told them that these words were part of a memory experiment. They then asked the participants, in a separate task, to guess whether the temperature of thirty unfamiliar cities was, on average, hot or cold. The researchers found that participants who were primed with angry words were far more likely to guess that a place was hot.

The fourth reason we avoid negative emotions is that we fear the social consequences of expressing them. You have an intuitive sense that if you mope around the office, or have unpredictable angry outbursts, people will hide in their cubicles until you walk past. Once again, there's a grain of truth in this belief, but our fears are much exaggerated. Our negative moods do have power over others. In a classic study, researcher Thomas Joiner examined whether the moods of roommates are contagious. What he found was that if one of the roommates was depressed at the initial assessment, it increased the likelihood that the other would develop depression over the subsequent three weeks. This was true even when Joiner controlled for baseline rates of depression and the presence or absence of negative life events. Not only was depression infectious, but, contrary to recent folklore, the depressed roommate is more likely to affect the other negatively than the happier roommate is to turn the depressed roommate's mood around. Yet another example of how bad is stronger than good.

Right now you may be surprised by the fact that we, the authors, haven't gone through the four major reasons people avoid negative emotions and debunked them, one by one. We can't. All of them have at least some validity. The important question is this: what purpose do negative emotions serve? As it turns out, they're an important part of our healthy emotional architecture. Although they can be messy, unpleasant, and sometimes problematic, negative emotions are also very useful. Emotions—all emotions—are information. Feeling good and feeling bad let us know about the quality of our progress, our interactions, our environment, and our actions. Simply put, your emotions are like a GPS monitor on the dashboard of your car, giving you metaphorical information about your location, the terrain in front of and behind you, and your rate of progress. People who try desperately to escape, conceal, and avoid negative states, miss out on all this valuable information. To be absolutely clear about this,

- you *want* to feel the prickle of fear in situations where physical harm is possible;
- you *want* to feel the thrust of anger when you need to stick up for your children;
- you *want* to feel frustration when you make inadequate progress in your guitar lessons; and
- you *want* to regret telling your children they aren't intelligent, attractive, or good people.

In each instance, these emotions signal that something isn't going right and needs your imminent attention. Immediately trying to tamp down the bad emotion of anger, or any other feeling, does little to shed light on why the anger has arisen and what course of action it might be pointing to. It's difficult to emphasize how important this is. *The reasons to avoid negative emotions seem legion*, you might be thinking, *but let me get this straight: there is only one reason they are good?* But even if there's only one, it is a really terrific reason. Just imagine living in a world in which no one really felt disappointment when they failed at a cherished goal. Or in which you could not access fear even in the presence of a fire in the home basement, or a dirty hypodermic needle floating next to you during an ocean swim. Without such so-called negative feelings, we would be living in a world devoid of fully functioning humans.

A Tour of Three Dreaded Emotions

Anger

Matthew Jacobs is a self-employed carpenter in his fifties. He lives in a San Francisco apartment-style co-op. He has a reputation for high-quality workmanship and enjoys playing football and reading nonfiction in his downtime. When he was younger, he did a stint as a military police officer during the Vietnam War. He describes his younger self as hotheaded but has long since cooled his jets and aimed to live a trouble-free life.

Late one night in May 2013, a female Vietnamese street vendor in the downtown corridor was handing Jacobs a bowl of *pho* when a large man approached and began screaming at her. The man—a total stranger—demanded a pen from the woman, and, when she said she didn't have one, he cursed at her using racial epithets. Also present were two high school girls who fidgeted nervously, obviously afraid of attracting attention to themselves.

As the newcomer's tirade got more and more heated, Jacobs realized that no one nearby was going to step up and protect either the vendor or the two teenagers. Drawing on one of his personal maxims—always offer two kind interactions before taking a more aggressive tone—he said quietly to the stranger, "Excuse me. Could you please lower your voice?" The man then turned on Jacobs and began berating him too. "I'd appreciate it if you could just move on," Jacobs calmly offered. "We're trying to eat in peace here; no one wants any trouble." In his own mind, Jacobs had just used up his second and final allotment of goodwill. Unfortunately, it didn't have the soothing effect he'd hoped for. Instead, the raging man stepped closer to Jacobs, screaming obscenities.

Jacobs carefully put down his bowl of noodles and ratcheted up the menace in his voice. "Where I grew up," he challenged, "this means you're looking for a fight. Well, here I am. Let's go!" The angry man stepped back in surprise, muttered a couple of face-saving curses, and walked away. Jacobs allowed himself a few deep breaths to calm down, grateful the confrontation had not come to blows, and that neither of the young people nor the food vendor had been hurt. He glanced at them, half expecting a nod of appreciation or a word of thanks. None came. Instead, he saw that they seemed as afraid of him as they had been of the abusive man.

This is a true story, not a dramatized account in which a brawl breaks out, or in which a damsel in distress rewards her rescuer with her undying affection. It's an example of negative emotions as they show up in real life. Negative emotions, anger in Jacob's case, often surface as a result of external circumstances (as opposed to "coming from nowhere"). They can be tremendously useful, even though costs (like turning off bystanders) might be incurred. As we see here, anger often dramatically alters other people's behavior, most often causing them to retreat, or compromise quickly. For this very reason, anger—and other negative feelings—are sometimes more appropriate than positivity.

Anger is in itself neither good nor bad; it's what you do with it that matters. Research suggests that only 10 percent of angry episodes actually lead to some form of violence, which is evidence that anger does not exactly equal aggression. Anger usually arises because we believe we've been treated unfairly, or that something is blocking our ability to accomplish meaningful goals. In our data, we coded 3,679 days when people reported feeling angry in everyday life. We discovered that 63.3 percent of these episodes were blamed on other people (as opposed to, let's say, on a computer keyboard). Anger is typically caused by what other people did, didn't do, or might possibly do.

The difficulty of navigating a complex, often unpredictable world of social exchanges that might include anger is precisely the reason why adult humans possess such hefty brains (47 times heavier than cat brains, and 19.5 times heavier than beagle brains). We have all been offended or hurt by another person. Despite your kind and compassionate vibe, you too have been nagged, teased, bullied, betrayed, lied to, and treated rudely. Positivity alone is insufficient to the task of helping us navigate social interactions and relationships. Anger is a tool that helps us read and respond to upsetting social situations. As for its benefits, research overwhelmingly indicates that feeling angry increases optimism, creativity, and effective performance, and that expressing anger leads to more successful negotiations and a fast track for mobilizing people into agents of change. Let's look at each case individually.

First, feeling anger is associated with a more optimistic outlook. In one study, participants were asked to turn over as many of thirty-two cards—each with a specific point value—as they wanted. Embedded within the thirty-two cards, however, were three bankruptcy cards that—if drawn—would cost the participants hundreds of points (far more than the meager number of points gained from other cards). In one condition, participants were allowed to choose how many cards they would risk turning over ahead of time, any number between one and thirty-two. Presumably, nobody would want to turn over all thirty-two because three of those cards would bankrupt them and stop the game. How many did they turn over? It turned out that people who had earlier been induced to feel mildly angry took bigger risks. Anger led them to feel more inclined to explore the boundaries of possibility.

This finding was also supported by a research team interested in how people make risk assessments. In this study, researchers asked participants questions related to—among other things—the perceived risk of getting a divorce, contracting a venereal disease, and an experimental treatment for a serious illness that would save many lives if it worked but would kill even more if it failed. When researchers put some of the participants in an angry mood, the participants were more likely to feel they had control over outcomes, believed a positive outcome was highly probable, and were confident that taking risks would pay off. It may be that anger—a high arousal emotion that prepares us to deal with threats—is helpful in prepping people for action in general. This may be why it is so common to see athletes psyching themselves up by getting mad.

Second, anger can help spark creativity. This is worth repeating in case it sounds too crazy to believe: yes, anger can help us be creative. In psychology, the study of creativity can be a lot of fun. Take this classic example: how many uses can you think of for a brick? Feel free to take a moment right now and write down as many as you can imagine. Chances are good that the most obvious uses come to mind first. You can easily envision building a wall with a brick. You can then get crafty and think of uses that have to do with the brick's weight, shape, and durability. Perhaps your list includes using the brick as a doorstop, as a paper weight, a small stepping stool, or a projectile weapon. Pretty good. But what about truly unusual applications for a brick? What about putting a brick in a backpack to get physically fit? What about using it to hold a hot kitchen pot, or wedged into a tire to provide a backup parking brake for a car on a steep hill? You might even use it as a prop for poking fun at first-generation mobile phones by holding it up to your ear and talking into it.

Psychologists adopt the uses-for-a-brick task as one measure of creativity. This task can assess fluency (how many ideas are created?) as well as originality (how many ideas do not commonly show up on other lists?) and flexibility (how many different categories of use can you generate?). In one study, researchers gave people either angry or neutral feedback on a different assignment and then had them complete the uses-for-a-brick task. It turns out that certain people—those with a high need to understand the rules of a situation and prefer a sense of control in a situation—performed better if they received angry feedback. By performed better, we mean that they outperformed a similar group of people who were given neutral feedback. The take-home message here is that in some cases anger led to more creativity. On the other hand, less grounded, rebellious people had their creativity dampened by anger. This is another illustration that context matters when it comes to anger, and that a general prejudice against it is misguided.

Finally, anger is selectively useful as a performance-enhancement tool. No one wants to live under a tyrant, but a little burst of irritation can send people scrambling to work. Parents know this is sometimes an effective strategy with their children, and many bosses know it as well. In a study of construction managers in the United Kingdom, researchers discovered that though some angry outbursts were regrettable and ineffective, others were the perfect prescription. One manager commented:

> Not too long ago in a project meeting, I had a rather emotional outbreak with the structural engineer, on the basis that they were trying to turn the tables contractually without any justification, and it had been going on for quite a while. . . . It [the meeting] concluded with an emotional outburst, I'm afraid. Retrospectively, did I regret it? Probably not, actually, because it resolved the matter.

What set regrettable spats apart from those seen as effective was not the amount of anger involved. It was, instead, a matter of context. However, even the managers who sometimes favored an angry word recognized that this was not—and couldn't be—a perennial approach to interacting with others. One summed it up nicely:

> It worked, it had the response I was hoping it would, everybody went out onto site and what hadn't been addressed was taken care of straightaway, so it all in all worked. I think if that happened often, you know, if you were always swearing at

people, eventually it would reach a point where it wouldn't have an effect. So if you use it every once in a while, I think it works.

Another context in which anger works well is negotiations. When two or more people are trying to come to a resolution, anger provides some leverage. In one series of studies, participants were given the task of negotiating for the highest price possible for a batch of mobile phones (and their real-world reward was directly tied to their performance). After the seller requested an initial price, the buyer responded with a series of counteroffers. For the purposes of the experiment, some of the participants were paired with an angry buyer, and others with a happy or neutral buyer. It turns out that, in the face of anger, people are far less likely to make strong demands. By the third round of negotiations, the person trying to sell phones to an angry buyer relented, giving a steep 20 percent discount, and by the sixth round, forked over 33 percent of their potential earnings. The researchers suggest that angry people are viewed as powerful and of high status in the moment. Thus, being angry by itself tilts certain kinds of competition in your favor. Happiness simply does not offer the same dividends.

That said, it may not be enough to simply adopt an angry stance in the hope of striking a favorable deal. Some of the same researchers caution—and the science is on their side—against faking anger. In one study, the researchers found that when a trained actor faked surface anger, as opposed to expressing deep anger, the ploy actually backfired. People in negotiations make higher demands of those who display fake anger, in part because they are seen as less trustworthy.

Take the real-world example of Barack Obama. Regardless of your particular political stripes, you have to admit that Obama comes across as mellower than most US presidents. He is a smooth speaker with an even-keeled deep voice. When the BP oil well spilled into the Gulf of Mexico in 2010, President Obama caught flack for his cool response. He later expressed anger on television, but this more emotional response had precisely the opposite of the desired effect: people perceived the president as being disingenuous.

Finally, anger has power in prompting collective action against unfair, inappropriate threats. In one autobiography after another, we found the same story: the initial prompt to fight against injustice was motivated by anger, like the spark that ignites the fuel in an engine. Martin Luther King Jr. said, "The supreme task is to organize and unite people so that their anger becomes a transforming force." It was anger that transformed W. E. B. Du Bois from a scholar—brilliant but ineffective in a world where exploitation and racism were rampant—into a powerful civil rights activist:

> At the very time when my studies were most successful, there cut across this plan which I had as a scientist, a red ray which could not be ignored. I remember when it first, as it were, startled me to my feet. . . . The news met me: Sam Hose had been lynched, and they said that his knuckles were on exhibition at a grocery store. . . . I began to turn aside from my work. . . . One could not be a calm, cool, and detached scientist while Negroes were lynched, murdered, and starved.

A bit later in his autobiography, Du Bois describes how anger eventually spurred him to action, and he founded the Niagara Movement, which later developed into the National Association for the Advancement of Colored People.

In recalling his activities on behalf of conscientious objectors to World War I, Bertrand Russell explains how he became "filled with despairing tenderness toward the young men who were to be slaughtered, and with rage against all the statesmen of Europe." Similarly, Helen Caldicott took her first steps as a peace activist when she "became indignant." Her indignation inspired a generation of social movements.

When anger arises, we feel called upon to prevent or terminate immediate threats to our welfare, or to the well-being of those we care about. Altruism is often born from anger; when it comes to mobilizing other people and creating support for a cause, no emotion is stronger. It's a mistake to presume that kindness, compassion, love, and fairness line up on one side of a continuum, and anger, rage, and dislike, on another side. Anger is a powerful element that is maligned by the mistaken notion that a healthy society is an anger-free society.

The deep prejudice against anger is largely unjustified. It is, admittedly, a strong and highly inflammatory emotion. Caution around anger is certainly smart, as is the knowledge that it should not be overused, or used with everyone. Anger is best wielded with an attitude of respect for the perspective of the particular person or persons who violated your well-being. Prepare for the fallout and it becomes easier to tailor the most effective expression of anger. With these caveats, the expression of anger—authentic anger—can be entirely appropriate with certain people in certain situations.

The Right Way to Get Angry

When you want to express anger, or any negative emotion, one way to do so is to start with what we call the *discomfort caveat.* Let other people know explicitly that you are experiencing intense emotions and because of this, it is more difficult than usual for you to communicate clearly. Apologize in advance, not for your emotions or your actions but for the potential lack of clarity in how you convey what you're about to say. Lead in with a statement such as "I want you to know that I'm feeling uncomfortable right now, which means it's not the best time for me to be expressing myself. But, under the circumstances, it's important for me to say . . ." The aim of the discomfort caveat is to disarm the person, to keep them from becoming defensive. When someone hears that you are uncomfortable and that the conversation is difficult for you, it increases the likelihood that they will approach what you have to say with empathy. After using this opening, you can then delve deeper into what bothers you, what you think and feel in the aftermath of whatever happened (why anger emerged instead of other feelings).

Consider using this discomfort caveat even if you are perfectly comfortable expressing anger or other negative emotions, so long as they're genuine. Remember, the aim is to trigger a change in what the other person is doing or feeling, to shift the momentum in a given situation so that it is more favorable to your message. Properly controlled, anger offers us a way to be proactive about removing threats and roadblocks. So don't be afraid to use small physical displays of anger, what we might call *micro-aggression*, to express the level of emotion you're experiencing. Push your hands forcefully into a table. Tighten your hands into fists. You get the idea.

If we haven't convinced you yet of the importance of expressing anger openly when you feel a looming threat needs to be quashed, then consider this. Dr. Ernest Harburg and his research team at the University of Michigan School of Public Health spent several decades tracking the same adults in a longitudinal study of anger. They found that men and women who hid the anger they felt in response to an unjust attack subsequently found themselves more likely to get bronchitis and heart attacks, and were more likely to die earlier than peers who let their anger be known when other people were annoying.

The obvious difficulty lies in figuring out how to put angry feelings to work, especially in relationships. First, we want to discourage you from making self-statements that push for trying to control or avoid anger, such as "I need to get rid of my anger," or "I need to keep this anger to myself," or "Why can't I be less angry?" Instead, recognize the difference between events that you can change and those that are beyond your ability to control. If you are on a trip and you lose your winter hat on the first day, there is nothing you can change, so there is no benefit in expressing anger. But if you are haggling with a shopkeeper at a flea market over the price of a hat and you're angry that you've been quoted a higher price than the last customer, you possess some control. Now, in this situation, how do you appropriately communicate annoyance or anger in a way that leads to a healthy outcome? Psychologist and editor of *Anger Disorders*, Dr. Howard Kassinove mentions that the key is to use "an appropriate tone without demeaning the other person."

Second, slow the situation down. Our initial tendency is to jump into a situation and act immediately, especially in cases where our blood is boiling. Instead, try thinking of anger as coming in both fast and slow varieties, when you want to scream versus when you want to motivate a person in a calculated way. When you're angry, give yourself permission to pause for a moment, even if someone is standing there awaiting a response. You can even let them know that you are intentionally slowing the situation down. Choose to make good decisions rather than fast ones. When you're angry, pauses, deep breaths, and moments of reflection more effectively exercise power and control than rapid-fire responses. If you feel less angry when you slow down, great, but that's not the goal. This is about giving yourself a wider range of options to choose from in an emotionally charged situation.

Think like a chess player. Before deciding on a course of action, imagine how the other person will counter and how the situation might look two moves from now. If it looks good, continue along your present path. If it looks bad, consider an alternative behavior, imagine how they will counter that, and evaluate this scenario. Keep checking in with yourself by asking, "Is my anger helping or hurting the situation?" When you're engaged in dialogue with someone else, there is no one-size-fits-all answer to this question because the emotions and actions involved are constantly shifting. At one point I might want to assert my dominance by telling a story, and a few minutes later I might want to increase the feeling of connection by ignoring an incendiary remark.

When we become extremely angry, it seems that if we don't go into attack mode we'll suffer serious consequences. Psychologist John Riskind, an expert in helping people with seemingly uncontrollable emotions, has come up with techniques for slowing down the speed of threatening events. Riskind has found that the experience of anger is not as problematic as the belief that the sequence of events triggering that anger is accelerating, that the danger is escalating, and the available window for taking action is quickly disappearing. This sense of impending danger pushes people to do something that might stop the immediate threat but in the longer term will make the situation worse (such as punching the person who cut you off in line at the grocery checkout).

The first step is to check in with yourself frequently to assess whether your anger is increasing, decreasing, or stable in the given situation. For a scrupulous self-examination, use a number and even a few descriptive words to capture the intensity of your anger, as you'll see in this speedometer example:

90 MILES PER HOUR AND ABOVE	BOILING, EXPLOSIVE, VIOLENT
85 MILES PER HOUR	FUMING, OUTRAGED
80 MILES PER HOUR	INFURIATED, ENRAGED
75 MILES PER HOUR	IRATE, EXASPERATED
65 MILES PER HOUR	BITTER, INDIGNANT
60 MILES PER HOUR	PISSED OFF
55 MILES PER HOUR	MAD, ANGRY
50 MILES PER HOUR	AGITATED, PERTURBED
45 MILES PER HOUR	ANNOYED, IRRITATED, FRUSTRATED
40 MILES PER HOUR	RUFFLED, DISPLEASED
35 MILES PER HOUR AND BELOW	CALM AND COOL, PEACEFUL, TRANQUIL

If your anger is well above the speed limit, you're going to need more time in order to retain maximum flexibility and control in dealing with the person who provoked or upset you. In this case, consider slowing the speedometer. At this high speed, you probably feel a bit out of control. Imagine putting on the brakes so that the way you're acting and the way others are responding goes from eighty-five miles per hour to sixty-five, and then from sixty-five to fifty-five. Create a visual image of what you would look like and how other people would appear to you. Notice how they no longer seem as physically close to you. Listen carefully to what the other person is saying, and read the underlying message in their body language. Use the lower speed to see whether the person bothering you is open to conversation or closed off, whether they're really looking to attack or are looking for a way out of this jam.

How does it feel when you imagine things slowing down? As Riskind says about anger, "You might think there are too many things to do and not enough time to do them." This exercise, focusing on the speed that threats are moving, gives us a little more psychological breathing room. Experiment with this tool. The overall objective here is to learn how to work with your anger.

Guilt and Shame

In contemporary society, people have come to think of guilt much the way they think of being fat—as a dreaded state that is both unhealthy and socially unacceptable. Perhaps this is why weight gain is often associated with guilt. In our culture, to guilt-trip someone is seen as underhanded; therapists offer guilt reduction, self-help gurus encourage people to let themselves off the hook, and life coaches scorn the use of the word *should.* By contrast, we want to remove the stigma from guilt. We aren't saying that it's always good to feel guilty. But at times it certainly conveys benefits, one of which is that when you feel guilty you're more motivated to improve your behavior than your less-guilt-prone peers.

Doug Hensch, a tad over forty years old, helps organizations develop stronger leaders, but his passion in life is coaching his nine-year-old son's American football team. His favorite coaching experience came when he was dealing with a fast, muscular, athletic player on the team named Zander, who had moved to the United States from Ghana. It was too bad that instead of applying those gifts to the football field, Zander was usually squirting other kids with water bottles or trying to jab a licked finger into someone else's ear. Fed up, Doug called a team meeting where he could speak to Zander and the rest of the team.

Doug was not looking forward to the conversation, and he didn't try to hide it when the time came. Beginning with a discomfort caveat ("I'm a parent, I'm your coach, but I also was a kid who played American football from the age of nine until I was twenty-one, just like most of you will. So I know team meetings with a frustrated coach are difficult;

please understand that it's uncomfortable for me, too"). Doug then proceeded to say,

> I want you to look at your teammates. I want you to think of all the effort each of your teammates puts in each week, getting hit, getting dirty, getting sweaty, getting out of breath, and sometimes wanting to puke. Now I want you to consider one question: *Is what you're doing helping or hurting the team?*

After sitting quietly for a full minute, Doug asked each player on the team to give an example from that day's practice of how they helped the team. Then he asked each player to come up with one example from that season when they had done something to hurt the team, even if it was minor. Everybody on the team had something to say, and after the last kid spoke, Doug said,

> When you do something that doesn't help the team, you are hurting your friends, kids who will protect you, fight for you, and risk getting hurt by someone twice their size on the other side of the ball so you can make the play. From now on I'm going to be asking you this question a lot, and when you see that you're hurting the team I don't want you to feel bad; I want you to do something about it. You got it?

When he saw the pack of heads nodding together, he asked them to huddle up, put their hands together, and scream the team name three times.

Zander lost his coveted spot on the starting team. Doug will tell you that the next time Zander started a game and got the ball he ran eighty yards for a touchdown, which led to the team's first win of the season. And when Zander saw that his teammates respected him more for actions that helped rather than hurt the team (even though some of his antics were really funny), he invested new energy in practice, cheered on his teammates from the sideline, and generally showcased a wholly different attitude. Doug's task with Zander was to help him transition into a responsible young adult, and by being transparent about his own discomfort and by inducing a bit of guilt, Doug succeeded.

We, the authors, have used this same question in university classrooms ("Is what you are doing helping or hurting the class?"), and while parenting our children ("Is what you are doing helping or hurting this situation?"). As socially awkward psychologists, we ask this question of ourselves when we're talking to other people ("Is what we are doing helping or hurting the relationship?"). We ask you to consider this question in regard to guilt: is it going to help or hurt you in the quest to become a better, stronger, wiser person?

For another example of how helpful guilt can be, let's turn to those who have been temporarily banned from society for their wrongdoings: jail inmates. According to the National Recidivism Study of Released Prisoners conducted by the US Bureau of Justice, of the 272,111 inmates released from fifteen states in 1994, 67.5 percent were rearrested for a felony or serious misdemeanor within three years. A new crime after release from jail is the norm, not the exception.

Hearing these statistics, you might believe that inmates are evil people. Or you may believe that most inmates are not much different from the rest of us—they want to find a place where they belong, find some semblance of meaning and purpose in their lives, and hope that their kids have a better life than their parents did. Either way, let's ask the key question: what prevents a jailed inmate from returning to illegal or immoral acts? June Tangney, a distinguished clinical psychologist, has spent nearly a decade asking whether moral emotions such as guilt are the secret sauce for preventing crime. In recent research, Dr. Tangney found that inmates who were prone to feeling guilty about past wrongs suffered more for what they had done, and in turn were motivated to confess, apologize, and fix the problems they caused. After being released from jail, these guilt-prone inmates were less likely to be arrested again for criminal acts. That is, inmates who tend to feel guilty for the harm they caused beat the statistical odds and stay out of trouble.

Guilt adds to our moral fiber, motivating us to be more socially sensitive and caring citizens than we might be otherwise, and these benefits of guilt extend to the noncriminal community. For instance, researchers have found that adults prone to feeling guilty were less likely to drive drunk, steal, use illegal drugs, or assault another person. If character is reflected in what you do when nobody is looking, then this moral emotion called guilt is one of its building blocks. By ignoring the value of guilt, parents and schools face a bigger uphill climb in cultivating good kids who will ensure the future of a healthy society.

The failed public relations campaign for guilt is a direct consequence of confusing guilt with shame. According to the *American Heritage Dictionary*, guilt is the "remorseful awareness of having done something wrong" and the "self-reproach for supposed inadequacy or wrongdoing." Shame is a different beast. When we feel ashamed, we don't just see our behavior as wrong or mistaken, we view ourselves as being fundamentally bad people. With guilt, this awareness of wrongdoing is limited to a specific situation, but shame is experienced as a negative metric of who we are. Guilt is helpful. As for its emotional cousin, shame, not so much. Guilt is local; shame is global.

There are helpful and unhelpful ways to feel bad for our failures and wrongdoings. To understand how to add helpful negativity to your psychological tool kit, let's take a look at the differences.

What is SHAME?	What is GUILT?
Focus on the entire self	Focus on the victim and the act that harmed them
Feel bad about who we are	Feel bad about what we did
Ask: How could *I* have done that?	Ask: How could I have *done that*?
Feel extreme distress and impairment	Feel moderate pain
Believe in no control over adverse outcomes	Believe in personal control over adverse outcomes
Desire to shrink, avoid, escape	Feel tension and remorse
Motivated to hide or attack (self or others)	Motivated to repair damage, make amends
Blame others (find scapegoats)	Take personal responsibility

People who feel shame suffer. Shamed people dislike themselves and want to change, hide, or get rid of their self. People who feel guilt are invested in learning from their mistakes and motivated to become better. Although they don't want their transgression on a placard hanging from their neck, guilt-prone people are less concerned about hiding bad deeds. The reason? They're ready to repair the damage and willing to work so it doesn't happen again. As for shame, let's take a look at the dark residue this emotion leaves. Remember that adults are more willing to pay exorbitant amounts of money to avoid reliving regrets. Let's explore why.

It has been fewer than six months since your last whiskey and one reason for this sobriety has been Alcoholics Anonymous meetings. As a newly sober adult, you are approached by strangers interested in hearing your story. Because it is typical to talk about personal problems at

AA meetings, you relent and even agree to be videotaped. Among questions about how you started drinking, how this has affected your relationships, and so on, the interviewer asks, "Describe the last time you drank and felt bad about it." It's a tough request that brings back painful memories, which you address honestly. You don't hear back from the interviewer for four months and when you do, they pull out a calendar and ask you to go back through every day since the interview to track how much you've been drinking. Because you are told this will be confidential and anonymous, you fill in the calendar.

This is exactly happened in a recent study. The interviewer was either Dr. Jessica Tracy or her graduate student Daniel Randles, at the University of British Columbia, and they did something creative. Dr. Tracy wanted to know whether displays of shame when discussing drinking helped predict which newly sober adults would lose their resolve and resume binge drinking. (If you want to detect shame in somebody's bodily movements, keep an eye out for slumped shoulders and narrowing in the chest area, as if he or she is curling into a fetal position.)

The results of the study might boggle your mind. Over the course of four months, newly sober adults who showed no shame during that interview had 7.91 drinks. Those who showed the greatest shame in those interviews (the top 10 percent)—get this—on average *consumed 117.89 drinks during the same period.* Those who had a shameful relationship with their drinking behavior found it much harder to recover from a slip-up.

Turning Hawks into Doves

Everyone makes mistakes. At work, you might assume responsibility for ordering flowers for a sick coworker and then forget to send them. At home, you might complain about your neighbor's lack of attention to their garbage and their garden, only to find out later that they have been bedridden with pneumonia. Feeling guilty, by definition, pushes us away from feeling happy. But although it comes at the expense of our immediate happiness, we've seen how guilt can help us in the long term; in addition, guilt benefits other people. As researcher Roy Baumeister puts it, guilt "makes us feel bad, but to avoid those feelings we do things that are better for our relationship partners and fellow group members." Attuned by guilt to the effect of our actions on someone else, we're prompted to act in more socially sensitive ways next time.

On the other hand, if you feel shame, expect your problems to escalate, and trying to get somebody else to change their behavior for the better by shaming them is not going to work either. We hope these words will be read by well-meaning parents who punish their child by making him or her walk up and down the block with a sign saying, "I watched pornography on the family computer." We hope they will be considered by those who think it's a good idea to make those undertaking community service wear high-visibility vests to mark them out as offenders. We hope this information reaches teachers who place a chart on the wall detailing how many times a six-year-old hit or bit another classmate. These tactics do not lead to improvement; they do not encourage people to become considerate, team players. The research on this is clear: the more shame a person feels, the more anxious, aggressive, and detached they become. Using shame as a form of punishment has the tragic paradoxical effect of increasing the behavior you're attempting to stamp out.

If you wish to motivate, choose guilt over shame. As Dr. June Tangney says, "We feel guilty because we care—an important message of reassurance for those whom we've hurt or offended." Flawed acts do not provide evidence that you are a flawed person. Take responsibility for your actions, feel the pain of harming other people when it happens, and draw your attention to no more and no less than the specific action that led to that harm. Experiment, make mistakes, fail, get upset, and then be more attuned to the welfare of other people in your next round of social interactions.

How to Escape the Shame Trap

Assuming that you are no stranger to compassion, we offer these suggestions for inspiring guilt without shame.

Keep the goal in mind. One common mistake in dealing with a guilty party is jumping straight into a personal attack. It's easy to quickly and even unconsciously conflate guilt with an absence of values, with stupidity, with greed, or any number of other character flaws. The problem is that nobody wants to be told they are bad. People are more open to being told that they have done something bad. You are more likely to get the point across if you reinforce the person's strengths and virtues (only if you see them, don't make them up) but still hold them accountable for their actions.

Start by establishing common ground. If someone did something wrong, show them, where possible, that you share their values and goals. Then point out how their behavior moves them away from those values and how alternative, healthier behaviors are more aligned with who they are. Another place to find common ground, as we discussed earlier, is by sharing your discomfort. These conversations are difficult, and sometimes it feels as if it would be easier to let bad behavior slide. It is typically just as uncomfortable for the person wagging a scolding finger as it is for the person squirming in regret about their misdeeds. If you want the feedback to stick and improve someone's future behavior, be honest up front about how the conversation makes you uncomfortable.

Instead of trying to control others, offer autonomy. Contrary to popular thought, people don't mind being told what to do. Consider this: you gladly take out the trash when asked, you turn in reports when deadlines loom, and when family members ask for something at the grocery store, you add it to your list. What people do mind is being told how to do something. No one wants advice on how to correctly replace a garbage bag, how to format a report they have been working on for weeks, or how to compare prices at the local supermarket. Scientists who study human motivation now know that one of our basic needs, right up there with physical survival, is the desire to direct our own life. When confronting a guilty party, do not give instructions about what they should do in the future. Instead, give them autonomy to come up with helpful modifications they can make. The aftermath of wrongdoing leads to the best outcomes when the plan to improve behavior is viewed as a collaborative, creative process between the perpetrator and victim.

Anxiety

Much has been written on the value of anxiety. In brief, too little anxiety suggests a situation that is boring and lacking in stimulation, effectively putting the mind into hibernation mode where attention, motivational priorities, and energy are shifted away from the current activity. As you might suspect, business managers are not excited by this prospect because employees tend to shift toward finding stimulation elsewhere by playing video games or bantering with coworkers. Too much anxiety suggests a situation that can be overwhelming, effectively paralyzing a person. As long as this experience of anxiety is brief, performance will take a dip, but in the end you will be fine. We all know the havoc prolonged periods of intense anxiety wreaks on our physical and mental health. When we experience too much anxiety too often, we age prematurely; we can see this at the cellular level when the telomeres that protect the ends of the chromosomes deteriorate. So authors, performance experts, and business leaders aim for people to experience the "just right" amount of anxiety, enough that they get the motivational butterflies without the out-of-control panic attacks and chronic stress. Sounds good and we agree wholeheartedly.

We just wonder why this has been the end of the story. In the early Sahara, our hominid ancestors living in small hunter-gatherer communities survived because of a specific set of anxiety circuits. Designed by natural selection, developed over the course of our evolutionary history, this specialized anxiety program operates largely outside our awareness, underappreciated for the nearly effortless way that it solves problems for us. Like us, you probably have been told that positive emotions expand your thinking and behavior in the moment, whereas anxiety narrows your thinking and behavior, causing you to miss the forest for the trees. To this we say that broader is not better than narrower. What is important is that you take advantage of each of these software packages installed in your brain. What happens when there is the possibility of danger and the anxiety mental program is activated?

Let's consider three problematic situations that would initiate your anxiety mental program. Somebody is tearing you down in front of a group of people in hopes that they get a boost in social status at the expense of yours. A person you have been romantically involved with is behaving oddly; he or she was late to your dinner date and there are long awkward moments during the evening that haven't arisen before. You get odd heart palpitations while talking to someone about a financial problem; you've never had this feeling before. In these situations, and many others that induce anxious thoughts and feelings, the ancient part of your brain associated with survival is already considering three courses of action: fleeing, fighting, or freezing. This process is taking place without any conscious contribution on your part. In fact, much has been made of the way the process can cause undue stress, given that survival is no longer the daily struggle it was when we shared the planet with saber-toothed tigers.

However, there are still surprising gems in that hardwired anxiety program, strengths that are hidden from us until that moment we feel anxious. In these moments, you get access to heightened perception, including amplified vision, being able to see things at a greater distance; and amplified hearing, being able to tune out random sounds to get greater clarity on the noise being made in a particular direction. You also get a bump in your ability to solve problems. To take an example from evolutionary psychologists John Tooby and Leda Cosmides, "Odd places that you normally would not occupy—a hallway closet, the branches of a tree—suddenly may become salient as instances of the category *safe* or *hiding place*."

Missing from prior discussions of anxiety are the ways it helps drive your success, and that of the family, romantic partnership, and the organization for which you may work. The surprising truth about anxiety is this:

- In some situations, you want to be a highly anxious person.
- You need an anxious person on your team.
- Without anxiety, small problems can easily end up morphing into a disaster.

We've discussed the fact that mistakes are a necessary part of becoming creative and innovative. Without mistakes, we don't learn and evolve. But let's not overestimate the value of mistakes; we want to catch them early enough so we can learn the lessons involved without anyone dying in the process. This is where the value of anxiety takes center stage.

When we're anxious, we serve the same function as canaries in a mine shaft; we're sentinels, helping other people by reacting quickly and vocally to early potential signs of danger. This works according to the five s's:

- *Scare.* Anxious people are on high alert for any slight shift in their environment. They are therefore extremely attentive to potential problems that might arise, especially in unfamiliar or ambiguous situations.
- *Startle.* Anxious people react quickly and strongly to the slightest cues that danger may be present (e.g., unusual sounds, disrupted rhythms).
- *Share.* Anxious people are quick to warn others about looming danger. They possess an unusually strong desire to tend and care for other people; this act of "getting out of their own heads" soothes them.
- *Scout.* If others are not immediately supportive, anxious people go into investigative mode and seek more data. They gather information with the intent of being more persuasive to others so that they can build an alliance to fend off impending danger.
- *Squat.* Anxious people suppress other important needs such as eating and sleeping to perseverate on the problem until it is resolved.

Yes, you do not want to be chronically anxious. Yes, you do not want a household or workforce made up only of anxious people. But as you can see, there are huge advantages to having a human alarm system. Non-anxious people often skip ambiguous cues that might suggest danger. Non-anxious people are more likely to ignore overt signs of potential danger because they don't deem the information as pressing as whatever else is on their minds.

In one fascinating research study, group members were led to believe that they had accidentally activated a virus that rapidly infected files on a computer. On their way to tell the person who owned the computer, they faced four obstacles that prevented them from warning others or seeking help. A person in the building asked them to complete a short survey; another person gave them the location of the building manager, but asked them to help with some photocopying as a favor; the building manager's door had a sign asking visitors to wait; and, finally, after being directed to a specific computer technician, they passed a student who "accidentally" dropped a stack of papers on the floor. Four social obstacles designed to trip them up. To get past the obstacles, they needed to be abrupt and assertive, two qualities that are not usually associated with people suffering from anxiety. Yet in the face of danger, the most anxious people slalomed through these detours with laser focus. Requests were refused, kindness was discarded, and they were more effective than their less anxious and happy peers at alerting others about the danger and getting immediate assistance.

Better Than Positivity

The advantages of being anxious are not available to those who typically live in the realm of positive emotions. Researchers found that being extraverted, sociable, and dominant were unrelated to the single-minded, gritty determination of anxious people. In danger zones, anxiety prevails over positivity. In situations when danger is a possibility but the cues might be obscure, complicated, or uncertain, anxiety prevails over positivity. In such cases, anxious people quickly discover solutions, and when there is a team around them (friends, family, co-workers), they share the problem and the solutions. Groups are more successful when they include a mix of personality types with different strengths—and at least one anxious sentinel.

EFFECTIVELY HARNESSING AND USING ANXIETY

1. Create a climate in which the sentinel response of anxious people is viewed as a psychological strength, not a neurosis to be excised. Be explicit in teaching other people about the inherent value of anxiety—a necessary balance within a culture devoted to maximizing pleasure, growth, and the pursuit of dreams and aspirations. The successful group has a mix of people with varying motivations, from pursuing aspirational goals to avoiding danger.
2. Ensure that listening to problems is encouraged regularly. Create information channels and be sure that whoever works at the hub of a group has the right combination of strengths—is responsive, articulate, persuasive, socially connected, and knowledgeable of the different strengths of different people (so they can find the quickest solution).
3. Create an incentive structure in which quieter forms of detecting and defusing problems are rewarded. This means that an antiterrorism task force foiling attempts to bring weapons into an airport is celebrated as much as the

agent tackling an assailant inches away from the detonating bomb. The media loves to label individual people as heroes because doing so sets up a simpler, sexier narrative arc. Organizations need to write their own stories, creating opportunities for sentinels to get the spotlight when they deserve it.

4. Instead of viewing threats as either present or absent, remember that the greatest threats often begin with slow, insidious, barely perceptible smoke signals that rapidly escalate. Recognize the beauty of early threat detection. Destigmatize this process and you might find a healthy side effect: people becoming comfortable in talking about friction and discomfort.

THE TAKEAWAYS

1. In not avoiding negative emotions, we gain emotional agility, the ability to use the full palette of emotional experiences.
2. Anger, guilt, anxiety, and other negative emotions are helpful in surprising ways. They give us more courage, regulate our behavior, keep us alert to our surroundings, and recharge our creative energies, among many other benefits.
3. Concrete strategies like slowing the speedometer can be used to transform so-called negative emotions into useful tools.
4. Abandon the notion of labeling emotions as exclusively positive or negative and instead, target what is healthy or unhealthy in a situation.

When you were a child, you probably pretended you possessed some kind of superpower (if you didn't you missed out). Perhaps you imagined that you could fly, or were phenomenally strong, or were invulnerable. When you think about your emotions in light of the benefits associated with all feelings—positive and negative—you realize that you don't just have one superpower, you have many. You possess a courage enhancer (anger), an unethical behavior derailer (guilt), and an alert sentinel standing watch over you (anxiety). In the next chapter, we'll take a look at your underappreciated lie detector (sadness). Because your feelings come and go, you always have a different power to draw from.

In the end, most prejudices against negative emotional experiences arise because people conflate extreme, overwhelming, problematic emotions with their more benign cousins. Guilt is not shame, anger is not rage, and anxiety is not panic. In each case, the former is a beneficial source of emotional information that focuses attention, thinking, and behavior toward a surprising number of effective outcomes.

CHAPTER 4

How Positive Emotion Can Lead to Your Downfall

If you observe a really happy man, you will find him building a boat, writing a symphony, educating his son, growing double dahlias in his garden, or looking for dinosaur eggs in the Gobi desert. He will not be searching for happiness as if it were a collar button that has rolled under a radiator.

—W. Béran Wolfe

As PSYCHOLOGISTS WHO FREQUENTLY TRAVEL for work, how we describe our careers to strangers in the airline seats next to us can determine the tone of the subsequent conversation for hours to come. For instance, the mere mention that we are psychologists prompts some people to open a book, don headphones, or pretend to fall asleep. In other cases, our expertise in mental matters seems to encourage our seatmates to unburden themselves. We can spend hours listening to the details of a failing marriage or a pet theory of motivation. Even pretending to be asleep doesn't seem to dissuade our seatmates from asking us to interpret their dreams. On the few occasions we actually risk the truth and own up to the fact that we are not just general psychologists but that we actually study happiness for a living, we can be guaranteed a near-desperate response: what can I do to be happier? There is a clear and nearly universal assumption that happiness is desirable and, being so metaphorically shiny, we should all be trying to stockpile it. As experts in the field, we know the surprising truth.

Let's pause for a second and explain what we mean by this so-called thing called happiness. When lay people are asked to define happiness, they often conflate potential causes of happiness with happiness itself. They say things like "happiness is family" or "happiness is being grateful." Although family and gratitude are undoubtedly important, they are fairly poor descriptions of what happiness itself actually is, what it feels like, and how we know we are experiencing it. When pushed for a more exact definition of the psychological experience, scholars, watercooler philosophers, and book group members agree on some broad commonalities. To begin with, happiness—at some level—has to be a feeling. Whether you call it joy, enthusiasm, or contentment, the basic truth remains: happiness is, at least in part, emotional, and is therefore experienced subjectively by the individual. When we talk about a happy person, we're describing someone who lives through frequent positive emotions and infrequent negative emotions.

Happiness also reflects a personal judgment about life. In 1965, Dr. Hadley Cantril, a pioneer in happiness studies, asked people to imagine being on a ladder with rungs numbered from zero at the bottom to ten at the top. The top of the ladder represents the best possible life for you, and the bottom represents the worst. On which rung of the ladder would you say you are standing at this time? On which rung do you think you'll be standing five years from now? The answer to the first question requires a mental calculation of positive thoughts in the present, and the answer to the second is a gauge of optimism about the future. Both contribute to your sense of happiness.

Happiness is a state of mind and, as such, can be measured, studied, and enhanced. You do this informally every day when you notice something about your spouse and ask, "What's wrong?" or when you ask your best friend, "How was your trip to Italy?" Scientists take this a step further by having people answer these same kinds of questions using a numbered scale. The astute reader might wonder whether such scales can truly be trusted. Researchers are trained not to rely on these self-reports alone, but also to ask friends and family members to rate target individuals. Occasionally we also use memory measures, reaction-time computer tests, daily diaries, and even biological measures such as brain scans and saliva cortisol samples. Taken together, these methods—even just a few of them—paint a reasonable portrait of a person's happiness.

The current fever for happiness is spurred on, in part, by a growing body of research suggesting that happiness does not just feel good but actually does good things for you. In a review of 225 academic papers on happiness, for instance, psychologist Sonja Lyubomirsky and her colleagues found that feeling upbeat is linked to all sorts of real-life benefits. People who feel frequent positivity

- engage in healthier behaviors such as wearing seat belts,
- make more money,
- have happier marriages,
- receive better customer and supervisor evaluations at work,
- are more generous, and
- end up being promoted more often by bosses.

Then there is the most compelling data of all: happiness is causally related to health, meaning that being happy actually makes you healthier. In one dramatic demonstration of this point, Sheldon Cohen and his colleagues infected willing participants with the rhinovirus (the common cold) after first giving them a cheerfulness questionnaire. Over subsequent days, the research team quarantined the participants in a hotel in order to control their diet and the people with whom they came in contact. During this period, participants had their temperature taken, their blood pressure measured, and were even asked to supply samples of their mucus. In addition, they filled out surveys regarding various symptoms such as headache, stiffness, and aching. What researchers found was that whether you observed the mucus consistency and immunoglobulin levels via biological samples (objective data) or asked participants how they felt (subjective data), happier people were 50 percent less likely to develop a cold than their unhappy counterparts. Thus, while happiness might not cure cancer, it does seem to promote better immune system function.

The research on the overall benefits of happiness is growing steadily. One common theory holds that happiness is humanity's natural resting state. Happy people are more likely to be social, exploratory, inventive, and healthy. It's a short logical jump from there to the idea that happiness provides an evolutionary advantage. It's no wonder that happiness is often touted as a panacea. In fact, happiness seems so valuable that it's sometimes difficult to imagine that it has any downsides.

One interesting red flag with regard to happiness comes from a recent study of the different ways in which Japanese people and Americans think about happiness. Yukiko Uchida, a researcher at Kyoto University, asked a question that would likely get her kicked out of an

American happiness club (yes, there are happiness clubs you can join). She asked people native to both countries to rate happiness on how positive it is and how negative it is, respectively. The Americans awarded happiness a very rosy 5.4 of 7 total possible points. The Japanese participants, on the other hand, gave it a respectable—but significantly lower—score of 5.1. More interesting is that the Japanese people rated happiness a 4.7 of 7 for being negative. The Americans, by contrast, gave it a 4.25 of 7, which, in statistical terms, was significantly lower. You might be scratching your head and wondering how happiness could be negative. Isn't it a *good* feeling? The two key negative aspects of happiness that Japanese people are sensitive to, and which Americans have a tendency to overlook, are *social disruption* (one person's happiness can interfere with that of another) and *avoiding reality* (can't happiness be a bit naïve?).

Perhaps this is merely a cultural quirk, a prejudice of Japanese people, so let's check their views against empirical research on happiness. We already know that happiness is widely beneficial. But are there downsides as well? One of the earliest published studies to identify a cost of positive emotion was published in 1991 by Ed Diener and his colleagues at the University of Illinois. They were interested in the uniquely American understanding of happiness: that intense jolt of enthusiasm you experience at a sporting event, the powerful rush of pride you feel when watching your child perform onstage, or the euphoria that comes with landing a new job. They wondered if all that cowboy-ish Yee-Haw might also make people just a bit saddle sore.

These researchers found several ways in which intense positive experiences can be costly. First is a *contrast effect* in which the experience of emotional highs makes other good events seem to shine less brightly. Winning a million dollars in the lottery, for instance, might make a subsequent win of one hundred dollars on an instant scratch ticket seem pretty ho-hum. Second is a *carryover effect*, in which people who mentally amplify their positive experiences also unwittingly amplify their negative experiences. For example, people who whoop it up in a big way after a win are also vulnerable to a crashing feeling of utter defeat after a loss. This 1991 study was an early and important cautionary note regarding happiness.

Has Happiness Been Taken Too Far?

The tendency is to overlook the fact that happiness itself is sometimes harmful. When most of us hear the phrase "positive emotions," we think of mental states that feel pleasurable and attract other people. When we hear "negative emotions," we think of unpleasant, unproductive states that repel other people (after all, who wants to eat lunch with a curmudgeon?). But positive emotions and thoughts are not always useful. Recognizing this happiness trap and taking advantage of it offers a 20 percent extra edge toward success in life. Here are several often-overlooked research results about a happy mindset that sound a warning:

1. Your happiness can interfere with long-term success.
2. The pursuit of happiness sometimes backfires, ending in unhappiness.
3. Sometimes people want to feel bad.
4. Someone else's happiness can impair your performance.

Let's take a closer look at these happiness caveats.

Research Finding 1: Your Happiness Can Interfere with Your Success

Psychologist Shigehiro Oishi and his international collaborators collected current dictionary definitions of happiness in thirty countries. They found that in twenty-four of those countries, happiness was deemed to be strongly related to fate, fortune, or luck. Notably, the United States ended up being part of the minority, a quirky country where happiness is viewed as a controllable, attainable state of mind. In fact, American collective views on happiness mirror a general attitude about life: if only we plan well and work hard, we can achieve the health, body, spouse, work, money, and recreation we desire. These views on happiness mirror our general take on life so closely that we often conflate happiness with success. This makes the notion that happiness can interfere with success particularly jarring for Americans, and yet a growing body of research suggests that happiness has some quantifiable drawbacks.

Happy people are less persuasive.

Before we get further into this happiness problem, let's spend a moment on a basic question. How do you go about persuading someone else to think or act differently? To buy your brand of toothpaste, to start using their seat belt, to vote for your candidate, to recycle? To get what we want from other people, we need to convince them that our ideas have merit and are better than the contrary ideas of the next person. Robert Cialdini's perennial bestseller *Influence: The Psychology of Persuasion* distills decades of research into a few principles for marketing ideas to other people. One principle is that people respect authority and are apt to follow the lead of experts. This can be seen in products advertised on television that use medical doctors as spokespeople. In fact, authority can be so persuasive that the doctor doesn't even need to be a real doctor! In a now-classic cough syrup commercial from the 1980s, a handsome leading man who played a medical doctor on a soap opera donned a lab coat and introduced himself to audiences by saying, "I'm not a doctor, but I play one on TV."

A second principle is to communicate the message in a concrete, detailed way. Interestingly, attention to detail is the type of thinking that characterizes unhappy moods. Happy people, by contrast, are more likely to overlook details in favor of the big picture—what we refer to as a superficial processing style. Extrapolating from this principle, unhappy people—with their tendency to pay more attention to and process concrete situational details—should generate more persuasive messages compared to the superficial, abstract approach of happy folks. Research shows this is exactly the case. When asked to construct persuasive arguments about issues that are germane to everyday life (using tax money to fund parks and playgrounds) and that are of the more philosophical variety (do soul mates exist?), unhappy people created stronger arguments than happy people. In three studies, judges rated the quality of unhappy people's arguments as approximately 25 percent more impressive and 20 percent more concrete than those made by happy folks. These remarkable numbers were based on participant conversations with a friend whom they were trying to persuade. When participants produced arguments to persuade a stranger to change views on a public policy issue, unhappy people were twice as effective.

Happy people can be too trusting.

Trust is difficult to establish with new people, given that there is no X-ray or CAT scan to gauge a person's underlying motivations, or to accurately predict how someone will treat you in the future. We must rely instead on our hunches regarding the character and honesty of the people with whom we come in contact. Dr. Joseph Forgas and his fellow Australian researchers wanted to determine how accurate happy people—with their more superficial processing style (paying greater attention to the gist, not the details)—are at detecting deceit, which requires paying close attention to facial expressions, eye movements, and the specific language people use. Researchers asked study participants to enter a room one at a time. Inside they found a movie ticket in an envelope. Once they were alone in a dark room with the envelope, they were given the option to take the movie ticket for themselves or leave the envelope alone: the experimenter emphasized that they—the researchers—would never know the truth. The participants were then instructed to deny taking the ticket if they did in fact take it. What's more, the participants were informed that there would be a reward later if they could convince everyone else in the research group that they had not taken the ticket for themselves.

After this brief opportunity to grab the loot, the participants were interrogated: did you take the movie ticket? Videos captured people denying the act. Unbeknownst to the observers, half of these denials were deceitful and half were honest. Forgas and his colleagues found that when people are happy they are able to detect whether someone is lying only 49 percent of the time, slightly worse than chance. When people were experimentally put into an unhappy, sad mood before watching the videotapes, they ended up being much more successful, accurately detecting liars 62 percent of the time.

Think about this in the real world. Imagine being able to boost your ability to judge the honesty of job applicants by 13 percent. Imagine being able to help resolve conflicts between adversaries, with their competing versions of the truth, by 13 percent. This is what happens when we stop holding rigidly to the idea that positivity must prevail as often as possible. This is that superpower we talked about in the last chapter, your built-in lie detector courtesy of the emotion called sadness (which, by the way, is not the same thing as depression).

You might be asking, how does this work? Should I be trying to make myself sad before work? We are not suggesting that you meditate on the suffering of victims of natural disasters to make yourself sad. We are suggesting, instead, that you honor the emotions that arise in you naturally at key decision points. When people are unsure whether someone is telling the truth, concerned about somebody's trustworthiness, or in the midst of evaluating someone, they are rarely in a flat-out happy mood. During these decision points, people often feel somber, even emotionally conflicted until the decision making is over. Just know that this state of mind is perfect for the task. Don't focus on the short game by trying to boost your mood. Instead, focus on the long game and pay attention to making good decisions instead of just feeling good.

HAPPY PEOPLE ARE LAZY THINKERS.

If happy people rely on cursory, superficial strategies to collect information from the outside world, then they are going to be more prone to using stereotypes and remembering fewer details than their unhappy peers. Researchers found support for both of these assumptions. After being given a list of fifteen words on a similar theme, such as *bed*, *rest*, and *tired*, and asked to remember whether the word *sleep* had been on the list (it hadn't), happy people were much more likely to take the bait and incorporate this misleading information into their memory. To get an idea of the extent of these false memories, happy people were 50 percent more likely to recall words they hadn't seen.

In another experiment, students sitting in a classroom watched a nervous woman walk up to the instructor and physically assault him. The altercation was staged to determine who was more prone to make eyewitness memory errors. When asked about the details of what happened, questions included false details ("Can you remember the young woman playing with her scarf as the instructor *gave her something from his wallet*?"—the detail in italics being false). Happy people were 25 percent more likely to recall false facts than unhappy people. Happy people, in their contentment, often fail to scan their environment and end up being blind to what's going on right before their eyes. Maybe there's a limit to how happy you want your police officer, firefighter, physician, and babysitter to be. If you prefer someone who is willing to pay close attention to details, choose someone who is at least a notch below happy.

The laziness of happy people extends to a reliance on stereotypes in stressful situations. Soon after the terrorist attacks of September 11, 2001, participants played a first-person shooter game in which they were told to kill any screen character carrying a gun. Ramping up the difficulty level, half of the targets wore traditional turbans and the other half didn't. If happy people are more likely to be driven by stereotypes, then do they end up with an itchier trigger finger against stereotypical Muslims? Compared with unhappy peers, they were three times more likely to shoot at Muslim than non-Muslim targets.

On average, happy people tend to be kind, feel grateful, and put a priority on being a good community citizen. But in aggressive situations, when negative stereotypes are activated, those benefits disappear. Happy people find it harder to escape deeply ingrained biases. Yes, the use of mental shortcuts is a wonderful time- and energy-saving device, but as shown here, in the wrong situations, failing to focus on details in the present moment can be destructive.

Taken together, these studies provide us with a new perspective on happiness. Although happiness can be beneficial, researchers have started to discover previously ignored drawbacks. When a task requires attention to detail, happy people are at a disadvantage compared with unhappy peers. When you're happy, the "keep the good times rolling" attitude compromises your ability to detect deception, and you become highly susceptible to judgment errors. By contrast, a slight tilt toward negativity enhances performance in several contexts, such as discerning someone's trustworthiness (for example, when we choose friends and business partners), when there is a pressing need to pay attention to details in a crisis (think of police officers), and when an effective argument is needed to change someone's opinion (what authority figures try to do daily). Thanks to scientists challenging the status quo, we have discovered that there are precise situations when deviating from positivity to feel and think negatively unleashes our potential to perform at our best.

Research Finding 2: The Pursuit of Happiness Often Backfires, Ending in Unhappiness

> *A great obstacle to happiness is to anticipate too great a happiness.*
>
> —Bernard le Bovier de Fontenelle

For months, you've been awaiting the release of what promises to be a blockbuster cinema event, the latest film in the epic retelling of J. R. R. Tolkien's fantasy classic *The Hobbit*. You read the book when you were a teenager and even now you delight in mentions of elves and dwarves. In anticipation of the big event, you've kept yourself in a media blackout so that you can experience every delight and surprise the film has to offer. You just know that the movie will be an awesome experience. What's more, you have an equally geeky friend who has promised to see the film with you on opening night. She has been following the production of the movie closely and knows that the director, Peter Jackson, split *The Hobbit* into three parts, each debuting at the theater one year apart. She also knows that Jackson will be drawing liberally from the book's arcane appendices to fill out the subplots. Who do you think is going to enjoy the movie more? You or your friend? Do you think your desire to be pleased will lead to more enjoyment, or will her detailed understanding of the many aspects of the film trump that? According to the latest scientific research, your friend is probably going to derive more happiness from the experience, in part because unlike you she is not trying to use the film to produce happiness.

Researchers have found that when you enter into a situation with the goal of becoming happier, you actually make that less likely to occur. To test this, Jonathan Schooler, Dan Ariely, and George Loewenstein randomly gave participants one of four sets of instructions before listening to Stravinsky's *The Rite of Spring*:

1. Try to make yourself as happy as possible when listening.
2. Listen as you normally do.
3. As you listen, move a dial to indicate how happy you feel and how your mood changes.
4. Try to make yourself as happy as possible and keep tabs on how your happiness ebbs and flows while listening (a combination of instructions 1 and 3).

Compared with adults using music as a tactic to become happier (instruction 1), adults instructed to just listen (instruction 2) ended up 4.5 times happier with Stravinsky's pleasant violins, a 450 percent better return on their investment. Clearly, the strategy of trying to use music as a means to an end backfired. Even more dramatic, people who tried to use music to become happier while also tracking how well they met their happiness goal felt 7.5 times worse than people just listening to the music. This finding is important because conventional wisdom regarding the pursuit of happiness tells us that people should understand what brings them happiness, create goals that will help with this overarching aim to be happy, and then work toward these goals, tracking the effort put in and progress made. We now have scientific evidence suggesting that this single-minded pursuit of happiness is akin to trying to grab a bar of soap in the bathtub. The more you reach through the water, the more the soap slips away, and the more difficult it is to lay a hand on.

In another example of the paradoxical effect of pursuing happiness, researchers Iris Mauss and Maya Tamir gave adults one of two doctored newspaper articles. One touted the latest science showing how happiness leads to better social relationships, health, and professional success. The other discussed the same benefits but attributed them to "making accurate judgments." Participants were then shown a comedy film. Mauss and Tamir explain that those people watching the comedy who overvalued happiness felt greater disappointment in how the film made them feel, because they had hoped they were going to end up much happier.

In another study, these same researchers gave adults a questionnaire asking them how much importance they place on attaining happiness and about the amount of stress in their lives. The same paradox emerged. Each day over a two-week period, adults with the greatest desire to be happy felt lonelier, more depressed, and less purposeful, and had fewer positive emotions, lower progesterone levels, and reduced emotional intelligence. This makes sense because that single-minded aim to be happy above all else is a selfish pursuit. It's about feeling good and having positive thoughts. The notion that other people matter is a secondary concern, which can interfere with the quality of one's relationships. Think about love in romance, family, and friendships. If only one of you gets an upgrade to that buttery leather seat in first class with treats from the ice-cream sundae cart, you give it up; love is about being willing to sacrifice your happiness to ensure theirs gets a boost. When someone shares a funny story, you often relish the experience because you know that your partner or friend will crack up during the retelling. Love is about adopting another person's perspective of the world, and when overvaluing your happiness gets in the way, it leads to unfortunate by-products such as loneliness.

The science, however, is clear that overvaluing happiness is only problematic in certain situations. Inaccurate theories about what leads to happiness only ended up being problematic in low-stress, seemingly pleasant situations. Listening to Stravinsky with the intent of being happy and monitoring how much happiness was felt throughout the song led to unhappiness. Makes sense and yet, if you happened to be listening to unpleasant music—such as one of the purported worst collaborations of all time, the Bee Gees with Peter Frampton—it shouldn't matter a lick whether you're trying to be happy, because those sounds are painful to all of us. Returning to the studies by Mauss and Tamir, if you recently experienced a flood of stressful events, being invested in trying to be happy did not lead to fewer positive experiences or pleasant feelings. This also makes sense. Our expectations about what will make us happy change when we're stressed out: now we have a ready-made excuse for why we fail to become as happy as we want to be. When life is relatively stress-free and positive, we expect to be really happy after trying hard to do so, and feel disappointed when we don't. Context matters.

Overvaluing happiness interferes with the extraction of pleasure from seemingly pleasurable events and has additional problems too. The experience of positive emotions perverts our expectations for whatever activity is next on the agenda. You win an award as the top sales performer for the month, and as your plaque is being put up on the wall, colleagues clap warmly and your feelings of joy, pride, and accomplishment surge. Returning to your desk after all the hoopla, going out for a movie with your wife no longer seems as exciting as it did earlier. And an e-mail from an unhappy customer writing in ALL CAPS about the ways in which you failed them seems more annoying than usual. Who is this person to think they can dampen your fantastic mood? Your positivity is now on a fast, systematic decline, and this pisses you off. Scientists have discovered that intense positive emotions feel good but that they change your baseline so that future positive events seem less enticing.

High, off-kilter expectations for happiness compromise the experience of happiness and success another way. Social situations are unpredictable. You could be incredibly polite, an interesting conversationalist, and a good listener, yet the stranger you've been chatting with on the train might get off at his stop without another word. We can control only our side of the conversation, never being sure of how other people will feel, behave, and respond to us. In the business world, the past is a poor predictor of what the marketplace will be in the future, which is why novices can outperform financial experts in picking stocks.

Similarly, happy people over-rely on their positive memories, often making the mistake of thinking that past success was their due (ignoring the role of luck and other people), and that their failures were due to circumstances outside their control, downplaying their role in the problem. While this optimistic bias is a great strategy for happiness and staying motivated, it also leads people to fail to learn from their mistakes and to walk into situations with inflated expectations.

We see this with entrepreneurs who tend to be more enthusiastic, excitable, and overly invested in trying to be happy. With this mindset, entrepreneurs often possess unrealistic positive expectations and fall helplessly in love with

- their ideas (and fail to seek or use feedback),
- their strengths (and fail to attend to weaknesses and the power of situations), and
- their grand vision (and overlook the details that require attention to avoid failure).

This is not unique to entrepreneurs. We see the same problem in happy students, happy romantic couples, happy parents, and happy leaders who get stuck in the past. They expect things to go well because of their bias toward remembering and overvaluing their accomplishments.

Research Finding 3: Sometimes People Want to Feel Bad

Have you ever watched a person at the customer service desk report a missing piece of luggage? Lost luggage, like broken merchandise and ill-fitting clothing, requires us to expend effort—often frustrating effort—and to advocate for ourselves. Despite the nearly universal feeling of hassle that comes with being separated from your suitcase, many people take the nice-guy approach: they offer the service representative a conspiratorial smile and a wink and say, "Hey, I know you didn't lose my luggage, you just work here." We are, after all, civilized. We can keep our cool and avoid hurting anyone's feelings. As we mentioned in the previous chapter, the people who "own" their feelings of frustration and can effectively communicate their anger about matters like lost luggage are often highly effective advocates. They persevere longer and are more likely to get customer service agents to use their position to override protocols and step up extra efforts to find the missing bags.

This is not hypothetical. One study shows that a little anger is a superior strategy when it comes to effectively returning a purchased item. The reasons for this probably change depending on who is having the conversation and the amount of money and time involved. But you can bet that anger works because the other person feels your discomfort. Your anger gets them to focus in the here and now on what you have to say, and they recognize that a problem will be highly likely and costly (to their job standing and mental health) if they don't act reasonably with you. By contrast, others who express disappointment but not anger are easier to brush off as insignificant. When emotions can lead to a better outcome, it's helpful to focus on what you want to accomplish rather than what you feel.

It turns out that people have an intuitive grasp of the function of negative emotions, and sometimes choose these psychological down states over happiness to achieve a goal. Building on the idea that anger promotes successful confrontations—to take a single example—researchers have shown that when given a choice of music to listen to before confronting a perpetrator (e.g., a person who ignored the no smoking sign), people didn't want to listen to the calming tones of Kenny Loggins or Frank Sinatra; instead, they showed a 33 percent greater preference for the angry hard-core sounds of Metallica and Rush. That is, people understand that "getting pumped up" emotionally equips them for confrontation in a way that being calm does not. Most important, when people believe that anger is useful in confrontations, then using music to amplify their anger *is* useful. They end up being more assertive, leading to a better outcome when confronting hostile, aggressive characters.

Certain situations call for feelings and behaviors that deviate from the happiness repertoire. Happiness motivates people to be friendly, to be helpful, and to try to connect with other people. Sounds good, except that other people are not always on our side. When somebody tries to sabotage you at work, you might want to seek help, creating alliances at meetings to ensure that your ideas aren't prematurely and unfairly shot down. This means convincing other people and figuring out strategies to neutralize adversaries. Expressions of sadness communicate to others that you are in trouble and need help; expressions of happiness signal to others that everything is fine. Thus, if your goal is to gain assistance, this is the wrong time to feel happy, express happiness, and minimize the unpleasantness of sadness.

Researchers have found that people intuitively know that sadness is beneficial when the goal is to persuade somebody to avert loss or failure. In one experiment, Maya Tamir and her colleagues instructed volunteers to collect donations in two scenarios that involved asking someone for help. In both cases, volunteers believed that feeling sad would be more useful in successfully collecting money from donors. To unlock the underappreciated benefits of negative emotions, you need to believe that unpleasantness is useful. To be more successful, know the situations when it is ideal to deviate from the experience and expression of happiness. Emerging research clearly establishes that

- *anger* trumps happiness when trying to confront a wrongdoer,
- *anxiety* trumps happiness when taking precautions against looming danger, and
- *sadness* trumps happiness when securing help to handle loss or personal difficulties.

Research Finding 4: Someone Else's Happiness Can Impair Your Performance Too

Victoria Visser and her colleagues conducted two studies looking at how displaying happiness or unhappiness in a leadership position (think CEOs, physicians, teachers, parents) affects how well the people under their watch perform. Business school students turned on a webcam to listen to the leader assigned to their team (an actor using a rehearsed script). The team leader encouraged everyone to do their best while giving instructions on how to complete two solo tasks: a sudoku puzzle (requiring analytical skills) and a brainstorming task in which they had to generate as many uses as possible for both bricks and pencils (requiring creativity). He gave the same speech to nearly three hundred adults, with one variation. Half the time his facial expressions and vocal inflection reflected a happy mood and half the time he acted sad.

Now, we mentioned earlier that happiness leads to big-picture thinking (think project managers) and unhappiness leads to detail-oriented, analytical thinking (think detectives). Building on this theme, Visser and her colleagues found that with a happy leader, followers performed 200 percent better on the creative task than they did for an unhappy leader, and when the leader displayed signs of sadness, followers performed 400 percent better on the analytical task. These numbers are staggering. The change in performance arose from simply watching the leader. This tells us that leaders can tilt other people's emotions enough to dramatically improve targeted performance goals if, and only if, they understand when happiness and unhappiness are most advantageous. Leaders who intentionally think about the nature of the task being given to someone and the best emotional state for that task get an extra leadership edge: the final 20 percent.

But this emotional agility goes beyond helping other people be more creative or analytical. Psychologist Seth Kaplan asked a group of people to complete what can only be described as an incredibly boring simulation of what air traffic controllers do every day. Research subjects were asked to sit in a chair and watch a radar screen carefully, and if they saw two planes en route to a collision they were to set off an alarm. What made this job so tiring were the high stakes involved and the tedium: 93 percent of the time the planes never came anywhere near each another. For fifteen minutes, subjects watched circles representing airplanes creep ever so slowly around a screen. While they were doing so, Seth Kaplan had one person serve as leader of the group, staying in the room with the air traffic controllers and adopting one of two management styles. In one group, the leader was a cheerleader, emphasizing how well each person was performing with a litany of appreciative statements ("You got this!"). In the other group, the leader commiserated, acknowledging how boring the task was but also emphasizing that together they would get through this painful ordeal.

In the research setting, staff with commiserating leaders not only performed better but also rated the task as more enjoyable. The take-home lesson is simple: do not create a culture based on the assumption that positivity must reign supreme. Instead, create a culture where everyone knows that it's safe to be real, and that depending on the situation, it's sometimes better to feel something other than happiness.

If Happiness Is So Great Why Aren't We Better at It?

If happiness is so beneficial, and if people frequently experience it (they report they do between 60 and 80 percent of the time), then why aren't we all better at being happy? Why do we move to a bigger house with the huge lawn to play football with the kids, and end up feeling less happy because it now requires an extra twenty minutes to visit our closest friends? Why do parents schedule their kids for after-school theater practice and maths tutoring, knowing that everyone will feel rushed, bicker, and argue more often? It turns out that we succumb to a variety of common biases that interfere with our ability to effectively choose what will make us happy. Even worse, these biases are often invisible to us.

Virtually all of our poor happiness choices hinge on a single psychological fact: we are typically in a different state when making choices than we are when we experience the result of that choice. Imagine, for instance, that you show up to a fancy restaurant famished. When your server takes your order, she informs you that if you want to order the chocolate soufflé for dessert the order must be put in immediately due to the long baking time required. Your stomach casts its vote and you go ahead with the soufflé. At the end of dinner, however, when it arrives at your table, you're full and you end up enjoying the rich dessert much less than you anticipated. The reason, of course, is that you did a poor job of predicting your future state, falling prey to what psychologists call *projection bias*.

A number of other biases lead us to make poor predictions of what will make us happy in the future, and the consequences can be much more dire than a half-eaten soufflé. A common one is known as *impact bias*. This happens when people overestimate the emotional intensity or duration of an event. For example, you might choose to retire to sunny Spain because you found it nearly perfect during a week-long getaway. Although you might not articulate it this way, your choice to retire there is based on the assumption that the weather, the pace of life, and the opportunity to be near the sea will improve your happiness. A wide range of research on sports victories and losses, political wins, and job success and failure shows that people consistently think that events will be more intensely emotional than they turn out to be, and that the emotional consequences of events will last much longer than they do. Where Spain is concerned, you might experience a temporary spike in happiness, but after a short period—perhaps a month—you will have adjusted to your new circumstances and be about as happy there as you were in your pre-retirement location.

A third happiness bias—*distinction bias*—is beautifully illustrated by researcher Christopher Hsee of the University of Chicago. Hsee points out that your mental state (rather than your emotional state) is often different from one time to another. To illustrate this, let's take a moment and—borrowing from Hsee's example—consider the purchase of a new television.

> You are in the market for a plasma screen television. You head to the electronics superstore, where you are confronted with

> two dozen dream TVs. This one has a larger screen; that one has a better warranty; both of these have bright screens that can easily be seen in a brightly lit room, and that other one has a special antiglare feature. Suddenly, your dream television is not a fantasy but a real-world dilemma and you have to make a choice—one among many—that you believe will yield the greatest amount of pleasure. You settle on a particular model, pay for it, and cart it home. There, in your basement, the TV largely lives up to its promise. You enjoy watching shows, but it isn't nearly the happiness jackpot you thought it would be.

In the TV example, you are likely the victim of the fact that you are using one set of information to evaluate the television in the store and an entirely different set to take stock of it at home. For example, at the store you were probably engaging in joint-evaluation, in which you appreciated your sixty-inch screen against the context of a neighboring fifty-eight-inch screen. Once you lug the TV home, however, that comparison vanishes and the sixty inches of screen is no bigger or smaller than anything else.

The single most toxic decision-making bias, where happiness is concerned, is the *wanting/liking bias*. When most people hear about this, they are shocked that they have gone their entire lives without having clearly understood it. This bias is based on the distinction between wanting something and liking something. You might want a pet dog, for instance, far more than you would actually like having a pet dog. Neuroscience research supports this idea that these are two separate psychological processes: wanting, which is an appetite, is associated with one region of the brain, whereas enjoyment, or liking, is associated with another. We won't bore you with terms like *ventral palladium*, *nucleus accumbens*, and *mesotelencephalic dopamine systems*, but please trust us that expert researchers—Kent Berridge foremost among them—have identified that wanting and liking involve two separate but related systems in the brain.

Craving something, whether it is a new job, a new toy, or a jelly donut, is often psychologically, and sometimes physically, arousing. We tend to want things really badly. Once we get them, however, we stop revving so high, emotionally speaking. We like whatever it is well enough, but not nearly as much as we once wanted it. In fact, the long meetings, tough commute, and nasty office politics at the new job may not be likable at all, despite the intensity of the craving to be offered the job in the first place. In this way, we often function a little bit like drug addicts, making purchases and other life choices based on a strong desire, without the ability or motive to really see the long-term effects.

Where happiness is concerned, the distinction between wanting and liking is of utmost importance because we often assume that these two are the same. If I want something, the intuitive logic goes, then I will like it if I get it. Not true. Trips to Mauritius, extramarital affairs, the regional manager position at work, a Rolex watch: we tend to want these things in the short term far more than we will actually like them in the long term. Everyone is prone to conflating these two experiences, and, as a result, we can make some really terrible decisions where happiness is concerned.

Taken together in the real world, these biases lead to billions of pounds annually in misspent money and impulsive decisions, none of which yield the happiness we expect. In psychology, we sometimes talk about an Icarus complex. According to Greek mythology, Icarus and his father, Daedalus, were imprisoned on the island of Crete. Daedalus fashioned two pairs of wings from wax and warned his son that as they flew away he should be cautious not to venture too near to the sun. But, once aloft, Icarus was so delighted by the experience of flight that he flew higher and higher until his wings melted, and he plummeted to his death. Not everyone suffers from an Icarus complex, but we are all prone to seeing happiness as unqualifiedly good, and this is an example of its backfiring in a big way.

A Playbook for Mild Unhappiness

Do not be mistaken, we are fully aware of the robust and widely confirmed findings on the benefits of positive emotions, positive thoughts, and happiness. In fact, we've contributed to the literature. But what's largely untapped is the potential we can draw from the fact that under certain predictable circumstances, being mildly unhappy seems to be better than being happy. This includes tasks that require detail-oriented, systematic, or analytical thinking, which counts for much of what we do at home (think of budgeting and designing weekend plans) and work (think of completing administrative paperwork and trying to determine trends and patterns from mounds of information). The key word is *mildly*, for serious unhappiness in the form of chronic loneliness and emotional disorders impair our ability to function, and in the worst-case scenario leads to thoughts of death and suicidal acts. Here, and throughout the book, we are not talking about emotional problems and disorders as hidden gifts.

The information-processing styles linked to mild unhappiness and happiness are not in competition: one is neither better nor worse than the other; each has its advantages in the right context. We all fall into the trap of using the terms *positive emotions* and *negative emotions*.

This language, this labeling, keeps us from being whole and able to function optimally, and fully.

THE TAKEAWAYS

1. When we're happy, our comfort with the status quo interferes with our ability to carefully attend to detail, and as a result we end up a bit more gullible, a bit less persuasive, and a little further from success.
2. Although happiness is widely beneficial, organizing one's life around it can lead to a great deal of effort and time being spent unwisely. Trying too hard to be happy interferes with the pleasure, engagement, and meaning we could otherwise find in the world.
3. Happiness agendas backfire. Short-term and long-term goals are connected to each other, and we often need to sacrifice short-term happiness to accomplish meaningful long-term outcomes. People want to feel bad from time to time, especially when these "negative" psychological states are seen as instrumental to achieving a particular goal, such as preparing for a confrontation or persuading another person to alter their opinions.
4. When a task is boring or requires detail-oriented or analytical skills, happy leaders can inadvertently squelch motivation and impair performance. The best leaders tailor their expression of emotions to what their followers are going through and what will inspire the best outcome.
5. If you want to be surrounded by productive, creative, satisfied people, create an environment where diverse feelings and behaviors are honored.

Peter Drucker once quipped, "Never mind your happiness; do your duty." Based on the latest science, we offer a similar recommendation that happy thoughts and feelings be viewed as a thermostat, a metric that offers insight into how things are going. When moving the thermostat becomes the objective of life, activities lose their intrinsic appeal and performance is compromised. If you want to be happy, get out of your head and into your life. Trying desperately to seek the positive and avoid the negative is not only a wasteful errand, it will also lead you to fail at what you desire most. The situationally aware person is ready to take advantage of fortuitous opportunities when they arise and prepared to tilt the expression of their thoughts and feelings toward happiness or unhappiness as appropriate. To claim the benefits of unhappy states described in this chapter, you must find, tolerate, and appreciate them. Put simply, you don't want happy people working as air traffic controllers.

CHAPTER 5

Beyond the Obsession with Mindfulness

The critical difference between the thinking of humans and of lower animals lies not in the existence of consciousness but in the capacity for complex processes outside it.

—Ulric Neisser

HEAD TO A BOOKSTORE and you will find a shelf, if not a whole section, with titles touting the benefits of developing mindfulness. Mindfulness, simply put, is conscious awareness. It's the ability to observe the world around you without fouling it up with internal dialogue, judgment, or other distraction. It's the ability to see a dress as red instead of cute, or of experiencing disappointment for what it is, rather than seeing yourself as a failure. Mindfulness is in vogue right now. Phil Jackson, who as a coach won the most NBA championships ever, was famous for advocating mindfulness techniques for his basketball players. Mindfulness meditation and mental focusing are being used in psychotherapy, sports training, and even business. These days, mindfulness is being touted as perhaps the optimal state of human functioning.

Mindfulness enthusiasts aren't just under the influence of some new age Kool-Aid. A growing body of scientific evidence supports the benefits of "gently observing" what is happening in the present moment, as opposed to judging it. A range of studies show that people with a tendency to be mindful in daily life report greater happiness, experience more meaning and purpose in life, have superior emotional intelligence, enjoy higher levels of self-compassion, and possess an enhanced ability to cope with chronic stress. Mindfulness, it turns out, is pretty cool.

If you want specific persuasive data, look no further than the two leading scientists who were both instrumental in popularizing mindfulness practices in the West, Jon Kabat-Zinn at the University of Massachusetts Medical School and Richard Davidson at the University of Wisconsin. The former is often considered the father of the mindfulness movement in the West, and the latter is well-known and highly regarded for his penchant for using fMRI and other brain-scanning devices to study the biological and physiological underpinnings of mindfulness. In a recent study, Kabat-Zinn and Davidson led an eight-week mindfulness course for employees working at a biotech company. After first exposing workers to a strain of influenza, Kabat-Zinn and Davidson discovered that employees in the mindfulness training showed a remarkable resistance to getting the flu.

As if better immune function wasn't benefit enough, the researchers also discovered actual changes in employees' brains after a mere twenty total hours of mindfulness training (two and a half hours per week). Researchers found a 400 percent increase in left-sided activation of the anterior prefrontal cortex. You're probably wondering, "Do I want my anterior prefrontal cortex increased?" The answer is yes. This is the brain region associated with positive emotions and with the willingness to view stress as a challenge to be tackled rather than a threat to be avoided. It only took these office workers the amount of time spent in watching four football games and in taking three trips to the supermarket to modify their brains in ways that promote greater success. It's safe to say that mindfulness isn't just cool, it's really cool.

If mindfulness is so helpful, why aren't we hardwired to do it more often? There's a reason why human beings evolved so that we spend an inordinate amount of time being mindless. Conscious thinking, which keeps us aware of what is happening in the present moment, is very limited in its processing capacity. Just think about the effort expended by our brain as we pass another person walking on the pavement. We estimate the distance from their body, calculate our speed and theirs, take stock of where our body ends and theirs begins so we don't bump into them, and at the same time we masterfully move one leg and then the other without stumbling over anything on the ground, or smacking into tree branches extending into our airspace.

When you look at someone's face, you quickly establish whether they are someone you know, and from their facial expression calculate whether the person is happy or unhappy, friendly or dangerous, or interested in stopping to talk. This task is all the more difficult because instead of being still, this other person's facial muscles shift into slightly different expressions every few seconds, requiring constant reassessment. If it happens that you do know this person, there are also higher-level functions to access. You must recall their name, the nature of your relationship with them, remember what you talked about during prior interactions, and set into motion the fine-grained motor skills of eye contact (not too much or too little), speaking volume, verbal content, and listening and encoding skills required to maintain a conversation. If you were only able to proceed with conscious, deliberate attention, you would never have the capacity to complete this overwhelming laundry list of activities.

Our conscious mind is simply unable to handle the complex, dynamic layers of data flooding us in each moment. One error in processing and you can step out in front of a fast-moving car, curse in front of your children, let slip a professional secret, burn your hand on the stove, or suffer a million small failures. By necessity, much of this mental processing happens at the speed of thought below the radar of conscious awareness.

In this chapter, we say *mindless* to offer a clear contrast to the cultural obsession with mindfulness as the answer to better health, relationships, and success. People often feel uncomfortable with mindlessness because it's the opposite of intentionality, strategy, and all those forward-thinking hallmarks of superior human intelligence. A long tradition of intellectuals argues that the good life is one that is thoughtful and planned. Mindlessness, by contrast, is the hallmark feature of, well, zombies. Interestingly, by turning to the example of zombies, we can find an illustration of the benefits of mindlessness.

Steven Yeun plays Glenn on the award-winning television series about a zombie apocalypse, *The Walking Dead*. Over four seasons, Steven's character transformed from an energetic hero to a jaded survivor as he and his friends escaped one flesh-eating zombie attack after another. You would think that, as an actor, Yeun would devote a considerable amount of mindful attention to the emotions, posture, and mindset of his character. This is especially true in tricky scenes where Yeun, as Glenn, pretends to stomp on a zombie during a fight scene. Yeun says that the secret to making it all look real is to think like a zombie; that is, to not think at all. Yeun cautions that if he gently attends to how many inches his foot needs to be from the head of the actor playing the zombie it will come across as choppy and artificial. Instead of thinking too deliberately and hard (brute concentration) or adopting a nonjudgmental observation of what is happening in the present moment (mindfulness), to do his job well, he must act with minimal conscious reflection—just as he would behave if he really did walk down the street trying to fend off a pack of zombies hungry for brains. He has to rely on automatic processing, which is about intuitive, instinctive decisions, and actions based on well-designed evolutionary hardware and years of training (which Steven Yeun has as an actor). At the heart of Yeun's stellar performance is the ability to lose himself—his conscious mind—completely, and become a different person, the character on television who is trying to survive the zombie apocalypse that becomes an alternative world that millions of viewers enter for one hour each week.

The pages that follow explore three areas where scientific research suggests that mindlessness can help you become more productive, creative, and better able to handle the hassles and ambiguous terrain of daily life. We might define mindlessness as a spectrum, from absent-mindedness to full immersion in the subconscious, but this would not do the topic justice. Instead, we detail three types of mindlessness that can propel you toward greater success and well-being: (1) harnessing autopilot, (2) taking impulsive action, and (3) trusting mindless decision making. The most psychologically flexible—and the most successful—people have the ability to switch back and forth between mindfulness and mindlessness, instead of becoming stuck in one mode. Intentionally using these unheralded paths offers the 20 percent edge that will be lost to those who remain wed to the idea that mindfulness is better than mindlessness.

Three Mindless Paths to Success and Well-Being

Conscious thought stays firmly under the searchlight, [whereas] unconscious thought ventures out to the dark and dusty nooks and crannies of the mind.

—Ap Dijksterhuis and Teun Meurs

Harnessing Autopilot

To save computing space in the brain, people rely on heuristic thinking, that is, the use of automatic—and therefore mindless—cognitive shortcuts. One common way we use heuristic thinking is in categorizing things. When you show up to your local post office, you don't begin your transaction by asking the clerk if she speaks the national language. You have already categorized her as a postal employee and, because she is, you can assume a great deal about what she knows (she will speak the official language, she will be literate, she will know the price of stamps, she will be able to answer questions about which forms of payment are acceptable, and so forth). Heuristics save time and valuable cognitive space by not troubling your conscious brain with unnecessary heavy lifting.

Research shows that people are able to make unconscious categorical judgments about others at amazing speeds. In a study on first impressions, participants only needed one-tenth of a second to reach conclusions regarding the personality of their target. In this brief window of time, people made judgments about trustworthiness, emotional stability, kindness, enthusiasm, carelessness, openness to new experiences, and other aspects of personality. To put this amazing, mindless personality detecting machine of ours into perspective, you took two hundred times longer than that just to read this paragraph. You might be wondering whether our assessments of other people lasting seconds are accurate. Across a wide range of studies, researchers have found that these "thin slice" observations are well above chance in accuracy (approximately 70 percent accurate). Pretty damn good for a blip of time and effort.

1. Mindless Detection of Sketchy Social Situations

One crucial aspect of autopilot thinking is determining whether a stranger is trustworthy. This difficult task is essential for effective social and business relationships, not to mention personal safety. Get this wrong and you could be swindled, attacked, or—at minimum—waste a great deal of time when you could be forming a satisfying, meaningful friendship with someone else. Many scientists believe that we give or withhold trust based on how other people respond to the cues we provide. Another person mirroring our behavior could signal that our needs, values, and well-being are of interest and concern to them.

Rick van Baaren and his colleagues at the Radboud University of Nijmegen found that when servers repeated customer orders (a clear sign that the waitstaff is being attentive) customers increased their tips by more than 68 percent. We are confident that customers did this mindlessly (not actively calculating how much money to put on the table based on whether a waitperson repeated their orders and requests for more water out loud). That simple act, repeating the order, is a subtle cue that the server is listening and can be trusted in the context of the restaurant.

High-maintenance social interactions can be painful, including conversations where you are out of sync with the other person, such as when you smile and lean close to tell a story and your parther doesn't move closer, too, or reveal any change in expression. An exchange without coordinated movements and some degree of mirroring feels uncomfortable. Researchers consistently find that we like people better when they mimic our mood and gestures—not when they make fun of us, but when they subtly mirror our posture, emotions, and even our ways of speaking. On the other hand, mimicry is inappropriate when we're competing with someone, or when we're asking a car dealer for advice on family sedans.

Psychologists at the University of Groningen, Duke University, and Yale University explored our reactions to "negatively tinged social cues." In one study, when participants were greeted by a very formal, stiff professional who tried to mimic them during a social interaction, participants literally got the chills, feeling two and a half times colder than when the same person did not mimic them. What about when participants were greeted by a friendly, playful person? Participants felt twice as cold physically after spending time with a friendly person who didn't mimic them, as if their body recognized the cool reception they were getting.

With this perspective in mind, imagine what happens in a study where strangers of different racial groups interact with each other, and afterward are asked to guess the room temperature. In a same-race interaction, the absence of mimicry by another person felt chilly, 2.04 degrees colder, to be exact; and when talking to a stranger of a different race, it was the presence of mimicry by that person that led the room to feel 2.47 degrees colder. These and similar studies are consistent with the idea that each of us has a gut feeling about situation-behavior mismatches. Mimicry is typically considered a sign of intimacy, so it's easy to see why, when a person doesn't expect intimacy, suspicions are raised by mimicry. Think of the psychological drop in temperature as an ever-so-slight signal on the fringes of conscious awareness that there are better, less threatening ways to spend our time than with the person sitting across from us.

We get this mindless form of self-protection courtesy of thousands of years of evolution. Asked about the practical takeaway, the lead author of the study, Pontus Leander, says,

> Perhaps, one shouldn't "try too hard" when trying to affiliate because it could easily backfire (for example, mimicking in a cross-race interaction). These studies highlight how some automatic processes are best left alone. I grew up in the South, and I often heard the phrase "if it works, don't fix it"; maybe that is especially true for mimicry.

We argue for a sequence as follows: (1) in a social interaction with new people or a conversation involving a hot-button issue, allow the near-mindless process to do its work; (2) make a conscious effort to notice any changes in your body; (3) reflect on whether your threat detector cast its net too far. Yes, we are talking about the complementary benefits of starting with mindlessness and then bringing present-moment mindful awareness into the situation between you and other people. We are not advocating the need for a battle between mindfulness and mindlessness. They work in tandem, in a particular order.

The first part of the sequence, harnessing autopilot, is what we, the authors, had never considered before. Before writing this book, neither of us used temperature estimates as a factor when making business deals with new people or talking to strangers in hotel lobbies. Now we do. We become mindful of this benefit of mindlessness. Besides gauging someone's physical attractiveness, intelligence, curiosity, and likability, we remind ourselves to be aware when there is a drop in physical warmth around another person. Before we may have blurted out, "damn, it's chilly in here," but now when we shiver, or feel compelled to find another layer of clothing, we privately take note. We become a tiny bit more skeptical, looking for any signs of threat or manipulation that we didn't consciously register before. With this extra bit of data that we previously ignored, just maybe we made a few better decisions in hiring employees and choosing taxi drivers in a foreign land.

2. Mindless Emotion Regulation

Interestingly, automatic processing also applies to emotion. Healthy emotion regulation—the attempt to control or alter the type, intensity, and expression of our reactions to the world—has been tied to almost every important part of living well. For example, researchers suggest that failures to effectively regulate emotions are partly responsible for individual problems such as depression, aggression, and infidelity, and, in the professional realm, poor performance, theft, and harassment of others. Knowing how important it is and how difficult it can be to regulate emotions like intense anger, fear, sadness, and embarrassment, it makes sense to ponder whether conscious emotion management consumes too much effort and is simply too slow to help us in strong situations.

By strong situations, we mean those times when we feel intense emotions and are pushed to do something, such as observing a strange man at the restaurant approach your daughter while she waits in line for the restroom, whisper in her ear, and slowly rub his hand up and down her bare arm. Think of the benefit of being able to regulate emotion mindlessly and automatically, before you even knew what you were feeling, dampening the tendency to engage in rash, ill-considered actions (in this example, grabbing a fork and making a mad dash to stab the man's hand, only to find out that he's your daughter's new boyfriend). What if your mind could be trained to effectively help before you even knew you needed help in a challenging situation?

In two studies, Iris Mauss at the University of California, Berkeley and James Gross at Stanford University asked participants to unscramble sentences, embedded in which were words related to emotion management such as *restrict*, *restrain*, and *cool* or to emotion bursts such as *unleash*, *boil*, and *explode*. The researchers wanted to know whether being unobtrusively exposed to these words played a role in how participants dealt with their emotions when an actor intentionally tried to piss them off. The actor asked them to quickly count letters from a blurry article while giving them feedback that they were incompetent in an increasingly irritated, impatient tone of voice. Participants primed to let their emotions out felt 42.2 percent angrier than those primed to stay in control. A second study showed that participants mindlessly primed with words that helped control their emotions reacted with a lower heart rate and lower blood pressure when approached by an obnoxious actor.

What are the takeaways from this research? First, very sophisticated goals, such as tolerating toxic people and our own distress, can be realized without any conscious, deliberate action on our part. Second, these mindless acts of emotion regulation appear to be cost-free, in that people show not only less distress but also less physiological damage. Third, simple, brief, low-cost interventions can push and pull us toward healthier reactions to difficult social situations. This tells us that a powerful mindless system is already at work regulating our emotions, and that by learning to influence it we can increase its benefits.

3. Mindless Creativity

Innovation is a big buzzword in business and education because it has the advantage of being tangible, measurable, the result of creative ideas, and can be physically implemented in the real world. Elon Musk, the genius behind Tesla electric cars and SpaceX, is a perfect example of how creative fire can be the centerpiece of business. In fact, businesses—especially so-called mature businesses—spend readily on innovation consultancy for their products and management, and another big lump of money on creativity training for their employees. At the heart of many of these trainings are improvisation, risk taking, and the acceptance of a little failure. No argument from us.

Also at the core of many creativity workshops is the idea that you can consciously perform creatively. The more mindful you are, the more receptive you will be to creative insights. Mindfulness is attractive because of the clear ties to effortful, deliberate, smooth action. This fits with the notion that a well-lived life should not and cannot be easy. The cultural message is clear but misleading. Researchers have been eager to depict how it is problematic when a person is unable to control their mind such that it wanders. Is it a cognitive failure when your child's mind wanders when the classroom teacher speaks? In an article on constructive mindlessness, psychologist Scott Barry Kaufman offers a counter to recent research and sentiments that dismiss mindless moments and mind wandering:

> This perspective makes sense when mind wandering is observed by a third party and when costs are measured against externally imposed standards such as speed or accuracy of processing, reading fluency or comprehension, sustained attention, and other external metrics.

> There is, however, another way of looking at mind wandering, a personal perspective, if you will. . . . We mind wander, by choice or accident, because it produces tangible reward when measured against goals and aspirations that are personally meaningful. Having to reread a line of text three times because our attention has drifted away matters very little if that attention shift has allowed us to access a key insight, a precious memory or make sense of a troubling event. . . .
>
> Pausing to reflect in the middle of telling a story is inconsequential if that pause allows us to retrieve a distant memory that makes the story more evocative and compelling. Losing a couple of minutes because we drove past our off ramp, is a minor inconvenience if the attention lapse allowed us finally to understand why the boss was so upset by something we said in last week's meeting. Arriving home from the store without the eggs that necessitated the trip is a mere annoyance when weighed against coming to a decision to ask for a raise, leave a job, or go back to school.
>
> From this personal perspective, it is much easier to understand why people are drawn to mind wandering and willing to invest nearly 50 percent of their waking hours engaged in it.

This point is echoed in an essay on sloth by author Thomas Pynchon, who said that

> what Aquinas terms Uneasiness of the Mind, or "rushing after various things without rhyme or reason," which, "if it pertains to the imaginative power . . . is called curiosity." It is of course

> precisely in such episodes of mental traveling that writers are known to do good work, sometimes even their best, solving formal problems, getting advice from Beyond, having hypnagogic adventures that with luck can be recovered later on.

Imagine if our minds were deprived of the ability to trail off. If we could not resist the pull of immediate tasks, would we be better off? Would we be happier and more successful with an authoritative hold on where our minds wander? Mindless pursuits are indispensable to self-awareness, reflection, and planning. An argument could be made that our brains require free-floating mental activity to uncover, discover, and consolidate information in the same vein as our physical body requires adequate sleep, exercise, and vitamin D.

Before investing in specialized training, consider the low-hanging fruit of reimagining these idle, mindless states as gestation for creative insights. After all, creativity has long been associated with unconscious incubation, a point often underscored by Nobel laureates and prominent artists. You are likely familiar with the idea of the aha moment, that burst of insight that suddenly solves a problem or delivers a relevant idea when it's least expected. There is, it would seem, something inventive about loose, unfocused attention. It turns out that research supports the idea of creativity sneaking up on us.

According to David Greenberg, author of *Presidential Doodles*, historical documents reveal that twenty-six of the forty-four presidents of the United States doodled while their minds wandered from whatever affairs of state (tax code reform?) were failing to grab their attention. Don't rush to dismiss this marginalia as a waste of tax dollars, though, because scientists have found that when compared with non-doodlers, people who doodle show a nearly 25 percent bump in remembering what happened while they were doodling. It may seem ironic that doing something distracting actually keeps you on task, but doodling only requires mindless attention, both keeping you alert and replenishing the mental energy that would otherwise be drained by boring speakers. Unfortunately, schoolteachers, parents, and managers often see doodling as disrespectful and therefore to be discouraged.

What if classroom teachers and middle managers started from a different premise? What if, instead, they encouraged mindless activities as a counterbalance to intensive focusing? You can already see an example of this in companies and universities that play soft background music while people work; research shows that this can aid concentration and provide a platform for calm, focused, long-lasting activity. A less obvious example can be found in policies that allow airline pilots to nap. Imagine that long flight from London to Sydney, Australia; you expect certain comforts—a pillow, a movie, a toilet that flushes, and a flight crew that's awake. Thankfully, nobody is telling you that the pilot was asked to take a twenty-five-minute nap in the cockpit seat while the plane cruises over the ocean. Don't worry, though. NASA researchers found that pilots who took naps in this study were 20 percent faster in their decision making and made 34 percent fewer mistakes after they woke up. The power of strategically turning the mind off to recharge cannot be underestimated. Where else can you gain a measureable 34 percent performance improvement in less than twenty-six minutes?

To find out more about why turning consciousness off is helpful, we turn to Dr. Andrei Medvedev, a professor at Georgetown University Center for Functional and Molecular Imaging. In 2012, his team monitored the brain activity of adults taking a midday nap. These researchers found that, during these napping periods, the right hemisphere of the brain—heavily associated with creative thinking—communicated frequently with the left side. Medvedev speculates that the right hemisphere is performing important housecleaning tasks when the body rests, such as helping transfer recent information and experiences into long-term storage.

This is like scheduling maintenance for your personal computer to autosave files and delete unnecessary information when you aren't using it, except that something unusual happens when this mental cataloging takes place. Accidental collisions with older memories result in original and even bizarre combinations. When we're asleep, the editor inside us is off duty, unable to declare some ideas off-limits, or to prematurely scratch them as impractical. It would be wonderful if each new combination of thoughts led to a creative breakthrough, but this conceptual soup is often inedible. This should be expected and honored. We shouldn't expect a steady stream of four-star ideas; all we need is one juicy one every once in a while.

Creativity arises from the oddest of mindless activities. When researchers inquired about the origins of the most creative ideas produced by 104 public relations specialists for organizations in the United Kingdom, the office turned out not to be the wellspring of originality. Commuting to and from work was the top-ranked muse for ideas, shower and bath time coming in a close second. We refer to these environments as accidental creative hubs, or ACHs. To be creative, we must take full advantage of these and other ACHs, like mowing the lawn, washing the dishes, going for a run, or taking the dog to the park.

A cautionary note: mindless activity is not, by itself, enough for creativity to occur. Otherwise we would all be Georgia O'Keefe or

Ernest Hemingway simply because we daydream while we're doing the dishes. Mindless activity is, however, the loamy soil where the best ideas take root. Researchers have found, for instance, that the most creative people, and those who are most invested in increasing their creative output, intuitively look to nonconscious states for inspiration. In particular, they are more apt to sift through their dreams, for example, and incorporate this material into their waking life. So plan for the unplanned by arranging to spend time away from activities where the mind is trying forcefully to create. And be ready to catch ideas anytime, anyplace, by always keeping a recorder within arm's reach.

Acting on Impulse

If you enjoy someone who is fun and outspoken, you might call them spontaneous, and if you don't, you might refer to them as impulsive. We have an ambiguous relationship with spur-of-the-moment activities. On the one hand we tend to see them as fun, but on the other they can seem foolish. One of the reasons impulsiveness gets a bad rap is that little attention has been paid to those situations when impulsive action gives rise to good results. So consider the following: you notice the forecast for the bank holiday weekend is non-stop rain and instead of spending yet another day at home with your three kids you click on that e-mail for weekend airline specials and book a family flight to Greece for some delicious, warm weather. Plucking an intriguing-looking hardcover book from a bargain bin, ducking into a new café on instinct, giving in to a spontaneous sexual encounter, striking up a conversation with an interesting stranger—it turns out that impulsive reactions and unplanned activities, while risky, can be hugely successful and enjoyable. This is precisely because they are unscripted and the outcome is uncertain, contributing to a mixed blend of anxious and curious emotions when we feel alive and fully ourselves—no false pretenses and none of the worries about making a good impression before taking a step forward.

1. The Liberating Effects of Losing Control

Imagine being dragged into a conversation on a controversial topic: legalizing marijuana, reducing the number of full-time firefighters and police officers to lower town budgets, deciding who gets what when Grandpa passes away. These topics are contentious because of their importance to the people directly affected. In the politically charged modern workplace, one of the most sensitive issues is diversity. Most modern, Western, industrialized countries accept that inclusiveness based on race, sex, sexual orientation, religion, national origin, or socioeconomic status is not only just, it is valuable.

Nicky Garcea, a business consultant in England, spent years running diversity programs. She would arrive at an organization, round up the workers, and launch into multihour workshops about the importance of appreciating differences. She quickly became disenchanted with this approach. "Pointing out how different everyone was," she confessed, "was pretty much a guarantee each worker would thereafter be pigeonholed as a woman, Indian, or gay."

Many of us walk a razor's edge between wanting to act as if there were literally no differences between people and talking about possible differences in sensitive, considerate ways. The problem with choosing words carefully is the sheer mental energy it requires. A white man, for instance, might spend lots of energy steering the conversation with a black woman toward innocuous, lighthearted, superficial fare. Both parties feel icky as they recognize the deeper truth that what is not being said is what matters. Two well-meaning people end up creating a high-maintenance interaction.

But what if you drained a person's energy prior to the conversation so that they lacked the oomph to hide, escape, or water down what they were thinking? To do this, you might have employees run a 5K race or complete a crossword puzzle before work. In one study, scientists asked subjects to do something intellectually or physically challenging right before a potentially sensitive conversation with a member of another ethnic group. Freed from effortful attempts to say the right thing, mentally exhausted people ended up being less inhibited in a conversation about personal differences with someone of a different race and enjoyed the interaction 25.4 percent more. They were also viewed as less prejudiced by black observers who watched videotapes of the interaction. Finally, the tired, uninhibited participants were 72.6 percent more likely to candidly discuss diversity and how to effectively handle this sensitive issue.

Additional support for the value of impulsive, or less regulated, action comes from an unlikely source: cognitive declines in old age that precede degenerative brain diseases. In one study, researchers informed younger adults (averaging nineteen years old) and older adults (averaging seventy-three years old) that they were part of a community initiative to counsel struggling teenagers. Everyone was led to believe that this community initiative was about giving advice to kids via videotaped interviews with everyday people who had lived through adolescence (instead of with professional therapists). Study participants selected their teenager from a slew of folders, unaware that the same information was in every one: a picture of an obese teenage girl along with information on how she struggles with insomnia, bullying, an inability to form friendships, and a lack of interest in school.

When participants were asked to think about what advice they wanted to offer, older adults demonstrated great candor in their advice, directly tackling the girl's weight and physical unattractiveness, as well as sharing stories about their own suffering as teenagers, how they coped, and what they learned from rejection and failure. Younger adults played it safe: 70 percent didn't even mention the girl's weight. Even more interesting, older adults with the worst cognitive functioning (as measured by a comprehensive neuropsychological exam) were the most open, 80 percent of them mentioning the girl's weight and providing the most advice.

Researchers then asked two distinguished physicians with expertise in obesity to watch film of the interviews and rate the quality of the advice being offered. Older adults with inferior mental capacity were viewed as giving better advice than younger and older adults with superior cognitive capacity. Their lack of inhibition made them more approachable, empathic, and helpful, despite their willingness to address the uncomfortable fact of the girl's obesity and its role in her social problems. In their article "The risk of polite misunderstandings," Jean-François Bonnefron and his colleagues conclude that

> Politeness taxes mental resources and creates confusion as to what is truly meant.
>
> While this confusion is functional in low-stakes situations, it can have untoward consequences in high-stakes situations such as flying a plane in an emergency or helping a patient decide on a treatment.

Giving advice and serving as a mentor are two fundamental leadership roles for a parent, teacher, or executive. Failure to tackle sensitive issues increases the likelihood that tasks fail, relationships erode, time is wasted, and money is lost due to poor communication. Lean into those feared conversations. Try them when you're a bit tired so that your natural defenses are down; this state can help you tolerate discomfort and draw on feelings that are less buttoned-down.

Making Mindless Decisions

We challenge you to go eight hours without making split-second decisions. Don't change lanes in traffic, don't invite someone to lunch on first meeting them, don't blurt out any thoughts until they're carefully weighed, don't send a hastily crafted e-mail, and certainly don't respond immediately to anything posted on Facebook. We won't be betting in favor of you making it successfully the full eight hours. We're guessing you could do this for one hour. If you happen to be at a shopping mall or watching television, we'll reduce that to two minutes.

People have a tendency to muscle important decisions. We're fond of laborious approaches to choice, such as creating cost-benefit analyses, consulting experts, and creating plans, when often sleeping on it is all we need. A more intuitive approach can seem almost new age, because it's predicated on the existence of the unconscious and the belief that this ghost in the machine can do some of the heavy lifting of judgment while our conscious minds are elsewhere engaged. According to the brain capacity principle, when there's too much data to digest, conscious thought is constrained by its process of attending to all the information, integrating it, retrieving relevant knowledge, and comparing and contrasting different choices until a final winner is selected. Mindless thinking has no such constraints because all its mental processing occurs outside conscious awareness. This leads to a counterintuitive rule of thumb: when complex decisions are required, after gathering some conscious information, avoid thinking about it consciously. Take your time and let the unconscious deal with the choice.

Nowhere is this rule more pronounced than in the research of Ap Dijksterhuis. This Dutch psychologist has studied the intelligence of the unconscious for years. In one compelling study, Dijksterhuis was interested in whether football fanatics, with their obsessive insight into the sport, are better at picking winning teams than uninformed adults who would rather use the newspaper sports section as cat litter than read it. He briefly exposed both groups to statistics on goals, assists, passing accuracy, interceptions, and arcane facts about several professional teams. Dijksterhuis wanted to see how the two groups used this information.

When given enough time to weigh this wide variety of metrics on team performance, the fanatics outperformed neophytes. No surprise there; fanatics used the data that they obsess over in their everyday life. But something weird happened when Dijksterhuis changed the rules. He let subjects deliberate for only two minutes, after which he prevented them from thinking about football by asking them to complete tough algebra equations. During these complex maths problems, Dijksterhuis interrupted them and asked for snap judgments about which teams would win upcoming games. Suddenly the neophytes outperformed the experts! Why? Because in the absence of pertinent data, the neophytes relied on whatever information grabbed their attention—such as high passing accuracy during rainy and wintry weather conditions, a statistic that experts might have glossed over. Neophytes based their gut reaction on unusual information right in front of them that their brain underlined, bolded, and bookmarked. Because experts had such a large repository of football facts stored in their brains, vital predictive information didn't stand out; it is very difficult to unlearn old facts and drop biases, which they needed to do quickly in order to absorb new facts.

Results from the football study aren't limited to the sports world. Gut instincts are just as relevant to injured people choosing doctors, obese adults deciding on a diet and fitness regimen, and medical practitioners diagnosing very sick patients. In a similar study, adults with advanced training in psychology were asked to determine from what, if any, psychological disorders a patient suffered. In one instance, these psychology experts read the case file of a patient and were then given four minutes to deliberate before making a decision. In another, they had to process the information from the file unconsciously while distracted with a word-search puzzle for four minutes. The experts made worse decisions when they reasoned more. In fact, experts making the more mindless decisions were five times as accurate as those making carefully considered decisions.

As we're seeing, there are distinct advantages to unconscious thinking, especially when it comes to the ability to dissect, manipulate, and synthesize large amounts of information. But, of course, there are also distinct advantages to conscious thinking. If you know that having a window overlooking trees and rolling green fields is essential to your quality of life at work, for example, then you need to consciously bring this to mind when you're offered a much bigger office with sleek ergonomic chairs but no view of the outside world. Otherwise you may get pulled in by the excitement of having so much space and be surprised by the precipitous decline in your spirits in the windowless months ahead. Where is the sweet spot between the two that helps you the most?

Take the problem of deciding on what flat to rent, a decision that can be overwhelming. It would be easy if a potential flat had every feature you wanted: low price, large bedrooms, nice bathtub, enough storage space, balcony, a neighborhood with great restaurants and parks, low crime, and nearby public transportation and shopping. And—oh yeah—make it pet-friendly while you're at it. In real life, finding a flat is an exercise in compromise. You get the walk-in wardrobe but not the public park, the updated kitchen but not the his-and-hers sinks. Most people try to engage in a mental shell game of swapping out the various parts in an effort to make a decision with which they can be happy.

In 2011, Dijksterhuis and his colleagues conducted an experiment in which participants had to find one or two ideal choices out of twelve possible flats. But just like the real world, there were no slam dunks; the best flats had eight positive features and four negative, and the worst had eight negative and only four positive. When people had to make decisions immediately after being given information on each flat, they arrived at the optimal choice a mere 15 percent of the time. When people were given four minutes to mindfully contemplate each flat, they arrived at the better choice 29 percent of the time. This indicates that being thoughtful trumps impulsive buying, but neither appears to be all that effective.

Interestingly, when the participants in a third condition were distracted with an unrelated word puzzle and then asked to make the decision, they did just as well, uncovering the best choice 30 percent of the time. What's really interesting is what happened when participants were able to spend two minutes mindfully contemplating each flat, and afterward their attention was diverted to irrelevant, difficult word games they had to complete for two minutes. Those who spent half the time consciously deliberating before making a quick, mindless decision after a tiresome word game arrived at the best choice a whopping 58 percent of the time. These folks spent half as long carefully analyzing each flat and their decision making was twice as good.

It is clear that mindful thinking alone is insufficient to help us reach the best decision in a sea of choices. We need to take advantage of the relative strengths of both conscious and unconscious thinking. An interesting but incomplete discovery, after all, where should we begin? Should our decision-making process start with conscious or unconscious thinking about the options in front of us? In a subsequent study, researchers discovered that the sequence of conscious and unconscious thinking matters. When flat seekers were given two minutes to deliberate on flats (conscious thinking) before being distracted by word games (unconscious thinking), they chose the best flat 57 percent of the time. When the sequence was reversed, their ability to choose the best flat dropped to 30 percent of the time.

No wonder there are so many books on mindfulness and irrational thinking! We're still learning how to function optimally as fully integrated, whole people. This fascinating line of research shows us that the most efficient and effective strategy for handling complex decisions is to flexibly use conscious and unconscious thinking, in tandem and in that order. In a cognitively demanding situation with a large number of options, the formula for optimal decision making looks like this:

1. Spend a small amount of time mindfully contemplating the situation.
2. Stop.
3. Skip over to another unrelated activity for an incubation period.
4. Render a decision.

Mindless Interventions

For decades, people have been looking to boost success by increasing self-awareness, but the researchers discussed in this chapter suggest a different approach. As an alternative, we offer the promise of (un)consciousness-raising strategies to help us all perform better at the goals we care about, and thereby live better. We offer the provocative notion that our behavior can be dramatically changed without any awareness on our part. Unobtrusive, unconscious information processing can lead us to be stronger, faster, and wiser in our decision making.

Consider the goal of increasing performance. At a call center, Gary Latham and Ronald Piccolo tested out a low-cost intervention on employees by giving them a photograph to view before calling customers. One photograph depicted three telemarketing reps smiling during a phone call (relevant accomplishment), another showed a woman triumphantly raising her arms as she crosses the finish line of a running race (irrelevant accomplishment), and a third portrayed the office building where they worked. Employees viewing photographs depicting accomplishments experienced a whopping 58 percent increase in the number of callers they persuaded to pledge money, whereas those viewing pictures of buildings showed zero improvement.

But that's not the amazing part. Get this: employees staring at the photograph of smiling telemarketers raised 85 percent more money than people staring at pictures of buildings. When asked how they ramped up their performance, not a single person mentioned the new, inspiring picture in their cubicle. Which do you think makes more sense: spending $10 for a poster and frame, or thousands on advanced trainings to improve employee morale, motivation, and performance? Here, researchers also found that subconsciously priming someone for high performance has an impact that lasts not seconds, or minutes, or even hours, but an entire work week.

Now let's move to bigger societal problems. Trying to convince people to stop using stereotypes about adults who are older, handicapped, gay, or of a different race has the unintended effect of making stereotypes easy to retrieve and therefore to use. In a similar vein, when smokers view antismoking advertisements, they end up smoking more. So when researchers corralled a group of white adults who admitted prejudicial views and a desire to avoid contact with blacks, the researchers wondered whether these views could be reconditioned without ever trying to convince their participants that prejudice and racism are bad.

When shown positive images and words about black Americans on a computer screen (picture a black child sharing her lunch with a hungry classmate), the white adults in the study were instructed to "approach blacks" by pulling a joystick toward them. When shown images and words of white Americans, they were instructed to "avoid whites" by pushing a joystick away from them. The idea was that repeatedly pairing subtle positive images of black people with the motivation to approach and appreciate them might revise the mindless habit of viewing black people as enemies who should be avoided. These researchers found that white adults trained to associate blacks with approach behavior experienced a 46.5 percent decrease in prejudicial beliefs compared with those who didn't receive any mental retraining. But does this brain rewiring influence how a white adult behaves toward a black stranger? The answer is an astounding yes. After being trained to mindlessly associate black faces with approach movements using a computer joystick, in a getting acquainted conversation, white adults moved their chair six times closer to a black stranger (a trained actor who was already sitting down when the participant walked in). Hot damn, the brain is an interesting organ!

For those of us already working toward a greater appreciation of diversity, we might not require reminders about the benefits of being around people who don't look like us or share the same values. But here's an important fact: all of us have an in-group, a circle of like-minded folks we reflexively view as more appealing than the rest of humanity. Whether it is religious people versus atheists, vegetarians versus meat eaters, feminists versus fans of pornography, or northerners versus southerners, we all have biases, some that we recognize and many more that are hidden to us. The latest science offers insights into how we can shift these biases. We now know that with repeated movements we can rewire brain patterns to change the mind for the better. Mindless mental training can be added to the list of strategies to enhance success and well-being.

Harnessing Mindlessness

We offer a contrast to the large amount of scientific and public coverage suggesting that mindfulness is better than mindlessness. Understanding how mindless thinking bolsters success will give you an edge over peers trying to log into a mindful state as often as possible. Even if you wanted to, it is physically untenable to always be mindful. To capitalize on unconscious thinking, we described the strengths of mindlessness in life areas as layered as goal pursuit, trusting people, creativity, prejudice, and complex decision making.

In certain situations, mindless thoughts enable us to be more objective. You might find yourself resisting this statement. After all, it seems intuitive that flash judgments on so-called unimportant simple decisions are fine, but that intense, focused deliberations are required for complex decisions. We are here to tell you that effectiveness is often jeopardized by beliefs about the superiority of mindfulness.

THE TAKEAWAYS

1. Mindfulness can be beneficial, but we are also naturally predisposed to mindlessness.
2. Automatic thinking helps conserve mental resources.
3. Mental depletion can lead to a productive form of disinhibition.
4. Mindless processing often leads to superior performance and better decisions, especially in complicated situations.
5. Subliminal prompts can push us toward greater goal effort.
6. Attempts to stamp out mindlessness are destined to fail.

Acknowledging the power of mindlessness is in itself an intervention. People can also be trained to take advantage of this underappreciated resource. Here are some additional shortcuts for harnessing mindlessness:

1. Set ridiculously short deadlines—ten seconds—in which to make decisions that you have already spent a few minutes paralyzed about what to do. In doing so, you force a mindless decision. There is always a reason not to take a

trip somewhere. There is always a reason to stick with the same grocery store purchases. Take ten seconds and then press submit, put the item in your car, or walk away without wasting any more energy on the decision.

2. Use cues or signals that represent your goals. Do you want to be cool and collected in a situation, or be candid and open to whatever you're feeling? Do you want to have big aspirations and be willing to take risks to achieve them, or be risk adverse, being sure not to make mistakes? Words and images can be taped in your room and on your desk that prime particular goals and motivational styles.
3. Schedule time for mental meandering. Mindfulness is a resource-intensive strategy; there's a reason we are not exclusively hardwired that way. When the mind wanders, our brain activity is almost the same as when we are resting. Ideas collide and creativity happens by accident. Households and organizations can be organized to encourage strategic mindless activity. This is one of many reasons that free play and physical activity during break time is the last thing that should be removed from school schedules.
4. Set rules for the use of intuition. When you have a simple choice to make, you will be better off with a logical, deliberate method. When you face a complicated decision, you will make it more effectively when you spend a few minutes contemplating the available information, give yourself an incubation period where you do something else ("sleep on it"), and then switch over to mindless, gut intuition.

Instead of choosing a winner between your two modes of thought, mindlessness and mindfulness, we argue for the relative merits of both. If you discount half of human thinking, half of human consciousness, then you create an artificially low ceiling for your success and well-being.

CHAPTER 6

The Teddy Effect

Can you imagine Barack Obama—or any head of state, for that matter—sneaking away from his security team to grab some private time? In this safety-conscious age, it's hard to picture. But that's exactly what Theodore Roosevelt did in 1903, only two years into his first term as president. While on an official visit to Yosemite National Park, he abandoned his retinue and stole away with a couple of park rangers and naturalist John Muir. Muir spent much of their stolen time together advocating for greater governmental preservation of wild lands. They spent the night among the sequoia trees and ventured to the magnificent precipice of Glacier Point before Roosevelt rejoined his bewildered staff in the hotel on the valley floor below. Now known as "the greatest camping trip in history," Roosevelt's ability to breach protocol was instrumental in what would later become wide-ranging legislation protecting wilderness areas.

If you think this act of rebelliousness and entitlement was a fluke, think again. In the modern era, can you imagine a government leader swimming naked in the Potomac River, the backyard of the White

House, to stay physically and mentally fit in the wintertime? Teddy knew how to manipulate his public image and other people. When William McKinley ran for president in 1900, he picked Teddy to be his running mate. They won and when President McKinley was assassinated, the world waited for Teddy to take the reins of power. The world would have to wait longer than intended because Teddy happened to be out of reach, rock climbing in upstate New York. Teddy had an inflated view of his superiority and potential for greatness, and felt he deserved special treatment.

The world needs more Teddies, and not because we need more nudity in the Potomac.

Roosevelt possessed bravado, daring, dynamism, and a willingness to embrace his negative side that few—if any—governmental leaders have had before or since. He won the Congressional Medal of Honor as a soldier. Catching malaria from an infected leg wound wouldn't stop him. He explored hundreds of miles of the Amazon rainforest; in fact, his party traveled farther down the Rio da Duvida (River of Doubt) than any travelers before them—a river later christened the Rio Roosevelt in honor of his awesomeness. Before a campaign stop in Milwaukee, he was shot at close range (the bullet passed through the handwritten speech in his breast pocket and lodged in his chest), but opted to give the hour-long speech in its entirety before seeking medical attention. As a statesman, Roosevelt won the Nobel Peace Prize for his foreign diplomacy. He is also seen as the father of the National Park Service, the first such system in the world to protect lands for widespread public enjoyment. By anyone's standards, Roosevelt was a great man and is commonly ranked as the fourth greatest American president (just behind Lincoln, FDR, and Washington).

How does one human being accomplish so many extraordinary feats? Is Roosevelt's success based on his indefatigable optimism and compassion? Evidence suggests just the opposite, the possibility that Roosevelt was that rare person with equal access to both the positive and negative sides of his personality. He made the most of being whole. Edwin Lawrence Godkin, editor in chief of the *Evening Post*, devoted many articles to Teddy's "bellicose temperament," claiming that his "value to the community would be greatly increased if somehow he could somewhere have his fill of fighting." But we see it differently: this aspect of wholeness, which we call the Teddy Effect, allows us to deal with the social aspects of discomfort, instead of avoiding them.

Curious about the adaptive nature of seemingly bad social traits, psychologist Scott Lilienfeld and his colleagues examined the leadership provided by forty-two US presidents by drawing on the expertise of 121 biographers, journalists, and scholars. Each expert was asked 240 questions about the personality profiles of these presidents, and this information was then compared with job-performance data from polls and other historical information. In particular, the Lilienfeld research team was interested in traits related to psychopathy, commonly defined as a personality dysfunction characterized by antisocial behavior, a diminished capacity for empathy or remorse, and poor behavior control. Without question, psychopathy in general, and psychopaths in particular, have a bad reputation. But psychologists referring to psychopathy are talking about a constellation of traits that include some very positive ones: being charming, being immune to the paralyzing effects of anxiety, and being physically fearless.

The researchers discovered that American presidents with more psychopathic tendencies—especially those associated with fearlessness—were better performers. Their psychopathy was directly associated with a huge range of enviable outcomes, such as being more persuasive, being more capable of handling a crisis, being more willing to take risks and to introduce new legislation, being viewed as a world figure by others, and maintaining better relationships with Congress. Of the forty-two presidents evaluated in the research, Teddy was ranked—by a landslide—as number one in fearlessness and number two in grandiose narcissism. Interestingly, in a series of follow-up studies headed by Sarah Smith, the Lilienfeld research team found similar results for psychopaths in university students and normal adults in the general population. Across these studies, psychopathy was repeatedly found to be associated with higher rates of altruism and more frequent acts of heroism.

If you have a brain in your head and a heart in your chest you probably don't want to be an evil jerk. That said, your likely default position of playing nice might be holding you back from that final 20 percent of the success you could otherwise be enjoying. Here we present a body of research that suggests strategic use of your negative emotions, including helpful behaviors that happen to be rule bending, dominant, cold, fearless, grandiose, manipulative, flamboyant, and self-absorbed. A minority might dislike you but nobody ever achieved great success or pushed the boundaries toward innovative change with a 100 percent approval rating. Not Plato, not Mahatma Gandhi, not Mao Zedong, not Nelson Mandela. If you were somehow able to match their fearlessness, unyielding determination, and undying devotion to excellence, just like them, you would be unable to escape criticism, jealousy, and enemies. As Teddy Roosevelt demonstrated, you do not have to sacrifice healthy relationships for successful accomplishments. Although his first wife died young, Roosevelt enjoyed a long and happy marriage with his second wife, and they had five children together. Socially uncomfortable behaviors can put you on the track to success without alienating your loved ones.

Throughout history, the Teddy Effect has been a legitimate way for leaders to acquire power and promote well-being. To motivate, improve performance, and survive you have to give yourself permission to engage in acts of dominance, aggression, strategic manipulation, and selfishness (putting yourself, family, and innermost circle first). This is as true for leaders with a capital *L* (as in heads of companies) or with a small *l* (as in anyone who is trying to influence someone else). By embracing the Teddy Effect, you access the 20 percent edge that you and the majority of society prematurely dismiss. As Teddy Roosevelt's life demonstrates, you do not have to sacrifice healthy relationships for successful accomplishments. Teddy was beloved by his wife, children, the soldiers under his watch, and an adoring public during his own time.

Let us be the first to admit that considering dominance and aggression as self-growth tools can seem off-putting. In our modern, hypersensitive world, many leadership experts refute the need for so-called dark behaviors, claiming that the success they offer is only short term. The modern positivity movement has placed an emphasis on gentle tactics by leaders who, according to Tom Rath of Gallup,

> deliberately increase the flow of positive emotions within their organization. . . . Instead of being concerned with what they can *get out of* their employees, positive leaders search for opportunities to *invest in* everyone who works for them. They view each interaction with another person as an opportunity to increase his or her positive emotions.

This approach is great for people who are less inclined to get angry, be assertive, or show toughness. It's the perfect approach when kids are intrinsically motivated to take out the garbage, mow the lawn, or do their homework. Studies show that leaders with virtuous traits can push people toward better performance while prompting them to feel good about themselves. However, almost all of this research has been conducted during times of prosperity, when the bottom lines are in the black, and families aren't so stressed over their finances. What happens during downturns? During these times, it makes more sense to consider adding the benefits conferred by the darker aspect of your natural humanity.

Understanding the Three Parts of the Teddy Effect

Without dismissing the potential damage of being emotionally detached or manipulative on a regular basis, we argue that attempts to pathologize certain strategies and eliminate them as options because they seem malevolent has led to leaders who struggle to communicate bad news, recover slowly from stressful events, and create employees and citizens unable to handle adversity. Just as negative emotions are often helpful, negative strategies can also make a surprising contribution. To gain insight into these benefits, let's peer inside the three parts of the Teddy Effect: Machiavellianism, narcissism, and psychopathy.

An astute observer of human behavior, philosopher Niccolò Machiavelli offered specific advice for decision making and leadership in his magnum opus, the five-hundred-year-old text, *The Prince.*

Machiavellianism, as his way of thinking and acting has become known, is about being emotionally detached when making everyday decisions so that the short-term pursuit of happiness does not derail our long-term plans. Machiavelli's rules are not about how to do good in an ideal world. Instead, they're about making the right choice, at the right time, for the right reasons in the real world. This means developing a heightened sense of situational awareness and the latitude to shift between honesty and deception, aggression and kindness: "He must stick to the good so long as he can, but, being compelled by necessity, he must be ready to take the way of evil." Machiavelli makes a powerful argument that the best thing to do cannot be divorced from the situation in which it is performed. This brings to mind Teddy Roosevelt's winning both the highest award for military combat and the most prestigious award possible for peaceful negotiations.

Machiavellianism is generally perceived as morally repugnant, and the same is true of narcissism. When psychologists consider it, however, they take into account that it has both positive and negative features. Narcissism is best defined by a grandiose sense of self-importance and entitlement. Narcissists do things in hope of winning the approval and admiration of other people, and they show little interest in people who can't provide such opportunities for them. On the plus side, narcissists idealize people they think they can learn from, showing deference as they absorb knowledge and skills. They also truly believe they are special in some way, which gives them a sense of entitlement—and therefore confidence—to pursue their own path.

According to Greek mythology, Narcissus was a young man renowned for his beauty. At one point, he gazed into a pool of water and fell in love with the face he saw there, not realizing that it was his own. Unable to tear himself away from his beloved, Narcissus did not drink, eat, or sleep, and eventually he died at the pool's edge. This tale warns us against the dangers of vanity. Although Narcissus might have been fixated on himself, this obsession was based on his legitimately superior physical beauty. Narcissus was extraordinary in this regard. That said, the superficial nature of this particular quality might be unappealing to the rest of us.

Does narcissism have any benefit beyond those rare instances when it is helpful to acknowledge extraordinary strengths in other people (beyond mere physical beauty)? Psychologist Roy Baumeister and his colleagues studied the potential upsides of narcissism and found that "people with a high sense of entitlement did not report stronger or weaker desires, but they reported less conflict about these desires than other people did." That is, when narcissistic people wanted something, they wanted it without regret, guilt, or second thought. The Baumeister team also concluded that "highly entitled persons apparently regard the fact that they want something as ample and often sufficient reason to do it."

In other words, grandiose people possess a willingness to pursue lofty aspirations that most people might dismiss as foolish, self-absorbed, or impossible. Rather than fantasizing about hosting a television show, for instance, narcissists are more likely to go out and try to do just that. The confidence of people who lean toward self-absorption derives from a sense of specialness. It's entirely possible that a feeling of uniqueness and a dollop of entitlement gave us the iPhone, the Human Genome Project, Microsoft Windows, an independent Israeli state, the Oprah Book Club, and *Exile on Main Street*.

In the minds of everyday people, the negative qualities associated with Machiavellianism and narcissism pale in comparison with psychopathy. Sensational accounts of psychopathic serial killers have blackened the reputation of this quality for the general public. People with psychopathy are considered incapable of feeling empathy for other people, and that such a life—devoid of any emotional connection—translates to the absence of guilt, to violence, and ultimately to murder. Research psychologists take a different view of psychopathy, one that offers a window into the benefits of small-stakes, situationally appropriate negative behaviors.

Simply put, the performance of psychopaths is unaffected by the fear and other powerful emotions that commonly paralyze nonpsychopaths. For most people, a knockdown drag-out fight with a romantic partner leads to impaired function of some kind, whether it's the ability to concentrate or even the ability to eat. In difficult circumstances, it can be very helpful to dial down the flow of emotions. Take the example of one dentist we know. When we jokingly asked him how he could tolerate the fact that he caused so much pain in his chosen profession, he had a ready answer.

> When I greet my patients, I feel human. I meet them in the waiting room, smile, and shake their hands. We are standing on a soft, shag carpet. Then, when we cross the threshold to the linoleum floor of the exam room I change. From that point forward, I turn my emotions off. Each patient becomes a set of teeth and a problem for me to fix.

The three elements of Machiavellianism, narcissism, and psychopathy (we call them the Dark Triad) each represent a tightrope. Lean too far one way and you hurt other people; lean too far to the other side and you become incapable of taking risks, or being truly effective. The Dark Triad lies at the core of every fictional antihero. In each case, they have flaws but also provide us a fantasy of a more successful self. Think Batman, James Bond, Han Solo, Severus Snape, Stringer Bell, and Tyrion Lannister. For female antiheroes, look no further than

Scarlett O'Hara, Madame Defarge, Scheherazade, Jessica Atreides, and Carrie Mathison. Their dispassionate cool makes them appealing, even when this attraction collides with our better judgment.

You've Been Naughty

Having restored some virtue to the Dark Triad, we're not proposing that you change your personality. Don't give up apologizing, volunteer work, or holding the door open for other people. Continue to be nice. We are suggesting, however, that you adopt Machiavelli's advice to be aware of situations in which the best possible outcome require the use of your inner Machiavelli, narcissist, or psychopath. If the Teddy Effect still feels repellent to you, then we would like to take this opportunity to remind you that you already engage in these behaviors to some extent.

Have you ever

- waited to press start on the dishwasher until your spouse walked into the room so he or she could witness your contribution to the household chores?
- tried to charm someone in order to win them over?
- delivered a "spoonful of positives" to help pave the way for a critique?
- fantasized about accepting an Academy Award?
- framed yourself as a victim when recounting an event in a bid to win support and sympathy from your friends?
- told a lie?
- pressed the lift button to close the door when you saw someone coming?

Perhaps you'll feel better knowing that we've all behaved "badly" for most of our lives. We know this from research on the honesty rates of children. Researchers Angela Evans and Kang Lee investigated the moral integrity of four-year-olds. Before leaving each child alone in a room, Evans asked them to resist looking inside a gift bag next to their seat. The children, of course, never suspected that they were being secretly observed, and 80 percent of them disobeyed to peek at the toy inside. When Evans came back into the room, she wanted to know whether the little swindlers would try to conceal their misdeed. To her surprise, 90 percent of kids didn't hesitate to say that they never opened the bag. Now get this: for every additional IQ point, the children were slightly more likely to lie. With greater intelligence, we become more analytical in our thinking, and more sophisticated in our strategies to outwit and successfully manipulate others.

Research suggests that you, like everyone else, think that you are better than other human beings. This so-called better-than-average effect shows that most people believe that they are above average, which, of course, is a mathematical impossibility. In one study, for example, 25 percent of respondents said they were in the top 1 percent when it came to getting along with others. In another study, 93 percent of respondents said they were above average in driving ability. When you ask romantic couples living together how much each one contributes to the overall housework, it always adds up to more than 100 percent. The average person lives inside a narcissistic bubble, a self-serving bias that gives most of us the confidence we need to face a complex and uncertain day.

In fact, research on the better-than-average effect is mirrored in other studies that suggest that narcissism—a heavy dose of me-focus—is on the rise. A number of studies by Jean Twenge at San Diego State and Keith Campbell at the University of Georgia suggest that the times, they are a-changin'. In one study, the Twenge team discovered that the use of collective pronouns such as *we* and *us* are decreasing slightly in everyday speech and that their cousins, the first-person pronouns of *me* and *mine*, are on the rise.

Similarly, this trend toward uniqueness can be seen in the naming of babies. In a study of more than a hundred years of baby names, the Twenge team found that parents are increasingly seeking highly individualistic names. In the days of yore, for example, 40 percent of boys were given names from the ten most popular baby names for that year (e.g., John, Michael) but today fewer than 10 percent are. Even we—the authors of this book (Todd and Robert)—have named our five children Violet, Chloe, Raven, Jayanti, and Jedi. Except for Chloe and Violet, which are very popular names at the time of this writing, we are pushing our kids off the grid. At this rate, kids in the future will be named after individual prime numbers.

Yes, narcissism is on the rise. You have spotted an increase in emotionally fragile, distrustful, antagonistic, admiration-seeking characters with a strong sense of entitlement on your work team. You have sensed a seismic shift in how people treat one another. No longer do two people fight, get it out of their system, and the next day pat each other on the back and move on with a bit more respect for each other. If you threaten someone's sense of superiority, they will often fight back. The difference is that more recently, when people feel attacked, they are relentless in their response. They will not stop until they win and you lose.

This phenomenon has become increasingly commonplace on the motorway. Think about how much time you spend each week defending your tarmac territory, inching toward the car in front of you so that the person to your left or right is boxed in and unable to cut you off. When you do this, have you noticed the additional physiological burden it places on your body, the increase in blood pressure, the elevated tension in your hands and feet? If this doesn't describe you, have you noticed how other road warriors box you in, somehow taking it personally that it requires a shift in lanes to get off at a motorway exit?

When you take a step back and observe this kind of human behavior, this narcissistic vulnerability, this antagonistic need to protect personal space as if a war has been declared, is bizarre. It's even worse online, where people can feel empowered by devaluing someone else and shredding their creations. It takes years to write a book, to film a movie, or to prepare for a world championship competition. It only takes a few minutes to write a scathing criticism of them. Such antagonistic rivalries and zero-sum games stress out all involved and are harmful to our mental health.

But as Twenge, Campbell, and others bemoan the imminent apocalypse, forgotten is that a healthy side of narcissism, dubbed *the striving for supremacy*, is also on the rise. This side of narcissism happens to be an unheralded strength. When the need to win the admiration of others is activated, this triggers the charming, self-assured, dominant behaviors that may result in various desired social outcomes:

- success,
- leadership positions,
- power and influence,
- attractiveness and popularity, and
- ability to bring grandiose fantasies to fruition.

Narcissists have grandiose visions of themselves, which result in the vigorous pursuit of goals where they get to showcase just how unique, visionary, and potent they think they are.

Sometimes good people act badly. Sometimes the Teddy Effect is responsible for bad behaviors. But if you hold on too firmly to this idea, you will miss out on a few surprises. Who do you think is most likely to help a stranger in crisis, a person scoring high on a measure of psychopathic tendencies or someone who lacks these so-called negative qualities (a positive person)? To find out, psychologist Mehmet Mahmut used trained actors to determine what it takes for a bystander to intervene.He didn't just have one actor cry for help; he set up a gauntlet for unsuspecting pedestrians to stroll through. First, pedestrians encountered an actor pretending to be lost, asking for directions. Then they ran into an actress who dropped a stack of papers on the ground. Finally, they came across an actor alone at a table with an arm in a sling unable to drink from a water fountain or jot notes on a pad.

When the stranger asked for directions, psychopathic pedestrians were less likely to stop and help. When watching a stressed woman pick up an unwieldy number of dropped documents, psychopathic pedestrians helped as often as their positive peers. On seeing the stranger with a broken arm struggling with daily tasks, psychopathic pedestrians were much *more* likely to step up and show kindness. When there was potential for heroism, when a display of virtue would look good to outsiders, when anxiety about what do is high, psychopathic characters stepped up, whereas more compassionate folks tended to walk by. Self-involved people are interested in the Big Stuff. Narcissistic people want to be admired, and this motivates them to take action in situations that will appeal to the outside world.

Under the Influence

The word *manipulation* is loaded with negative connotations. We tend to think of con men as manipulators, or of the psychic who bilked one of our family members for a huge sum of money. Manipulation actually means to control or influence, much in the way that beer companies influence you by making a funny commercial that gives you a jolt of well-being. Or much in the same way a driver following close behind you is urging you to switch lanes and let her pass. Or much in the same way that retired San Joaquin County Sheriff Robert Merk would occasionally flash his badge when he was pulled over for speeding and say, innocently, "I should have known better than to be driving so fast since I work in law enforcement." Every day we all exercise influence.

One reason the word *manipulation* lands poorly on our ears is that it can suggest gaining power over another person. When we read accounts of slimy sales tactics—lowballing, bait and switch, the foot in the door—these strategies seem ugly. In one account of car sales techniques written by psychologist Robert Levine, for example, the sales process seems freighted with trickery. One salesman Levine interviewed admitted to offering absurdly low prices simply to get people to visit the car lot. Once they arrived, the salesman suddenly received a phone call and passed the customer off to a colleague, who then explained that the first guy had made a mistake and that the cars were actually more expensive than the customer had been led to believe.

When we hear about these tactics our blood boils. We get so offended, in fact, that we forget a simple truth: the customer is actually looking to buy a car and the salesman is actually looking to facilitate that process. Getting the customer on the lot through trickery may be dishonest but it is—in all honesty—an indispensable part of the car buying process, and one that will serve the customer.

One relatively innocuous instance of positive manipulation is when nonprofit organizations solicit contributions. Just like advertisers of food products, charitable organizations have a stake in manipulating people to fork over cash. They think hard about how best to do this. A science has even emerged around soliciting funds. Take a single study by Daniel Feiler, at Dartmouth's Tuck School of Business. He was interested in examining the different types of appeals used by charitable organizations. One type is known as egoistic appeal (giving money will help you feel good) and another is known as altruistic (giving money will help provide food to the poor). When presented with one or the other type of appeal potential, donors to a university alumni association donated about 6.5 percent of the time. When presented with both appeals, however, that percentage was cut in half. It appears that people don't mind being appealed to, but too much appeal feels like manipulation, which is a turnoff. This study underscores what is, perhaps, the only rule in the game of social influence: it's okay to manipulate as long as you don't get caught.

Another positive example of manipulation and influence comes from police work. Every day, police officers are faced with situations in which they must influence others in the interests of public safety. They coax potential jumpers back from ledges, convince naked people to put their clothes back on, encourage partners in domestic arguments to cool off, and negotiate to free hostages. The police have a wide range of physical interventions at the ready—guns and tear gas and tasers and handcuffs—but they are also trained to use their body language and words to de-escalate tense situations. Effective police officers must be master manipulators.

In 2008, the city of Portland, Oregon, had contracted one square block of the city center known as Pioneer Courthouse Square to a private security firm. The square, affectionately known as "Portland's living room," is an open plaza where businesspeople have lunch, where folks can play chess with strangers, and where the town's towering Christmas tree stands in the winter. Its security guards, much like those at shopping malls, were primarily meant to serve as a preventive measure, intended to ease the burden on the police. In the event of a major crime, Portland's finest could have been on the scene quickly, but otherwise they wanted to be free to patrol high-crime areas. However, the criminal element noticed the relative absence of uniformed police officers, and before long the dispatcher was receiving between thirty and thirty-five calls a day reporting instances of drug dealing in the square.

Enter Adam Morengo. He and his partner, dressed in plain clothes, arrived at the square to gather intelligence regarding the drug activity. After a half hour of observation, Morengo had identified the lead drug dealer and his five runners, and had figured out the specific nuances of the drug-selling operation. There was no question that enough heavily armed police officers could eventually apprehend the six criminals, but likely not without a foot chase and a possible shootout or other dangerous consequence.

Morengo opted for the soft touch. With his hands and body visibly relaxed and open, he walked right into the middle of the pack of drug dealers. He identified himself as a police officer and immediately reassured the group that he had no intention of arresting anyone. The primary dealer became very aggressive toward Morengo, saying at one point, "You can't do anything to us. We could have you gunned down in the street." Morengo persevered.

"Guys," he said, "I am not here to disrespect you. I am not accusing you of anything, and I am not mistreating you. I am here for one purpose only, and that is to see if we can work together." This threw the drug dealers for a loop. They went from posturing to watchful. Their curiosity, it seems, was getting the best of them. Morengo explained his proposition.

"Really, all I care about is that this square is safe. People bring their kids here, and I just want to know that no one is going to get hurt. Now there is no way I can arrest all the people here who are breaking the law; I simply don't have the resources." This drew wide grins from his audience. "So," Morengo continued, "I want to brainstorm with you guys on how we're going to work together to make this square safe."

The leader loomed over Morengo. "Are you giving us a free pass?" he asked in disbelief.

"Absolutely not," Morengo said. "You know that when we see illegal behavior we have to act on it. You know that the more obvious and persistent the behavior is, the more we are obligated to take care of it. So if you deal drugs I can promise you that you will get arrested. But we have an opportunity right now to avoid trouble and arrests. So what can we work out?"

It may have been that Morengo was using de-escalation techniques such as keeping his hands in plain sight, speaking with a soothing voice, answering questions, and not smiling (which, as we've seen in the studies on mimicry, can be misinterpreted). It may have been that he was treating the drug dealers with a degree of respect they were unaccustomed to from police officers. Whatever the case, the drug dealers suggested a solution. "We could move out of the square and take our business somewhere else."

Morengo told them that he would sincerely appreciate that, and that he was happy that they had all worked together to keep things safe in an important part of the downtown corridor. Without showing his weapon, or even raising his voice, Morengo had convinced a large, tough, and well-armed group of criminals to walk away from a lucrative location. As it turned out, all the men were arrested within twenty-four hours of setting up their drug operation in a new location. There, just as Morengo had suggested, conspicuous drug dealing drew a phalanx of heavily armed officers who didn't mind arresting the group of young men in this less populated area.

Morengo's story is suggestive of the wide range of techniques—from open discussion to armed response—that we use to influence others. When we, the authors of this book, think of influencing others, we generally sort this into two categories: hard and soft approaches. Hard approaches are more overt, dramatic, and sometimes coercive. A perfect example of this can be seen in the way that Ronald Reagan handled a nationwide strike of air traffic controllers. In a three-minute speech delivered in 1981, the former president declared, "They are in violation of the law, and if they do not report for work in forty-eight hours they have forfeited their jobs and will be terminated." This was not a warm hand extended in understanding or an offer to sit down at the negotiating table. It was a tough stance and it was no bluff; Reagan went on to fire more than eleven thousand air traffic controllers.

Hard approaches to influence are admittedly one of the reasons why people have such a negative view of so many Teddy Effect strategies. In thinking about hard approaches, it's important to look beyond a long history of con men using shady dealings to fleece public trust and money. You can see more pedestrian examples of hard approaches in the grandstands of virtually any major professional sports event.

Die-hard fans—those with face paint and wearing official team merchandise—are well-known for both their support and opposition. They cheer on their hometown favorites and jeer at their opponents. Basketball fans sitting behind the glass backboard, for instance, wave what are called thunderstix to distract visiting players attempting to make a free throw. So common is this practice, in fact, that the Dallas Mavericks have experimented with waving the stix in unison, on the advice of a neuroscientist who suggested that it would be a more effective visual distraction than random waving. In their first two coordinated attempts, Maverick fans were able to drop the number of successful rival free throws by approximately 20 percent.

Hard influence—especially related to aggression—has also received scientific support for being effective. In one study, mini-crowds of ten people watched various athletes perform. The crowd was instructed to cheer in some conditions, to jeer in others, and to be silent in a control condition. The jeering worked; athletes performed worse than when they were supported or when the spectators kept quiet.

In another and more compelling study, researchers tracked the effects of booing in real basketball games at the University of Illinois and at Kansas State University. Here the researchers were interested in the performance of both the home and visiting teams in the five minutes that followed fifteen sustained seconds of booing. Interestingly, in only half of all games were there instances of such extreme displeasure. When this type of booing did occur, however, it had an immediate impact. Home teams immediately started scoring more, committing fewer fouls, and maintaining better control of the ball (committing fewer turnovers). Visitors, by contrast, scored less, lost the ball more, and committed more fouls in the five minutes after the jeering occurred. Notably, the seventeen thousand fans packed into the Assembly

Hall basketball arena at the University of Illinois are not a selection of sociopaths; they are normal people who can access their Teddy Effect when it serves their needs.

Take another example of a hard manipulative approach. If you're a commuter crossing the state line from northern Virginia into Washington, DC, by going over the Teddy Roosevelt Bridge, stop at the first red light and turn your head to the left. You will see a man in a two-button three-piece petrol-gray suit. In his clean hands is a haphazardly ripped piece of cardboard with the words "Need Money for Cocaine." He is smiling, beckoning you to put a few bills in his velvet hat. Many people hoot at him contemptuously, waving him off. Five yards farther on stands another man. He has a shaggy beard with what looks to be dirt and bits of egg shell embedded in it. A dirty, plaid blanket is wrapped around him, and his eyes plead for compassion as he holds up his own sign that reads "Help Me, Need Food." Drivers roll down their windows and hold out one- and five-dollar bills for him to grab. By the end of the day, his pockets are filled with cash.

We spoke to these two men. As you probably suspected, they work as a team. They used to work alone until they started comparing notes about what behaviors increased their revenue. They switch roles every few days and thoroughly enjoy it. They also earn a lot of money, far too much to stop and start working for minimum wage at a fast-food chain. What's their favorite part? Some people call them out on the scam, smile, and then give them money anyway for the entertainment.

They are unapologetic about their manipulation. As two adults with a combined education of thirteen school years, and a long history of physical and emotional abuse by caregivers, they found a tiny niche that works for them. You have to hand it to them for their ingenuity.

They're a perfect example of how manipulation can become an art, both literally and metaphorically, and how the best work makes other people feel good, right, or both about what they are doing. You simply cannot have a genuine conversation with another person and influence them without temporarily switching your perspective to theirs in order to understand what they want and what motivates them to take action.

Soft approaches to influencing others are more subtle. These approaches, often based on charm and seduction, might include hints, smiles, or seemingly casual mentions of other people to show off, or incite rivalry. Soft approaches are ultimately defined by their nonconfrontational nature and their evocation of both pleasant and unpleasant feelings in the target.

If you're turned off by hardball tactics, then consider a typical soft approach: guilt. As we saw earlier, guilt-tripping is a surprisingly common method of influencing people. It involves three common strategies: (1) telling a person about your many self-sacrifices (to activate a feeling of reciprocity); (2) reminding a person of their obligation to the relationship (to activate feelings of personal responsibility); and (3) pointing out a time when a person behaved in a desirable way (to activate knowledge of how easy it is to change). Think about those times when you've said "No, you go ahead and enjoy your movie; I'll stay home and clean the kitchen" or "I'm pretty sure your sister would be willing to do this, if you won't." These are usually instances of coercive manipulation.

Interestingly, guilt-tripping is not a strategy reserved for mean-spirited mothers or self-serving best friends. Activating another person's guilt can serve as a tool for good. When Grandma complains that "no one ever comes to visit me," she isn't a villain. She is, instead, reminding you of the very real and very typical social obligation we all take on to fulfill duties and maintain relationships. Similarly, when the new head coach of the Portland Timbers soccer team, Caleb Porter, explains how much he hates losing, it puts pressure on his players not to disappoint him. It worked. Porter turned a bottom-of-the-barrel team into the Western Conference champions in his very first season with the club.

Another example of the soft approach can be seen in this anecdote told by Rachel Barnett, of Portland, Oregon.

> I was seventeen years old. It was Christmas season and I was going to the local mall. I was driving on the highway with a few friends in the car going about seventy miles an hour and we passed through a construction zone with a thirty-five mile-an-hour speed limit. There was a motorcycle cop there and he signaled me to pull over. He came to my door and I immediately started crying. I was legitimately freaked out because this was the first time I had ever been pulled over. Even so, I didn't try and stop myself because I knew it would be helpful in dealing with the cop. The officer asked me if I would stick to the speed limit from now on. I cried some more and finally said yes, and he let me go.

Rachel's story is instructive because it's simultaneously authentic and manipulative. She was truly upset. She's no psychopath pretending to cry when she's not really upset. On the other hand, she also wasn't in any rush to say to the officer, "Please don't mind my emotional state. I was speeding and you should give me a ticket despite the fact that I'm crying." In fact, she knew that her distress would likely provoke sympathy and therefore serve her well.

Soft approaches are often intended to grease the wheels of social interaction through flattery, name-dropping, or reciprocity. These approaches are commonly used, and sometimes for the most altruistic reasons. For example, a charity might enlist the aid of a well-respected celebrity to help drum up interest in their cause. Similarly, people often use soft persuasive tactics to resolve conflict, especially in the case of friendships or romantic relationships. Consider, for instance, a boyfriend who wants to console his partner and says, "That must be really hard for you." The empathy can have the intended effect, which is to lower the level of emotional distress in the room, a move that protects him as well as his partner. Of course, this depends on how convincingly the words are said, and genuineness cannot be underestimated here. It also might be an intentional strategy intended to replace his knee-jerk impulse to offer advice with an expression of empathy. In this instance, it is both genuine and strategic.

All the World's a Stage

Shakespeare claimed that all men and women are players in one great, unfolding drama of life. He suggested that they have their entrances and exits and that they play many roles. Psychologists agree. In fact, psychologists often describe social interactions in terms of roles and scripts. When you interact with the cashier at your local grocery store, for instance, you follow a fairly predictable sequence. You might inquire as to his or her well-being, and the answer almost always indicates that things are good. If there is additional time, you might make small talk about the weather, the current holiday season, or the relative number of customers at the store. Whether you feel comfortable admitting it or not, a huge amount of your behavior is conducted with the idea that others are watching. Case in point: while observing cloud formations on your way to the postbox, you trip over your shoelaces and start to jog a few steps, as if that's what you were planning to do all along. Delightful to watch and fascinating when we think about why this happens.

The idea that the world is a stage and that the people around you are an audience creates an opportunity you can manipulate to your advantage, and for the gain of others. In business negotiations, international peace talks, and legal mediation there is always some degree of stagecraft. In sensitive talks between disputing governments, for example, there is often a mutual agreement not to make public statements about the ongoing process. To do so would be to entrench one's position and—potentially—inflame the other parties in the discussion.

Jeff Dahl, a lawyer who worked personal injury claims in Florida for more than a decade, illustrates the ways that stagecraft—while manipulative—can be in everyone's best interest. Florida, like many other states, likes to see lawsuits handled through mediation rather than cluttering up the court system. One time Dahl was serving as mediator between a thirty-year-old plaintiff, who had been injured in an automobile accident, and an insurance company. Dahl put the plaintiff and his lawyer in one room, and the insurance representative across the hall in another room. Both rooms had glass walls and afforded a full view of the opposing party.

Dahl spent the better part of the next two hours moving from one room to the other, patiently hearing out each side and validating their concerns. The insurance company agreed to pay seventy thousand dollars, which Dahl knew was exactly the figure the plaintiff wanted, so Dahl expected to conclude the deal. Unfortunately, when the plaintiff received the offer he became temporarily intoxicated by the prospect of money and indicated that he wanted to hold out for more. Dahl knew that the insurance representative was not authorized to pay additional money. Fearing that the mediation would devolve into a bitter lawsuit, Dahl opted to engage in a little drama.

Dahl marched into the room where the insurance rep sat waiting to hear that the plaintiff had accepted his offer. Instead of relaying the fact that the plaintiff now wanted even more money, Dahl said, "I need to know you are serious about this seventy thousand dollars and that it's your best offer. If this is truly the case, you can communicate that to me in earnest by packing up your briefcase and leaving. After all, there is nothing more for us to do here." At Dahl's suggestion, the rep began packing to leave.

Dahl used this opportunity to rush, panicked, to the plaintiff across the hall. "Oh no!" Dahl warned, "The rep is leaving and taking his offer with him! You'd better agree to the deal quickly, so that everyone can go home happy." Minutes later, the parties got together to sign the papers. It's important to remember that while what Dahl did was manipulative in the purest sense of the word, it was also intended to benefit all parties equally—and it succeeded in doing so.

How does this type of artifice apply to you and your success? You might—just might—be timid about lying, for instance. Some folks have a black or white attitude about lying. This, oddly enough, is why so many people are such atrocious storytellers. How many times have you heard a friend feebly try to relate a true story, only to have the factual details derail the whole process? "I was in my calculus class that started at nine o'clock . . . wait, no, I think it was at ten o'clock." One of the positive benefits of a bit of psychopathy is the ability to be fluid socially by not getting hung up on minor and—quite frankly, irrelevant—points of accuracy. Psychopaths can see the big picture and engineer situations to serve the larger outcomes. Sidestepping the truth can be difficult for other people, especially because it can smack of betrayal or other immoral motives. If you can balance the notion that the truth is a gray area with the idea that your actions should promote the welfare of others, psychopathy can suddenly seem like a more attractive tool.

But what is it that makes Dahl and others like him so good in these tense situations? Dahl is kind and mild-mannered, and no one who meets him would think of him as a psychopath. He's not, yet he does possess some of those skills: he's a quick thinker and he has a superhuman ability to remain calm in stressful situations. The same emotional detachment that we sometimes associate with serial killers is also helpful for mediators—and for A&E doctors and hostage negotiators. In fact, this is another element of stagecraft: knowing your lines. People with psychopathy feel that what they are doing is right in the same way that actors gain confidence by memorizing their lines. When things aren't going well, you can also draw on another skill common to both actors and people who can draw on psychopathy: improvisation.

Another way you can use stagecraft to your advantage when attempting to influence others is to act as a director and to cast people in a particular role. Social psychologists have long known that the roles people fulfill—daughter, husband, lifeguard, boss, volunteer—have real-world impact on their behavior. Classic evidence for this comes from Phil Zimbardo's famous Stanford Prison Experiment, in which

Zimbardo took a group of Stanford undergraduates and assigned some to be prisoners and others to be prison guards. The scenario extended over several days and the guards became increasingly abusive. They forced prisoners to do large numbers of push-ups; they interrupted their sleep and isolated them. Remember, these "guards" had been right-minded undergraduate students only days earlier.

Roles can be incredibly powerful, and not merely in ways that leads to poor behavior. Take the inspiring example of Lin Hao, a Chinese schoolboy. You might recall young Lin walking with basketball player Yao Ming to lead the procession during the opening ceremony of the Beijing Olympics in the summer of 2008. Only months before the games, Lin Hao's home in the province of Sichuan was struck by a massive earthquake, which flattened buildings and killed nearly seventy thousand people. Lin, only nine years old at the time, gained renown for saving two of his second-grade classmates from the rubble of his school. When asked about his heroism, Lin referred to his role. "I am the hall monitor," he pointed out, as if saying, "heroism is my job."

One of the easiest ways to manipulate people into being the hard-working world-changing folks you want them to be is to assign them roles that bring out their best. When Peter Lindberg, an American expatriate, took a job teaching English in Taiwan, he noticed that a huge change came over his students when they adopted English names. These reserved and soft-spoken children suddenly became as outgoing as if they were Americans. Modern businesses increasingly draw on the power of roles by assigning titles such as director of learning or director of fun. Although these roles can seem kitschy, they also serve as a permission slip to act in a certain manner.

Two Narcissists Are Better Than One

Interested in the effects of narcissism in a group setting, Jack Goncalo and his research team at Cornell University created teams of four people who were told they were serving as organizational consultants for a company with serious problems to solve. Their objective was to generate innovative action items that could be realistically implemented. Not only did the members of the teams want to succeed, they were also under the added pressure of knowing that two experts in organizational psychology would be independently evaluating their ideas in search of the top performers.

Seventy-three teams were given several weeks to complete this group project. Before starting, all 292 consultants were evaluated for narcissistic traits; after the project, they were asked about group dynamics such as debating ideas and considering all possible alternatives before making decisions. Defying the notion that narcissistic leadership is inherently bad, researchers found that too few or too many narcissists led to suboptimal group dynamics and creativity (as determined by experts' rating solutions for the company). Two narcissists were better than one or none, in terms of both the group process and the quality of the product.

You might be asking, why do I want narcissists on my team? The reason two narcissists performed so well is that norms and rules often get in the way of creative thinking. To be creative, people need to challenge assumptions of how things are supposed to be. Narcissists, with their sense of being special and their grandiose fantasies, have little interest in being socially appropriate. Ideas that might otherwise have been prematurely ruled out as absurd or unfeasible become fair game. In his *Harvard Business Review* article, Michael Maccoby came up with many examples of successful narcissists, people who can get people to stop talking and start doing.

> Throughout history, narcissists have always emerged to inspire people and to shape the future. When military, religious, and political arenas dominated society, it was figures such as Napoléon Bonaparte, Mahatma Gandhi, and Franklin Delano Roosevelt who determined the social agenda. But, from time to time, when business became the engine of social change, it, too, generated its share of narcissistic leaders. That was true at the beginning of this century, when men like Andrew Carnegie, John D. Rockefeller, Thomas Edison, and Henry Ford exploited new technologies and restructured American industry. . . . Leaders such as Jack Welch or George Soros are examples of productive narcissists. They are gifted and creative strategists who see the big picture and find meaning in the risky proposition of changing the world and leaving behind a legacy. Indeed, one reason we look to productive narcissists in times of great transition is that they have the audacity to push through the massive transformations that society periodically undertakes. Productive narcissists are not only risk-takers willing to get the job done but also charmers who can convert the masses with their rhetoric.

Narcissists want to do something daring and attention grabbing. They also tend to be trendsetters: when they break the rules, other people follow suit. The first rule of creativity is that you must be able to risk being wrong, risk making mistakes, and risk public scrutiny. One narcissist in a group gets stares and snickers. Two narcissists are a powerful minority faction that can no longer be ignored. They inspire the kind, compassionate, selfless (non-narcissist) members of the team to change tactics, to fight the status quo, and to aim to do something worthy of admiration.

The Teddy Effect helps creativity in another way, by making a person argumentative. The problem with creative people is that they have a tendency to fall in love with their own ideas. This is partly because creativity is experienced as a pleasurable epiphany, and what feels good is often mistaken for what is good. See New Coke, the oddly shaped Suzuki X90, and Fiery Habanero Doritos for examples of products that must have sounded terrific in the boardroom. Some amount of critical pushback, or so-called depressive realism, acts as an antidote to falling in love with our own ideas. Hans Eysenck, one of the pioneers of intelligence and personality testing, was famous for saying that the only useful brainstorming sessions are ones that involve fierce criticism. Why do so many parents, teachers, and organizations ignore his advice?

Organizations desire creativity but often want it controllable. It is a long-standing problem for managers that highly resourceful problem solvers also have a hard time following rules and completing detailed work. What's more, businesses love new ideas but hate the lack of certainty that accompanies them. Is there a way to deal with this paradox? Thankfully, we can turn to more than a decade of creativity research by Jennifer Mueller at the Wharton School of Business and her colleagues.

Imagine yourself in one of her research situations. You're working hard when a colleague announces a new influx of capital in the company. You're told you might receive some of this money, but, to avoid long debates about who contributed most and is most deserving of an unexpected cash bonus, distributions will be determined by random lottery. You feel excited, anxious, and uncertain. After this research dynamic has been established, everyone is asked a few questions on a computer. What the researchers want to know was this: when you're in a mental state of uncertainty (being told the money you receive has nothing to do with merit, it's going to be randomly determined) does your attitude change about the status quo? In particular, when you feel uncertain, are you more prone to crave certainty and therefore less open to novel ideas?

The researchers knew it would be useless to ask everyone point-blank whether they valued creativity. Nearly everyone knows that the "right" answer is yes and will likely skew their responses accordingly. To get around this, Mueller and her colleagues used computer reaction-time tests—famously tough to fake—to check whether people had unconscious biases against creativity. The results could not have been clearer. When put in a state of high uncertainty and asked whether they valued creativity, 95 percent of participants said, yes, creativity rocks! Yet, when the computer test measured automatic mental associations, people in a state of uncertainty linked creativity with words like *vomit* and *agony*.

Here we move closer to that 20 percent edge. When we want to get rid of uncertainty, we harbor negative attitudes toward creativity. To be open and receptive to creative ideas, we need to be open and receptive to discomfort. From what we learned about the Teddy Effect, narcissism might be helpful in overcoming this kind of discomfort. At this point, you won't be surprised to hear that entitled, grandiose people are better at facing uncertainty. They experience fear openly, without the fear of fear, because they are busy moving in the direction of the grandiose kind of life they most want to live, feel they deserve, and are willing to work toward. With this final thought on the value of the Teddy Effect, we ask you what you would be doing with your time if you were not busy managing your [insert whatever difficult feelings, thoughts, urges, or memories that bother you here]? What have you given up, how has your life space narrowed over time, in an attempt to feel less social discomfort?

Is the Teddy Effect a source of evil in the world? It can be. But it can also be a source of beauty, happiness, meaning, and growth, and when you can extract these benefits, you emerge as a stronger, more resilient, and agile leader. The darker behaviors described in this chapter are part of our genetic blueprint, and we find evidence of their existence in children as young as four years old. These darker behaviors are built into the very society that likes its leaders to be unrelentingly positive—from teachers to athletes to surgeons to police officers to the soldiers we ask to fight our wars. In the right context, we can all draw on Machiavellianism, narcissism, and psychopathy to keep a level head in tense situations, to charm others, and to believe in our ability to pursue big dreams. Acknowledge this part of your psychological repertoire, be willing to access it when needed, and you've just gained the 20 percent edge that you will need in that final lap. Everyone has these tools at their disposal, and yet too many people won't use them for the sole reason that feeling comfortable in the moment is more important than doing what the situation requires for fulfillment *and* success.

The message here, supported by scientific research, is to encourage you to deviate from a kind, compassionate approach when situations warrant. Sometimes you have to be assertive and manipulative, not only for your sake but also for the sake of those around you, whether they are direct reports, colleagues, or members of your family. By learning both hard and soft strategies for dealing with other people, you gain an edge you will need to make your work, and your life, complete.

THE TAKEAWAYS

1. Everyone, without exception, manipulates others.
2. Doing so effectively is a matter of dosage and timing.
3. It is essential to separate the malevolent parts of the Dark Triad from the benevolent parts of psychopathy, such as fearless dominance, and the benevolent parts of narcissism, such as grandiose self-assuredness, that stimulate courage, creativity, and leadership ability.
4. Some of the greatest leaders in history had these qualities and with them were willing to take risks and be disliked in the pursuit of personally valued, ambitious goals.
5. A little narcissism, psychopathy, and Machiavellianism (underutilized skills in human relationships) can be extraordinarily effective in winning others over, creating great experiences for friends and customers, motivating other people, and accelerating a sense of intimacy and comfort.

CHAPTER 7

The Whole Enchilada

There is no coming to consciousness without pain. People will do anything, no matter how absurd, in order to avoid facing their own Soul. One does not become enlightened by imagining figures of light, but by making the darkness conscious.

—C. G. Jung

WE LIVE IN an unusual time. In the past, it was the toughest people who succeeded: warriors who showed their mettle on the battlefield, or players who proved their athletic prowess on the football pitch. Things have changed. Nowadays geeks run the show. They're the ones creating the computer gadgets the rest of us ooh and aah over. It's tech and maths folks who number highest among today's billionaires. It's the science fiction crowd that creates the superhero blockbusters we flock to each summer. Where in the old days, mention of *Star Trek* might get you crammed into a high school locker, now a Star Trek emblem on a T-shirt is a badge of retro-nerd cool. The same kids who argued over whether *The Empire Strikes Back* was better than the original *Star Wars* are now making business decisions that affect the way we drive, invest, communicate, and recreate.

This trend toward nerdiness is exactly why we think it's appropriate to bring up an unusual example of wholeness: Aquaman. In case you have resisted the allure of comic books, let us get you up to speed. In brief, Aquaman is a superhero who pals around in the same imaginary universe as Batman, Superman, and Wonder Woman. Ruler of the aquatic kingdom of Atlantis, he can breathe underwater, swim like a fish, communicate mentally with all sea life, and—above all—has an awesome gold outfit. These abilities make Aquaman pretty badass when a shark goes wild, when a boat capsizes, or when an earthquake dumps a whole city into the sea. Unfortunately, 100 percent of bank robberies, ethnic cleansings, and—in the comic book world—supervillain takeover attempts happen on land.

This is why Aquaman has the reputation among comic book aficionados as the lamest superhero of all time. Spider-Man is a wisecracking kid with super strength and spidey-senses. Wolverine is the bad boy loner with metal claws. Wonder Woman is principled, beautiful, and can even take down Superman. But Aquaman? A really swell swimmer who breathes underwater? Sounds more like Michael Phelps than Tony Stark.

Aquaman, however, is much cooler than first impressions might suggest. Let's start with the fact that his territory covers more than 70 percent of the planet. The brooding, neurotic Batman, by contrast, confines his vigilante prowls to a single city. Aquaman also communicates with pinnipeds, such as seals and walruses, who can, of course, help fight crime on shorelines, atolls, and sandbars, as long as they stay wet. With his helpers factored in we can comfortably claim that Aquaman is the primary guardian of 80 percent of the earth's biosphere. Awesome—but, of course, that leaves 20 percent of the earth unprotected.

To expand his range to the full 100 percent, our trident-wielding super swimmer must dig into his emotional, cognitive, and social agility. Let's take that last one first: Aquaman is a charmer. As king of Atlantis, he knows how to play host to his super-colleagues. In doing so, he maintains strong relationships and can extend his crime-fighting reach. In a story arc called "The Trench," Aquaman demonstrates his flair for social gamesmanship while being interviewed by a blogger in a seaside restaurant. The blogger rudely asks him, "How does it feel to be nobody's favorite superhero?" Instead of arguing, Aquaman tips his waitress enough to put her kids through university ("Now I'm *somebody's* favorite superhero, so there!"). Where he got the tip money, or where on his skintight outfit he keeps it, we have no idea.

When he recognizes threats outside his limited aquatic range, Aquaman doesn't brood in an underwater cave. Instead, as a member of the Justice League, he influences and persuades an assembly of the world's greatest superheroes, including Batman, Superman, Wonder Woman, Flash, and Green Lantern, to risk injury and even death. Possessed of sufficient cognitive agility to recognize his own vulnerability and sufficient social agility to scaffold his weaknesses (through strategic alliances), Aquaman taps into the 20 percent edge.

Although it might seem silly that we're lingering so long on make-believe superheroes, we hope you appreciate that Aquaman is symbolic of the major theses of this book. He is a terrific example of the way that all of us tend to focus on the 80 percent of our world that is familiar and comfortable. He is also a good illustration of how we can tap that additional 20 percent to extend our effectiveness. In this book's various chapters, we have taken you on a tour, steeped in science, to show why our culture's approach to personal happiness requires radical revision and how we need to go about it. The salient facts are these:

- Comfort addiction results in lower immunity to negative experiences (chapter 2).
- Negative emotions are an underappreciated resource (chapter 3).
- The pursuit of happiness can weaken you (chapter 4).
- Mindlessness is beneficial, especially when alternated with mindfulness (chapter 5).
- Machiavellianism, narcissism, and psychopathy give you an edge in tough, complex dealings with other people (chapter 6).

Now it's time to shift from the obsession with happiness to adopting a broader definition of success. Let's give Aquaman his due.

Recognizing Your Positivity Bias

It's worth reiterating that you might have a blind spot where positivity is concerned. Don't worry, so do we. If you hail from the United States, England, Canada, or Australia, you likely have leanings toward positivity about which you are not even aware.

This *positivity bias*, as psychologists call it, is the tendency to artificially inflate the goodness of, well, just about everything. This is especially true when we make evaluations of broad and abstract categories. For instance, when asked by researchers to rate their satisfaction with education or their social life, people from the western hemisphere are significantly more likely than their Asian counterparts to give an enthusiastic head nod. This is because it's difficult to rate your educational experience as a whole. How do you derive a single number from zero to a hundred to capture the quality of your entire education or every aspect of your social life? Put in this position, we reflexively rely on our cultural script, which is typically upbeat.

Our collective leaning toward the positive is reflected in our optimism. Researchers at the University of Michigan led by Dr. Edward Chang found that, when compared with the Japanese, Americans were more likely to believe that good events were on the horizon. When asked about common positive events such as bumping into an old friend, and common negative events such as failing a test, Americans thought that they were nearly twice as likely as their sibling to experience something good and 1.5 times less likely to suffer misfortune. What a difference from the Japanese, who were 2.5 times more likely to think that bad events would occur in their lives compared with their siblings. This pessimistic bias is exactly the type of sky-is-falling negativity that we avoid, but the University of Michigan's Dr. Chang points out that optimism can backfire. Expecting the worst, sometimes called *defensive pessimism,* can be beneficial.

Defensive pessimists, according to Dr. Julie Norem at Wellesley College, "hope for the best but expect the worst." It might sound as if these characters need to be fixed or improved or optimized, but hold that thought. Defensive pessimists do not necessarily wear dark glasses all the time or expect to fail in every life situation. But even if they were successful in the past, they know this time could be different. So when Mom has an upcoming plane trip with three small hyperactive children, she might burst out a defensive pessimism strategy that could include

- lower expectations for how things will turn out (the six people sitting near us will hate us, which is fine, because I will hate my life for two hours); or
- vividly detailed imagining of all the things that could go wrong (the kids will pull off someone's toupee and toss it like a Frisbee, the pilot will come on the overhead PA system and ask passengers to look at my row so they'll know who to blame if the plane crashes, and so on).

Rather than firmly holding a perpetually sunny outlook and avoiding negative thoughts and feelings, defensive pessimists allow themselves to imagine how they will feel if things turn out badly. Julie Norem found that having burst through the stranglehold of positivity, defensive pessimists cope extremely well with the threat of failure and disappointment. By imagining worst-case scenarios, defensive pessimists transform their anxiety into action, implementing plans that can mitigate disaster.

You might be wondering, isn't it better to perform well and be in a good mood than perform well and be in a bad mood? Norem and Chang's research teams have found a provocative rebuttal to that thought. When strategic optimists and defensive pessimists threw darts, they did equally well overall but were most effective under differing conditions. Before throwing darts, some people listened to relaxing tapes ("hear the gentle rolling of waves on a sun-sparkled ocean"). Others imagined themselves throwing darts and missing their targets. When they actually threw their darts, the strategic optimists were about 30 percent more accurate when they relaxed instead of imagining negative outcomes. But the opposite was true for the defensive pessimists: they were about 30 percent more accurate when they thought about negative outcomes instead of relaxing or picturing perfect performance. Norem's research suggests that "positive mood impairs the performance of defensive pessimists." When they're in a good mood, they become complacent; they no longer have the anxiety that typically mobilizes their effort. If you want to sabotage defensive pessimists, just make them happy.

What's more, initial research evidence indicates that these types of people don't experience negative moods as intensely as people who are more routinely upbeat. That is, their lowest lows aren't so bad. In fact, research shows that defensive pessimists perform better than optimists in stressful, challenging situations. In Singapore, when the government warned the public about an outbreak of severe acute respiratory syndrome (SARS), defensive pessimists were more worried than optimists, yet they engaged in more preventive efforts, and this somber outlook helped protect them and their families more efficiently and effectively.

What about the value of positivity when it comes to big societal issues, like the well-known gender gap in many science, technology, engineering, and maths disciplines, in which men outperform women? About 60 percent of this gap can be attributed to prior background and preparation, but that leaves 40 percent, much of which is due to the psychological hazards of feeling inferior, devalued, and even hardwired to fail. Being reminded that you are a woman before taking a test activates this negative feeling, leading women in this situation to perform even worse. But here's an amazing finding. For women who engage in defensive pessimism, who imagine taking the test and failing, the negative gender stereotypes bounce off like gumdrop bullets. Their test scores are unaffected.

We see much the same scenario when we look at negative stereotypes about the intellectual ability of black students compared with white students, and the underperformance of minority students in education. In predominantly white universities, where stereotypes about the alleged intellectual inferiority of minorities can paralyze black students, researchers took a close look at defensive pessimism. They found that black students who used defensive pessimism in the classroom ("I try to picture how I could fix things if something went wrong," "I often start out expecting the worst, even though I will probably do OK") were less likely to drop out and had better grades. The overall point here is that simple psychological strategies for seemingly entrenched social problems can be effective, if and only if you are willing to deviate from the limited perspective of positivity.

Even optimists strategically use pessimism; they just don't know it. In a little twist of mental trickery, optimists, but not pessimists, are likely to engage in what is known as *retroactive pessimism*. This occurs when a person fails at a task and unwittingly protects themselves from the psychological sting by mentally reaching back into the past and reevaluating it. In the new, revised version, they are far more pessimistic about their likelihood of success. In fact, as they consider the matter further, it becomes obvious that circumstances conspired against them, and failure was all but guaranteed.

Here's how researchers discovered this phenomenon. They presented participants with a scenario such as a description of someone taking a job as an assistant in a science lab. The scenario included some negative and some positive elements, such as coming up with great lab research ideas but also breaking a few pieces of important equipment. The researchers asked people to judge the likelihood of success in such an endeavor, as described. They then fed participants a final line that pronounced the hypothetical situation either a booming success or a miserable failure. In the failure condition, the optimists were far more likely to write off failure as inevitable. Framing an event as an inescapable failure makes it easier to digest.

Research on the benefits of pessimism, as well as studies on positivity bias, offer an important lesson: it is high time that we reevaluated long-held beliefs about what is negative and what is positive, psychologically speaking. It is time for a new way of understanding what it means to be mentally healthy and successful, to see both positive and negative as part of the larger, and more viable, whole.

This, then, is the Holy Grail of psychology: wholeness. Medicine is not about penicillin, or setting bones; it is, fundamentally, about health. Science fiction films and novels often depict a future in which gadgets and pills can alter DNA to repair damaged cells and promote long life and perfect health. In this same vein, psychologists are ultimately engaged in the quixotic search for *wholeness*, which goes by many names, including *empowered* and *self-determined*.

Wholeness is a concept that has crept quietly into every corner of life. It is known by many approximations and comes in many derivative forms. In the workplace it is in vogue, for instance, for managers and leaders to speak about *optimal performance*, *full engagement*, and *fitness for duty*. In parenting, we know it as *identity formation* or *maturity*. Wholeness is to psychology what enlightenment is to spirituality.

Modern psychological scholars are not naïve about neurosis, hardship, and the darker half of human nature. The real travesty comes in dismissing these as ills needing to be cured in the same way that cancer needs to be treated. In fact, most modern scholars differ from their lay counterparts in that they view uncomfortable states not only as an inescapable aspect of self-growth, but also as tools for success in their own right. Roy Baumeister, a trailblazing psychologist at Florida State University, deviates from his peers and their obsession with healthy self-esteem and other forms of positivity to adopt a more inclusive view of the light and dark sides of human nature. He says, "I see the world far more in terms of trade-offs than a lot of other people. Good actions are often tied to bad actions. People do things that are corrupt. They take money out of the system. But it's usually toward supporting their families and relatives." The famous Swiss psychiatrist Carl Jung put this condition poetically when he wrote, "A whole person is one who has both walked with God and wrestled with the devil."

Take, for instance, a new study by Alison Wood Brooks of the Harvard Business School. She noticed, as others had before her, that people tend to get wound up about all sorts of performance-related issues such as singing karaoke or taking tests. Anxiety is so common in these situations, in fact, that many universities allow special exam accommodations for students who suffer from severe test anxiety. Brooks noticed that many people attempt to deal with the high-rpm experience of anxiety by calming down. They take deep breaths, listen to soothing music, or relax their muscles, strategies reminiscent of the World War II motto we mentioned earlier: "Keep calm and carry on." Brooks is clever, and she realized there might be another approach. As we suggested in chapter 3, anxiety is, above all else, a highly aroused emotional state. Brooks was curious to see whether, instead of trying to lower this arousal, people might use this amped-up state to their benefit.

In one study, Brooks forced nearly a hundred participants to sing karaoke. In particular, she had them belt out the first few lines of Journey's hit song "Don't Stop Believin'." If you are anything like us, just running these words in your head gets your heart pumping. Brooks randomly assigned her participants to practice, in earnest, a self-statement before singing. In one condition, people admit to feeling anxious; in another, they reframe this state as "I feel excited." Interestingly, while there were no differences in the amount of anxiety members of these two groups felt before singing, those in the excited group gave better performances. Singing accuracy, gauged through a sophisticated software program, was 80 percent for the excited group, but only 53 percent for the anxiety group.

Brooks went on to apply the same research approach to fear of public speaking, in which excited (versus calm) speakers were judged as more persuasive, more competent, and more confident. Brooks knocked it out of the park by replicating these findings yet again with maths performance. In the end, Brooks concludes that your relationship with your internal experience matters more than you think. For people who are able, even artificially, to reframe anxiety as excitement, there is a subtle but powerful shift away from the internal state and toward the situation. Brooks calls this an *opportunity mindset*.

We would like to suggest that viewing the dark half of human nature in terms of opportunity is a radical, healthy stance. To recap the basic thesis of this book—divorcing yourself from the so-called negative aspects of your natural psychological architecture limits your potential. By not only accepting but also actually embracing the less comfortable aspects of your being, if only for brief periods, you maximize your chances for true success and becoming whole. This, and not some feeble-minded happiness, is the true Elysium.

It's Complicated, but in a Good Way

We were once on a radio show on which the host claimed to have been perpetually happy for decades. He bragged openly about this seemingly impossible achievement, as if he had achieved the highest possible psychological state, a kind of emotional enlightenment. To us, he merely seemed out of touch. Had no loved ones died? Had he never experienced a setback? Had he not witnessed an injustice? We were less concerned with how he managed to be happy in the face of hardship than we were with why he would even want to. We think the good life is certainly a pleasurable and happy one, but it is also more than that. True happiness must be more than fleeting feelings of pleasure. Below we present a matrix that we believe is essential to a successful and happy life, the type of life for which most people strive.

Just as in real life, this matrix of experiences is rich and varied, and occasionally even in conflict with itself. We present two primary dimensions of a good life: (1) pleasure/meaning, and (2) novelty/stability.

Simply put, people want to experience pleasure and meaning, and they want to balance some degree of fresh experience along with a modicum of predictability. There are certainly individual differences in how much a given person seeks each of these desirable states, but they apply in a general way to all people. It's not that this is the empirical truth and that no other important dimensions exist, but these two dimensions capture a huge range of everyday life experiences. In the two sections that follow, we deal with each of these in turn.

PLEASURE ←——————→ MEANING
NOVELTY ←——————→ FAMILIARITY

Balancing Pleasure Now with Meaning Later

It's one thing to encourage you to wrestle with the devil and quite another to support you in doing so. In the preceding chapters, we supplied a parade of studies and discussed a mountain of results that have hopefully convinced you that there might be more to those pesky negative states than meets the eye. Skeptics will accuse us of promoting anger, turning away from rational thought, and advocating the manipulation of others. It will be easy to paint us as cynical, selfish, and mean to people who have not read this book yet. You, however, know better. Here we would like to build on your newfound goodwill by providing you a few how-to suggestions with regard to living a whole life and enjoying more success at work and home.

As we've seen, wholeness is predicated on a series of skills, all of which are based in psychological flexibility. We have described these as mental agility, emotional agility, and social agility. The basic idea is that psychological states are instrumental. That is, they are useful for a specific purpose, such as finding your car keys, being physically safe in a parking garage, negotiating a business deal, or arguing with your child's teacher. Rather than viewing your thoughts and feelings as reactions to external events, we argue that you ought to view these states as tools to be used as circumstances warrant. Simply put, quit labeling your inner states as good or bad or positive or negative, and start thinking of them as useful or not useful for any given situation.

One of the best places to make this case is in one of our areas of greatest expertise: happiness, that delicious and elusive state for which we all strive. In scientific circles, the topic of happiness is super hot and equally divisive. On the one hand is a long tradition of researchers who have studied what is known as *hedonia*, described by philosopher and historian Richard Kraut as "the belief that one is getting the important things one wants, as well as certain pleasant affects that normally go along with this belief." Hedonia is that sense of well-being you get on seeing the first finished copy of your new book, crossing the finish line after running a marathon, after a bout of great sex, on hearing you're getting a good pay raise at work, and while enjoying a party where everybody feels comfortable enough to sing, dance, and be silly. Sounds fantastic; sign us up!

On the other hand are those scientists who have fixated on *eudaimonia*, a term made famous by Aristotle that translates, essentially, to behaving virtuously and striving toward the full development of our potential. Eudaimonic activity is volunteering time to help somebody else, persevering at a valued goal in the face of obstacles, expressing gratitude to somebody who has been helpful, and striving for excellence in the development and use of one's talents—whether surfing ocean waves, being honest, or being fully present when someone speaks. Sounds fantastic and profound; sign us up for this, too!

Somewhere along the way to compiling wisdom, a kind of academic cage fight started around these two types of happiness. Some people, quite understandably, are ill at ease with the idea that life is all fun and games. For these folks, fun is superficial, whereas being authentic and pursuing goals that are bigger than the self offer a deeper and truer form of well-being. On the surface, relishing pleasures (hedonia) seems to be an inferior shortcut to the quest for meaning and purpose in life. As for us, we are unimpressed with the idea of auditing pleasures and deciding which deserve praise and which deserve ridicule.

We are reminded of several conversations over the past year in which people mention what they know of a great television show such as *Breaking Bad*, or an inspired novel such as *A Confederacy of Dunces*, before proudly claiming, "But I don't watch TV or read fiction. I don't have time to waste." Our typical response is something along the lines of, "So you're saying that good stories, interesting characters, and creative ideas are a waste of time, right?" At this point, they usually recant, saying, "Actually, there is one show I really like. . . ." Far too often, people assume that their source of happiness is superior to others, despite the infinite number of possibilities out there. To us, nothing is cooler than being passionate about whatever it is you are passionate about—and doing so with reckless abandon. Especially if that passion is aligned with who you are, what you are intrinsically interested in, and what you want your life to stand for.

This said, we hope you are not so quick to dismiss pleasure as a trivial pastime or as a selfish pursuit. Pleasure is wonderful. In fact, we recently conducted a study of pleasure with a sample of a quarter million research participants from thirty nations. Pleasure is a universal phenomenon, and people from around the world enjoy thrills, relaxation, good food, music, sex, and other common pleasures. In fact, when people recount some of their best moments, they are often the small pleasures of everyday life. Sipping coffee in the morning, getting a massage, watching the sun set, going rock climbing, and cuddling with your children under a warm blanket: these are activities that can be deeply enjoyed without being saddled with any pretense of plugging into a deeper truth, or experiencing some kind of spiritual growth.

Unfortunately, the either/or dichotomy of pleasure and meaning misses the larger truth that people are rarely only hedonists, or only immersed in meaning. We would do better to ask, "When should I experience meaning, and when should I experience pleasure?"

One way of answering this question is by charting the times you already feel each of these desirable states. This is exactly what psychologist Jinhyung Kim and her colleagues at Seoul National University did in a recent research program. In several studies, the Kim team asked people to pull out a calendar and make a schedule of all their activities for the current week (here and now) or the same week next year (distant future). People were able to write anything they wanted into their calendar. Entries included things such as hanging out with friends and dancing with them until late night, watching an entertaining TV show, going to a water park, playing the piano confidently in front of many people, listening to friends' troubles, keeping a regular schedule by getting up early, and working out at the gym. Afterward, the research team coded each activity as pleasure seeking, in pursuit of meaning or purpose (such as attempts to be virtuous via self-sacrifice, honesty, integrity), or neither. The researchers discovered that people made 34 percent more meaning-and-purpose-related plans in the distant future. The preference for meaning over pleasure gets stronger as we focus more on the distant future.

This research dovetails with a recent publication by Roy Baumeister and his colleagues. Using a sample of nearly four hundred adults, these researchers mapped the experiences of pleasure and meaning. They found that pleasure was heavily associated with present-oriented thinking, and that meaning was more strongly associated with thinking about the past, as in the case of grandparents recalling raising their own children, or thinking about the future, as in the case of planning important goals.

The point here is that pleasure and meaning work like a seesaw, and it's important to have both in your life at different times (and occasionally even at the same time). People often sacrifice short-term pleasure, such as having dessert, or going to a party, in favor of that future-oriented meaning, as in the example of competing in a triathlon or graduating from university. Often when you willingly and temporarily give up pleasure, it is replaced by an activity that sort of sucks: studying for an exam, running on a rainy afternoon, working on a report late into the night. In these cases, you opt for unpleasantness. Although you wouldn't want them to dominate your life, they do make you stronger, and often lead to more success.

The trick is to change your basic thinking from what you like to feel, to what is functional. You want your life to stand for something important, but you also want to enjoy yourself along the way. Becoming a pleasure- and meaning-person depends on your time perspective. Consider the following questions:

- For the next hour, would you rather experience a pleasurable life without meaning, or a meaningful life without pleasure?

- For the next week, would you rather experience a pleasurable life without meaning, or a meaningful life without pleasure?
- For the next month, would you rather experience a pleasurable life without meaning, or a meaningful life without pleasure?
- For the next year, would you rather experience a pleasurable life without meaning, or a meaningful life without pleasure?

When researchers asked people exactly these questions, they found a predictable trend in the trade-off between pleasure and meaning. People were attracted to the notion of short-term pleasure and long-term meaning (see the figure below). It's as if people are saying, "I care about meaning, I just don't care about it right now!" We are, it turns out, short-term hedonists and long-term saints. What's more, nobody can be accurately categorized as an exclusively pleasure-person or meaning-person.

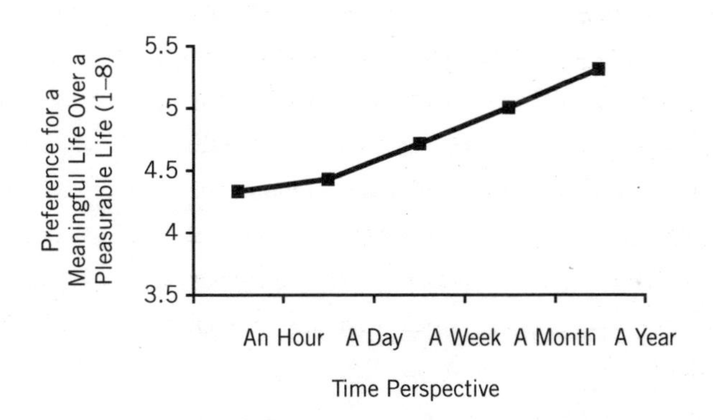

A life of meaning that is devoid of pleasure is, frankly, no fun. On the other hand, a life fully given over to the pursuit of pleasure may miss out on the benefits of having objectives that we aspire to accomplish, or to become, namely, a purpose in life. If you want to envision a person who is whole, imagine that person with one foot rooted in the present, mindfully appreciative of what they have, and another foot reaching toward the future with its undiscovered sources of meaning. As a formula, that dynamic would look like this:

$$\frac{\text{Pleasure}}{\text{1 hour}} + \frac{\text{Growth + Sacrifice}}{\text{1 month}} = \text{Wholeness}$$

So let's put an end to the struggle between pleasure and meaning. Go ahead, invest in profoundly meaningful goals and seek out the ultimate purpose of life, the nature of human existence, and the larger universe that we reside in. (Be forewarned—Douglas Adams, author of *The Hitchhiker's Guide to the Galaxy*, may have been correct—the ultimate purpose may simply be forty-two.) At the same time, let pleasure loom large in everyday life; enjoy the sensory, social, and intellectual delights available to you—as long as there is no mismatch with your deepest values. Instead of succumbing to what you ought to be, allow yourself to become whole and live well.

Balancing Novelty with Stability

When you think about retirement, it's fun to imagine yourself engaged in various pleasurable pastimes. Snorkeling with tropical fish. Swinging in a hammock in the Costa del Sol. Having a glass of wine with your spouse. It's tempting, in fact, to view retirement as an endless string of idle but rewarding pastimes. The tendency is to forget that the garbage still needs to be taken out, the lightbulbs still need to be changed, and the dry cleaning still needs to be picked up. Researcher Shigehiro Oishi and his colleagues asked retirees and nonretirees to rate the importance of novelty and familiarity in a retirement location. The nonretirees placed a premium on novelty. They wanted retirement to be full of opportunities to meet people, uncover hidden talents, and test-drive never-before-tried hobbies. The actual retirees, by contrast, favored familiarity. They wanted to continue interacting with family members and friends on a regular basis. They wanted to stick with physicians who knew their medical history. In fact, for retirees, the idea of being exposed to novelty and challenges to grow as a person, develop their full potential, and expand their social circle had nothing to do with being happy.

This study highlights another seesaw relationship. All humans are motivated to seek out the psychological rewards of both novelty and stability. On the one hand, novelty is fresh and exciting. Our personal evolution requires complex, mysterious, uncertain, and challenging experiences. Without them, we stop learning and growing. On the other hand, stability leads to predictability, which can be soothing. When we feel knowledgeable and in control, which is what stable situations offer, we feel safe and free to be ourselves.

Both ends of this seesaw are necessary for the good life. To illustrate this point, consider the following thought experiment. Which of the following two scenarios would you prefer? In scenario A, you must keep your living room as it is for the rest of your life. You can never rearrange items, purchase new furniture, display new photos or artwork, or spruce the place up with flowers. It must stay exactly the same. In scenario B, your living room will change every single day for the rest of your life. One day it will be modern, the next Bauhaus, and the third art deco. Day in and day out you can expect something new to adorn your walls. On Tuesday, eighteenth-century Korean screens take center stage. On Wednesday, each side of the room will be a sheet of transparent glass. The question is, which of these two lives would you want? The answer to this question speaks to your individual leanings; you might be an adventure seeker or you might crave stability. Regardless of your particular preference, you can see that either scenario might become oppressive after a while. Both change and predictability are necessary for a good life.

Novelty and stability also have downsides. When things are familiar, this sense of calm encourages you to let your guard down and requires fewer mental resources. But too much stability and you begin to feel like a caged animal, pacing back and forth; we often construe this state as boredom, and we feel bored when the current situation is monotonous, low intensity, and rather meaningless. Here again, in the case of boredom, we see an emotional experience that people shy away from. Not only because it is difficult to find any semblance of pleasure or meaning in boredom, but also because it can be viewed as a personal flaw. There is a tendency to believe that people with sufficient intellectual ability or internal drive don't stay bored; they can entertain themselves ("if you're bored, then you're boring").

In fact, a recent study by Brigid Carroll and her colleagues found that dozens of CEOs, general managers, and other senior leaders viewed boredom as counterproductive in the workplace. They saw boredom as indicating a lack of strong ambition in subordinates. A smaller number of leaders, however, recognized the adaptive value of boredom.

How could boredom be beneficial? In Hindu and Buddhist traditions, boredom is described as a precursor to insight and discovery. Parents sometimes want their children to be bored because they have an intuitive sense that grappling with this uncomfortable state is how kids discover what they're interested in, quiet their mind, and find outlets to channel their energy. We wish more parents would trust that when their kids get bored, they'll find the way out on their own, resisting the temptation to schedule activities from morning to night to keep boredom at bay. But don't just take our word for it. The American Academy of Pediatrics released a 2007 consensus statement on how child-directed, exploratory play is far superior when it comes to developing emotional, social, and mental agility than structured, adult-guided activity.

Edward O. Wilson describes the value of boredom in his autobiography, *Naturalist*:

> Adults forget the depths of languor into which the adolescent mind descends with ease. They are prone to devalue the mental growth that occurs during daydreaming and aimless wandering . . . often I just sat for long periods scanning the pond edges and vegetation for the hint of a scaly coil, a telltale ripple on the water's surface, the sound of an out-of-sight splash.

How we react to this internal state determines whether boredom becomes a healthy or unhealthy influence. For instance, you can try to eliminate boredom with the ubiquitous availability of smartphones. Any time your interest level wavers, or you feel an emotion you don't want to feel, you can immediately start texting, e-mailing, and calling people; if nobody responds, you can surf the Web, play video games, and avoid the self completely. But by trying to be entertained at all times, we are stuck in a cycle of experiential avoidance in which we are playing defense and hiding from discomfort. By force-feeding ourselves stimulation whenever boredom arises, we never experience the serendipitous growth opportunities that arise when the mind wanders without planned destinations.

As with other states of mindlessness, something special can happen during periods of boredom. When the brain is left to wander, at best it's a springboard to creativity and growth, and at worst it encounters a brief period of discomfort. Boredom can also be a state of low energy, signaling that work is complete and acceptable. That is, nothing is left to do so a person feels aimless, but this lack of direction is association with the satisfactory completion of tasks. Last, boredom can have motivational impact, pushing a person toward novelty, providing the mental gun to the head that helps people shift out of complacency into the uncertain, challenging zone where safety and success are not guaranteed.

Like the oppressive boredom that occasionally comes with stability, novelty also has a negative aspect. Too much novelty provokes anxiety. The constant change involved in an ongoing product test, or a divorce, or even a whirlwind trip through South America is difficult to manage. The nervousness that people feel when it's all just too much is an emotional signal to slow down and hunker. Boredom and anxiety, though unpleasant, are highly functional. Both signal that you have spent too much time confined to either the novel or the familiar side of life.

Once again, the key to understanding the interplay between these two concepts is time. Just as we saw that pleasure is a short-term phenomenon and meaning is a long-term one, so too are novelty and stability. Novelty is primarily about fast time. That is, novelty is experienced in an intense, absorbing way that makes time slip by quickly. We lose ourselves in the enthusiasms of the moment. It is neither a negative or positive state, but an emotional blend that brings a sense of vitality such that we feel fully present and alive. Stability, by contrast, is all about slow time, in which opportunity to reflect, react, assess, and judge what is happening is ample. This can be pleasant, as when we appreciate what we have, or unpleasant, as when we notice that life is becoming too repetitive.

You can use your perception of time to understand whether you need to speed up or slow down. In the instances when time seems to crawl to a stop, what in German is called *langeweile*, you cease to distinguish between past, present, and future. There is simply too much time when you're on the cusp of boredom. On the other hand, when life comes at you too quickly and you feel bombarded by nonstop sensory overload, you edge toward panic.

The beauty of slow time is that it offers enough psychological space for making decisions about how you want to view familiar people, activities, and surroundings. Can you find the unfamiliar in the seemingly familiar? Can you see what is unique in this moment, even though on the surface everything is in exactly the same place as it was the day before? You can't always be happy, but you can almost always be profoundly aware and curious.

The beauty of fast time is that you're energized. The trick is in harnessing this energy to what you care most about, in accordance with your values. If you want to understand value-based living, think of a GPS system. When you use a GPS system and make a wrong turn, it supplies redirection without judgment. The GPS system doesn't scold you. You only receive information, an instant indication of which path to take if, and only if, you want to continue the initial journey. Value-based living works much the same way. Just as a GPS doesn't force you to take the route you first programmed, knowing your values or purpose in life doesn't mean that's the only path you can take either. For example, your deepest value might entail being a loving, attentive, affectionate parent to your kids, and yet there will be times that you want desperately to escape their presence so you can enjoy solitude, adult conversation, or a ninety-minute body scrub and massage by a Korean man in black latex underwear (yes, it's awesome!). Deviating from your values or purpose doesn't nullify them. We cannot hold ourselves to the unreasonable position of always being on the right path (after all, as we saw in the last chapter, we're all hypocrites some of the time).

Mahatma Gandhi was often a harsh, judgmental, neglectful father to his sons, and yet his purpose—inspiring people to be compassionate even to their enemies—remained intact. He was a great man but had difficulties and flaws just like the rest of us. Instead of being sacrilegious, this depiction of Gandhi is liberating. Tushar Gandhi, his great-grandson, puts it this way:

> Gandhi has become a hostage to his mahatmaship. It is easy to say that we cannot emulate someone like him when we put him on a pedestal. What we should be doing is seeing him as a normal, frail human being who strove to achieve something. We should emulate people like him, but not worship them.

Listening to Tushar takes the pressure off the rest of us. There's no need to try to keep love, work, and play in perfect balance. Perfect balance is not what it means to be whole. Being whole is about being open and accommodating of all parts to your personality: the light and dark passengers, the strengths and weaknesses, the successes and failures. To this we add the combination of a pleasurable and profoundly meaningful life, and the embrace of both novelty and stability. Acknowledging seemingly contradictory aspects of the self will increase the power and influence you wield in the present, and the vitality, agility, and perseverance you can bring to the life tasks that lie ahead.

Broad Strokes or Fine-Toothed Comb?

When airliners hit New York City's twin towers on the morning of September 11, 2001, people recognized that the world had just changed. To document these events and their impact, reporters from the *New York Times* and other media outlets trolled the streets, stopping locals for a person-on-the-street interview. In the days that followed, two interviewees responded very differently:

> My first reaction was terrible sadness. . . . But the second reaction was that of anger, because you can't do anything with the sadness.

> I felt a bunch of things I couldn't put my finger on. Maybe anger, confusion, fear. I just felt bad on September 11th. Really bad.

If you had to guess, who do you think is better at tolerating stress and working toward their goals despite the presence of pain? With amazing precision, the first person points out a sequence of intense sadness followed by a surge of energy and the desire to use their anger to approach someone and do something. The second person struggled to describe what was bubbling inside, and in the end could only state that they did not feel good, they felt bad.

Now imagine that this one moment, caught on tape by a news reporter, is typical of how these two New Yorkers put their feelings into words. Like us, you probably assume that people with greater understanding and clarity of what they are feeling are less overwhelmed in stressful situations. And you're right. The first person, who can clearly identify what she is feeling during times of stress, gains access to the response tendencies that are activated (guilt pushes her to be a better person next time, shame pushes her to hide from other people). This knowledge can be used for intelligent decisions about whether to stick with a situation or improve it. If a person is unsure whether she is feeling guilty, ashamed, angry, or afraid, it's going to be more difficult to manage discomfort. She may be more prone to knee-jerk responses in order to feel better, such as consuming copious amounts of alcohol, or smacking the guy who repeatedly interrupts in order to change the subject. Research from our laboratory has shown this to be true.

Being able to clearly differentiate emotional experiences is a valuable skill in your toolbox, and the best news of all is that you can be taught to apply it better. You might, to take an unusual example, be fearful of spiders. Or, like most people, you might find a spider with a four-centimeter purplish, bulbous abdomen to be disgusting. If there is anything that psychology has mastered it is the treatment of spider fears. The gold standard for treatment is exposure therapy. How does it work? It's simple. You slowly walk a person from one step to the next, helping them become comfortable in situations that were once terrifying. In the first session, you might be reading *Charlotte's Web*, looking carefully at the illustrations of Charlotte settled in her web. Once this is mastered, you might move on to a documentary film, observing how spiders crawl up walls and use their weblike slingshots to trap and feed on crickets, grasshoppers, and butterflies.

Then we move up the hierarchy of fears, starting with a live spider in a closed jar kept behind a closed door, then inside the same room but twenty meters away, and then a little bit closer, and closer. Finally, the person holds the closed jar, and then when ready, opens the jar, and after a few more sessions that spider will be crawling over their arms and legs. After four to six weeks, we might even get fearful clients to the point where they can drive around an empty parking lot while dozens of spiders are let loose on the front seat and dashboard (we kid you not!). This process sounds worse than it is because we haven't sufficiently stressed that we never move to the next step until your anxiety stabilizes at a low level and you commit to the next, more demanding, test. Exposure therapy works. In fact, several research teams, including our own, have found that using this approach can knock out someone's fear of spiders in less than three hours.

We've also found a way to improve on this therapy, using a process called *emotion labeling*. Now why would you try to improve on a technique that is this effective? Because we psychologists have learned that emotion labeling rocks. Here's what three psychologists from UCLA did. They had people who were afraid of spiders take part in exposure therapy, just as we described, except some of them were given additional strategies to use, such as thinking optimistically ("sitting in front of you is a little spider and it's safe"), engaging in experiential avoidance ("hey, when was the last time you flossed?"), or clarifying and labeling the emotions being felt. In emotion labeling, people describe each distinct feeling they experience, such as curiosity about how spiders cling to sheer walls, disgust at the hairiness of a spider, and fear that the spider might crawl on them or bite them.

In evaluating which intervention worked best, folks trained to deal with their fear of spiders by learning to think optimistically, or to engage in experiential avoidance, ended up worse than when they started. And folks trained to label their emotions showed the greatest improvement over time. Emotional labeling supercharged their ability to handle spiders: they reported less fear (18.1 percent drop) and showed less physiological reactivity (27.5 percent reduction) when shown a spider, and they climbed more steps in their fear hierarchy, switching from a threat mindset to an opportunity mindset.

What's so impressive about these findings is that emotion labeling is a simple, trainable skill that many of us have overlooked. Why? Because we think it is child's play. You can walk into a kindergarten classroom and find a wall poster showing how a sad facial expression differs from angry, frustrated, lonely, suspicious, and perplexed. Well, we're here to tell you that we adults need to improve our emotional literacy as well, especially if we want an additional edge when it comes to improving our success and well-being. Yes, it's useful to distinguish between positive and negative emotions and aim for a higher frequency of positive emotions in everyday life. But you already know this. Our goal in this book is to bring you to the next level.

Beyond the obsession with feeling comfortable, how we relate to, describe, and distinguish emotions matters. When asked how you feel right now, you might give simple answers similar to those of a child: awesome, okay, horrible. When people struggle to put their feelings into words, relying on little more than good versus bad, they are more easily overwhelmed by stress, which often translates into health problems. When we become more adept and precise in differentiating what we feel in a given situation, negative emotions are no longer so problematic. Here are some specific supportive findings from our research laboratory:

- When stressed out, people who can describe what is being felt in nuanced, precise ways consume 40 percent fewer alcohol drinks each time they go to a bar or head to a party than people who have difficulty clarifying what they feel.
- When angry at someone, people who can label their feelings using a rich vocabulary of emotion words are 40 percent less verbally and physically aggressive to the person who pushed their buttons (the bully or provocateur) than people who have difficulty clarifying what they feel.
- When rejected by a stranger during a ball-toss game, people show less activity in brain regions tied to physical and emotional pain (the insula and anterior cingulate cortex) when they are adept at describing and differentiating what is being felt in a given moment. That is, people who can clarify and differentiate their emotions show equanimity in emotionally upsetting situations, and we can observe this in their neural activity.

What we have discovered is that by understanding and distinguishing negative emotions, we transform them and detoxify our mind and body. We become less susceptible to unhealthy emotion regulation strategies such as binge drinking and eating, aggression, and self-injurious behavior. Knowing whether someone is experiencing a great deal of negativity does not tell us whether they are going to be successful. *That depends on whether they are effective at differentiating what they're feeling.* This is an evolutionary step beyond the notion that positivity is good and negativity is bad; it depends on your attitude toward the emotions being experienced and the degree to which you can identify what is being felt.

You might be asking, wouldn't it be problematic if people ruminated more on their negative emotions? The answer depends on whether this thinking becomes obsessive. Ruminators can get stuck dwelling on the origins of negative thoughts and feelings, and in these cases rumination can pull us down into the depths of pain, preventing us from doing something more fun or productive with our lives. But ruminating, or obsessive thinking, is very different from emotion differentiation, which is about observing and describing what is being felt or thought without getting tangled up with these mental events. Because we are just looking at emotions as information, emotion differentiation allows us to become smarter, wiser, and more empowered in everyday situations. This mirrors the theme of the entire book.

One reason people do not naturally engage in emotion differentiation tactics, even those that would be helpful, is the natural tendency to think of things in categorical terms. You save space in your brain by clustering together objects in your daily experience based on shared features. You think of trees, for instance, or city employees, or men. In each case, members of the category share some essential feature. The concept of essentialism can sound a bit like a puzzle game. Could an elephant ever be a pine tree? The answer is no, because elephants and pine trees possess a distinct essence that does not allow for overlap. The question "Could a doctor ever be elderly?" does have overlap, because both doctors and aging involve people.

It turns out that people also lean toward clumping emotions

together. Just try it out for yourself. Could anger be embarrassment? People who tend toward essentializing emotion—that is, believing that negative emotions cluster together—are far less likely to differentiate between them, and, as a result, far less likely to experience the full palette of emotions throughout the day. As Nietzsche said, "Language dictates consciousness."

We propose a new way to view prematurely dismissed aspects of the self. With this information, you have the opportunity to broaden your sense of self. No longer do you need to choose between positives and negatives, because either/or approaches are too rudimentary to capture the complexity and beauty of the real world. Allow yourself to be as differentiated as your emotion, and you will gain access to the joys of higher peaks and the skills to handle deeper valleys.

Beyond Happiness

All of us have an almost overpowering urge to improve our quality of life. Ambition, health, knowledge, legacy: so many of our highest goals center on maximizing wins and successes. In recent decades, this natural leaning toward improvement has become conflated with the desire for comfort. There's been an uptick in the sheer volume of discussion on the value of positivity, people seeking to avoid pain and double down on pleasure. Blogs, magazines, consultancies, and books all tout a feel-good mentality. Positivity leads to better outcomes at work and makes it easier for people to connect interpersonally. Folks skeptical of these approaches dismiss them as mere Pollyannaism, rightly understanding that an unquestioning devotion to positivity has little connection to the uncertain, complex challenges that each of us face in everyday life. Each of us, in Jung's words, walks with God and wrestles with the devil.

You cannot banish the devilish, unflattering qualities of your personality. Nor would doing so be healthy or useful. Suppressing experiences is psychologically destructive because it divorces us from the full richness of real life. To progress on your journey of personal growth, love, and meaning and purpose in life, you need to become aware of all aspects of yourself, including your darker tendencies, and be agile enough to integrate them into your behavioral repertoire as needed. Do not repress, ignore, or hide the darker gifts. Be aware of them, appreciate them, and when you're ready harness them. When you do this, you'll find that you've gained greater access to well-being. To do otherwise is to be enslaved by fear, to set an artificial limit on what you experience and accomplish in this, the one and only life we know for sure that you'll have. Make the most of it. Become whole.

ACKNOWLEDGMENTS

THIS BOOK IS THE CULMINATION of a lifetime of experiences. I lost my mother when I was a young teenager. She never had a chance to know me as an adult, but when I learn about her personality and interests, there is no doubt that I am her direct descendent. My grandmother had the unfair task of trying to tame my rebellious nature on her own. Both of them are missed, and everything that I do is a pilgrimage to them.

Because my biological family was small, I decided to create a larger one of my own. For more than a decade, I have been fortunate to lead hungry, intelligent, deviant students in my Laboratory for the Study of Social Anxiety, Character Strengths, and Related Phenomena. I would be less productive, less creative, and derive far fewer rewards from everyday tasks without William Breen, Patty Ferssizidis, Nina Farmer, Leah Adams, Evan Kleiman, Alex Afram, Kevin Young, Jessica Yarbro, Fallon Goodman, Sam Monfort, Daniel Blalock, Kyla Machell, and many others. For this book, Kevin Young and Fallon Goodman were indispensable in bouncing around ideas, synthesizing research, and helping me think like a human instead of a scientist.

Being a scientist and writer requires a great deal of time alone. As rewarding as these moments are, I am grateful for the vitality, support, brilliance, wisdom, and playfulness of friends and colleagues who have allowed me to be effortless myself over the years.

I didn't have sufficient space to list the large number of scientists who contributed to this book by sharing their unpublished research and answering a barrage of questions via e-mail, phone call, and face-to-face conversation. I also don't have space to express my gratitude for the friends, relatives, acquaintances, clients, and students who unknowingly provided essential ideas, stories, and criticisms that improved this book.

I have been fortunate to have a number of supportive colleagues and administrators at George Mason University who let me follow my wide-ranging passionate pursuits to become a fox instead of a hedgehog. But there are three people at George Mason University who have quickly become some of the most important characters in my life, forming the basis of my wise council.

Nance Lucas, the director of the Center for the Advancement of Well-Being, is the exemplar of primal, resonant, emotionally intelligent leadership. I smile every time I see her, I am inspired every time I listen to her, and I am in awe of how she brings out the best qualities of everyone she meets. There is something beautiful about witnessing what greatness looks like in a single domain, and the world would be a better place if there were more leaders like her.

Gallup has found that if someone can check "yes" to the statement "I have a best friend at work," he or she is going to be engaged and productive. With Patrick McKnight at my side, I have been able to check "yes" for years, and, in turn, stressful events bounce off me like bullets made of gumdrops. Our 7:00 a.m. brain-storming sessions are as meaningful and pleasurable as any Saturday night party.

Paul Rogers is my soul brother. If every person was as loving, interesting, intelligent, open-minded, and value-driven as him, I would never get any work done. He commands respect when he speaks and he is the greatest father I know. If I die before my time, he is the only man who I would want to raise my kids. There is no stronger statement to be made.

Thanks to my editor, Caroline Sutton, and the entire team at Hudson Street Press for supporting this project, with full allowance of the pain and pleasure of the serpentine road taken. This book has little resemblance to what started, and we are grateful for the opportunity to evolve as needed.

Thanks to my other editor, Peter Guzzardi. His intellectual challenges, creative contributions, and editing have transformed this book. It cannot be understated—the best elements of this book do not exist without Peter.

Then there is my beloved agent, Richard Pine. He is tough. He is insightful. He is dependable. He is encouraging. He provides the secure foundation that allows for great explorations, risk taking, and discoveries. I refuse to accept the notion that there is a better agent out there. This is our second book together, and I suspect we will be linked from here on out.

Anyone who writes a book knows that the process is fraught with the highest of highs and challenges that induce nausea in every cell of the body. I was fortunate to write this book with one of my closest friends, Robert Biswas-Diener. Despite spending more time talking to him than any other human being over the past two years, our only fight lasted 3.3 minutes.

There are a few additional members of my wise council who keep my life in perspective. Barry and Marilyn Spitz are my second set of parents. Unconditional love is easy to proclaim, hard to enact. Barry and Marilyn are great parents, even better grandparents, and will always be part of the inner sanctum.

As for my wife, Sarah, none of this happens without her. She taught me how to be a man, a father, and a healthy influence on the world. She senses the emotions of those around her, anticipates what others need, satisfies them, and, in turn, other people are drawn to her; just as I am. When I watch her raise our three girls, I am at peace knowing that they have full access to everything that they need to be happy, fulfilled, and, above all else, whole.

I wrote this book for my three girls, Raven, Chloe, and Violet. With them, I am stronger and more agile, with a better understanding of what matters most.

One of my life ambitions is to help them find the same.

—Todd B. Kashdan

This book was many years in the making and would not have been possible without amazing support and guidance from others. First, I would like to acknowledge my coauthor, Todd, for helping to create something far better than I could ever make alone.

I would also like to extend my gratitude to Caroline Sutton and the entire team at Hudson Street Press. Caroline, you saw a diamond in the rough and I thank you for your willingness to polish it. Similarly, Peter Guzzardi provided excellent editorial direction. Peter, you have a gift: you can tell me everything I do wrong and get me to smile and thank you for it! I also need to acknowledge Nadia Lyubchik for her invaluable help with our references.

I would also like to thank Richard Pine, agent extraordinaire, for his help in crafting this book and helping it to see the light of day.

Finally, I would like to acknowledge my wife, Keya, who has supported my writing with absolute faith for many years. Thank you!

—Robert Biswas-Diener

NOTES

Introduction

viii **This is what psychologists refer to as *distress tolerance*:** Zvolensky, M. J., Bernstein, A., & Vujanovic, A. A. (Eds.). (2011). *Distress Tolerance: Theory, Research, and Clinical Applications.* New York: Guilford Press; Zvolensky, M. J., Vujanovic, A. A., Bernstein, A., & Leyro, T. (2010). "Distress tolerance theory, measurement, and relations to psychopathology." *Current Directions in Psychological Science*, 19(6), 406–410.

ix **There will always be experts:** Seligman, M. E. P. (1998). *Learned Optimism How to Change Your mind and Your Life.* New York: Pocket Books; Seligman, M. E. P. (2002). *Authentic Happiness: Using the New Positive Psychology to Realize Your Potential for Lasting Fulfillment.* New York: Free Press.

ix **We believe—and new research supports—the idea that every emotion is useful:** Tamir, M. (2009). "What do people want to feel and why? Pleasure and utility in emotion regulation." *Current Directions in Psychological Science*, 18(2), 101–105.

ix **Research shows that only rarely does anger:** Kassinove, H. (1995). *Anger Disorders: Definition, Diagnosis, and Treatment.* New York: Taylor & Francis. Also see: Potegal, M., Stemmler, G., & Spielberger, C. D. (2010). *International Handbook of Anger: Constituent and Concomitant Biological, Psychological, and Social Processes.* New York: Springer.

x **Simply put, people who are able to use the whole range of their natural psychological gifts:** Kashdan, T. B., & Rottenberg, J. (2010). "Psychological flexibility as a fundamental aspect of health." *Clinical Psychology Review*, 30(7), 865–878.

xi **In our study, we had more than a hundred participants:** This study was conducted by Todd Kashdan and his Laboratory for the Study of Social Anxiety, Character Strengths, and Related Phenomena. See: Kashdan, T. B., Adams, L., Farmer, A., Ferssizidis, P., McKnight, P. E., & Nezlek, J. B. (in press). "Sexual healing: Daily diary investigation of the benefits of intimate and pleasurable sexual activity in socially anxious adults." *Archives of Sexual Behavior.* Also detailed here: Kashdan, T. B., Adams, L., Savostyanova, A. A., Ferssizidis, P., McKnight, P. E., & Nezlek, J. B. (2011). "Effects of social anxiety and depressive symptoms on the frequency and quality of sexual activity: A daily process approach." *Behaviour Research and Therapy*, 49, 352–360.

xiv **If positivity and optimism account for:** We would like to emphasize that our 80:20 ratio should be interpreted as a useful rule of thumb presented in a popular book rather than as a scientifically exact description of human psychology. Across many types of studies researchers find approximations of an 80:20 ratio and we argue here that it is a useful generalization regarding the amount that people are—or "should be"—in positive versus negative states. In this book we describe the 80:20 ratio using the metaphor of a race in which the beginning, middle, and end require distinct mindsets to achieve overall success. The mathematically inclined reader will realize that the 80:20 ratio represents fifths while our race metaphor is divided into thirds. Take heart, we make no claim that the three portions of the race are equal. Therefore the final portion of the race could constitute only 20 percent.

Chapter 1: The False Nose of Happiness

1 **In sixteenth-century Denmark, Tycho Brahe was:** *Wikipedia*. (2014). "Tycho Brahe." Retrieved from: http://en.wikipedia.org/wiki/Tycho_Brahe.

2 **In fact, in a study of more than ten thousand participants from forty-eight countries:** Diener, E., & Oishi, S. (2004). "Are Scandinavians happier than Asians? Issues in comparing nations on subjective

well-being." In F. Columbus (Ed.), *Asian Economic and Political Issues: Vol. 10* (pp. 1–25) New York: Nova Science.

3 **Happiness researchers have linked positive feelings to a host of benefits:** Lyubomirsky, S., King, L., & Diener, E. (2005). "The benefits of frequent positive affect: Does happiness lead to success?" *Psychological Bulletin,* 131(6), 803–855. Also see: Cohen, S., Doyle, W. J., Turner, R. B., Alper, C. M., & Skoner, D. P. (2003). "Emotional style and susceptibility to the common cold." *Psychosomatic Medicine,* 65(4), 652–657; Pressman, S. D., & Cohen, S. (2005). "Does positive affect influence health?" *Psychological Bulletin,* 131(6), 925–971.

The potential benefits of happiness are, in our opinion, one of the most exciting developments in happiness scholarship. For millennia, people have asked, "What makes a person happy?" That is, attention has largely been focused on the causes of happiness. It is only recently, and through the scientific method, that we have been able to shift our collective focus to the consequences of happiness. A growing body of evidence indicates that happiness is good for individuals and societies.

3 **Some researchers, like Barbara Fredrickson from the University of North Carolina:** Fredrickson, B. L. (2001). "The role of positive emotions in positive psychology: The broaden-and-build theory of positive emotions." *American Psychologist,* 56(3), 218–226. For greater depth, see: Fredrickson, B. L. (2006). "The broaden-and-build theory of positive emotions." In F. A. Huppert, N. Baylis, & B. Keverne (Eds.) *The Science of Well-Being* (pp. 217–238). New York: Oxford University Press.

3 **Examining data from the European Social Survey:** Huppert, F. A., & So, T. T. C. (2013). "Flourishing across Europe: Application of a new conceptual framework for defining well-being." *Social Indicators Research,* 110(3), 837–861.

It is hard to accurately gauge how many people are flourishing, in part because the answer to the question is complicated. One body of research suggests that most people are mildly happy most of the time, not perfectly happy, of course, but feeling mildly good and satisfied. Another suggests that anxiety and depression are being experienced at record numbers and that—perhaps—too few people are feeling that life is truly exceptional.

3 **Eight statements with which you may agree or disagree follow:** Diener, E., Wirtz, D., Tov, W., Kim-Prieto, C., Choi, D. W., Oishi, S., & Biswas-Diener, R. (2010). "New well-being measures: Short scales to

assess flourishing and positive and negative feelings." *Social Indicators Research*, 97(2), 143–156. Additional psychometric data on this scale continues to be published, as detailed in these publications:

Hone, L., Jarden, A., & Schofield, G. (2013). "Psychometric properties of the flourishing scale in a New Zealand sample." *Social Indicators Research*, 1–15. doi: 10.1007/s11205-013-0501-x.

Silva, A. J., & Caetano, A. (2013). "Validation of the flourishing scale and scale of positive and negative experience in Portugal." *Social Indicators Research*, 110(2), 469–478.

Sumi, K. (2013). "Reliability and validity of Japanese versions of the flourishing scale and the scale of positive and negative experience." *Social Indicators Research*, 1–15. doi: 10.1007/s11205-013-0432-6.

5 **Let's begin with the research of Barbara Mellers:** Mellers, B. A., & McGraw, A. P. (2001). "Anticipated emotions as guides to choice." *Current Directions in Psychological Science*, 10(6), 210–214. Also see: Mellers, B. A. (2000). Choice and the relative pleasure of consequences. *Psychological Bulletin*, 126(6), 910–924.

5 **We overestimate, for instance, how happy we will be if our favored political candidate:** Gilbert, D. T., Pinel, E. C., Wilson, T. D., Blumberg, S. J., & Wheatley, T. P. (1998). "Immune neglect: A source of durability bias in affective forecasting." *Journal of Personality and Social Psychology*, 75(3), 617–638.

5 **Take, for example, the study in which Mellers and her colleagues:** Mellers, B. A., & McGraw, A. P. (2001). Anticipated emotions as guides to choice. *Current Directions in Psychological Science*, 10(6), 210–214. (See figure 2c for details.) Some of the data are unpublished and the results are being written up for publication. Results are available upon request to Todd Kashdan (who due to the generosity of Dr. Barbara Mellers, has access to the original data set).

6 **Most damning of all when your pursuit of happiness is concerned:** Mauss, I. B., Savino, N. S., Anderson, C. L., Weisbuch, M., Tamir, M., & Laudenslager, M. L. (2012). "The pursuit of happiness can be lonely." *Emotion*, 12(5), 908–912.

8 **Students who are confused but work through the confusion:** D'Mello, S., Lehman, B., Pekrun, R., & Graesser, A. (2014). "Confusion can be beneficial for learning." *Learning and Instruction*, 29, 153–170.

8 **Centenarians—people who are a hundred years old or older—find that negative feelings:** Martin, P., da Rosa, G., Margrett, J. A., Garasky, S., & Franke, W. (2012). "Stability and change in affect among centenarians." *The International Journal of Aging and Human Development*, 75(4), 337–349.

8 **Police detectives who have themselves been victims:** Eskreis-Winkler, L., Shulman, E. P., & Duckworth, A. L. (2014). "Survivor mission: Do those who survive have a drive to thrive at work?" *Journal of Positive Psychology, 9(3), 209–218. doi: 10.1080/17439760.2014.888579.*

8 **Spouses who forgave physical or verbal aggression:** McNulty, J. K. (2011). "The dark side of forgiveness: The tendency to forgive predicts continued psychological and physical aggression in marriage." *Personality and Social Psychology Bulletin,* 37(6), 770–783. For additional adverse consequences, also see: Luchies, L. B., Finkel, E. J., McNulty, J. K., & Kumashiro, M. (2010). "The doormat effect: When forgiving erodes self-respect and self-concept clarity." *Journal of Personality and Social Psychology*, 98(5), 734–749; McNulty, J. K. (2010). "Forgiveness increases the likelihood of subsequent partner transgressions in marriage." *Journal of Family Psychology*, 24(6), 787–790.

9 **Workers who are in a bad mood in the morning:** Bledow, R., Schmitt, A., Frese, M., & Kühnel, J. (2011). "The affective shift model of work engagement." *Journal of Applied Psychology*, 96(6), 1,246–1,257.

9 **"We argue that it is the balance of being able to endure phases":** Bedlow, R., Schmitt, A., Frese, M., & Kühnel, J. (2011). "The affective shift model of work engagement." *Journal of Applied Psychology*, 96(6), 1,254.

10 **According to the National Mental Health Foundation:** Mental Health Foundation. (2014). "Mental Health Statistics: Anxiety." Retrieved from: http://www.mentalhealth.org.uk/help-information/mental-healthstatistics/anxiety-statistics/.

12 **Psychologists call this disqualifying the positive:** First mentioned by Aaron Beck in his seminal work: Beck, A. T. (1976). *Cognitive Therapy and the Emotional Disorders*. New York: International Universities Press. A resurgence in these ideas has been led by Justin Weeks: Weeks, J. W. (2010). "The disqualification of positive social outcomes scale: A novel assessment of a long-recognized cognitive tendency in social anxiety disorder." *Journal of Anxiety Disorders*, 24(8), 856–865.

12 **Not to mention Fritz Strack's famous study:** Strack, F., Martin, L. L., & Stepper, S. (1988). "Inhibiting and facilitating conditions of the human smile: A nonobtrusive test of the facial feedback hypothesis." *Journal of Personality and Social Psychology*, 54(5), 768–777.

14 **Karl Wheatley, a researcher at Cleveland State University, argues:** Wheatley, K. F. (2002). "The potential benefits of teacher efficacy doubts for educational reform." *Teaching and Teacher Education*, 18(1), 5–22.

15 **In 1995, a Swedish adventurer named Göran Kropp:** Kropp, G., & Laagercrantz, D. (1999). *Ultimate High: My Everest Odyssey*. New York: Discovery Books.

15 **A week later, members of several expeditions:** Krakauer, J. (1997). *Into Thin Air: A Personal Account of the Mt. Everest Disaster.* New York: Villard.

16 **People with specific goals have a yardstick by which to measure:** Emmons, R. A. (2003). *The Psychology of Ultimate Concerns: Motivation and Spirituality in Personality.* New York: Guilford Press.

16 **Legendary boxer Muhammad Ali once quipped:** Muhammad Ali. (2014). *Muhammad Ali Quotes.* Retrieved from: http://www.muhammadaliquotes.org/.

16 **In fact, researcher Eva Pomerantz of the University of Illinois:** Pomerantz, E. M., Saxon, J. L., & Oishi, S. (2000). "The psychological trade-offs of goal investment." *Journal of Personality and Social Psychology,* 79(4), 617–630.

Eva and her colleagues demonstrate that when people are heavily committed to a goal, this commitment can lead to either happiness or anxiety. It turns out that the people who feel good have a natural tendency to focus on their progress toward the goal. Folks who worry, by contrast, are those who focus on the potential negative impact of possible failure.

17 **In a psychological phenomenon known as *sehnsucht*:** Scheibe, S., Freund, A. M., & Baltes, P. B. (2007). "Toward a developmental psychology of Sehnsucht (life longings): The optimal (utopian) life." *Developmental Psychology,* 43(3), 778–795. Also see: Kotter-Grühn, D., Wiest, M., Zurek, P. P., & Scheibe, S. (2009). "What is it we are longing for? Psychological and demographic factors influencing the contents of Sehnsucht (life longings)." *Journal of Research in Personality*, 43(3), 428–437.

19 **Psychologists Jonathan Adler from the Franklin W. Olin College:** Adler, J. M., & Hershfield, H. E. (2012). "Mixed emotional experience is associated with and precedes improvements in psychological well-being." *PloS one,* 7(4), e35633.

19 **Consider this description from a client after a few sessions:** Ibid.

20 **Dacher Keltner, a psychologist at Berkeley, claims that:** Keltner, D. (2009). *Born to Be Good: The Science of a Meaningful Life.* New York: W.W. Norton.

21 **Kim is unusual among academics in that she gets out of the laboratory:** Kim, E. C. (2012). "Nonsocial transient behavior: Social disengagement on the Greyhound bus." *Symbolic Interaction*, 35(3), 267–283.

23 **For instance, Dutch psychologist Ap Dijksterhuis had students engage in a writing:** Dijksterhuis, A., & Van Knippenberg, A. (1998). "The relation between perception and behavior, or how to win a game of Trivial Pursuit." *Journal of Personality and Social Psychology*, 74(4), 865–877.

23 **For example, researchers in one study subtly primed some participants—but not others—with the smell of cleaning products:** Holland, R. W., Hendriks, M., & Aarts, H. (2005). "Smells like clean spirit: Nonconscious effects of scent on cognition and behavior." *Psychological Science,* 16(9), 689–693.

23 **In the so-called "sleep on it" phenomenon, people who are distracted—and therefore not mindful:** Dijksterhuis, A., Bos, M. W., Nordgren, L. F., & Van Baaren, R. B. (2006). "On making the right choice: The deliberation-without-attention effect." *Science*, 311(5,763), 1,005–1,007.

Chapter 2: The Rise of the Comfortable Class

25 **This is exactly the question posed by psychologist Shigehiro Oishi:** Oishi, S., Seol, K., Koo, M., & Miao, F. M. (2011). "Was he happy? Cultural differences in the conceptions of Jesus." *Journal of Research in Personality*, 45(1), 84–91.

26 **Christie Napa Scollon, a researcher at Singapore Management University:** Scollon, C. N., & King, L. A. (2004). "Is the good life the easy life?" *Social Indicators Research*, 68(2), 127–162.

27 **We are stampeding toward comfort and convenience:** Convenience is a conceptual cousin to comfort. Convenience, defined as being able to proceed without effort or difficulty, is simply a mental rather than a physical aspect of comfort. As technologies such as airplanes and microwave ovens and smartphones make the basic tasks of daily life more convenient, people are becoming less patient. You can see evidence for this in road rage, the inability to deal with the frustrations of traffic, or in angry outbursts at the airport following a delayed flight. The comedian Louis CK famously takes aim at the way people take modern comforts and conveniences for granted. In one bit he criticizes people who complain about flight delays. After the hypothetically delayed passenger groans about sitting on the runway for forty minutes, Louis CK puts it all in context: "What happened then? Did you fly through the air like a bird, incredibly? . . . You're sitting in a chair in the sky! You're like a Greek myth right now!" To which his hypothetical target continues complaining, "But [the chair] doesn't go back very far and it's sort of squishing my knees."

27 **According to Juliet Schor:** Schor, J. (1998). *The Overspent American: Why We Want What We Don't Need.* New York: Basic Books.

27 **This sudden desire for air-conditioning is particularly interesting:** Maslow, A. (1954). *Motivation and Personality.* New York: Harper & Row.

Maslow's theory is, arguably, one of the most well-known theories in all of psychology. Lay people are likely to accept the bottom tier—basic needs—rather uncritically. It is, in actuality, very difficult to determine how basic a need is. To take just a single example, the need for thermoregulation—keeping the body warm—is fundamental but can be achieved through fire, clothing, the sun, central heating, or shared body heat. At the lower boundary of this need, people slip into hypothermia and can die. But even beyond dangerous cold, people are motivated to seek a comfortable level of heat. This is why so many spouses fight over the household thermostat, a likely extension of this basic need.

29 **In the last twenty years hospital admisisons for food allergies:** Allergy UK. (2014). "Allergy statistics." Retrieved from: http://www.allergyuk.org/allergy-statistics/allergy-statistics.

30 **To be, or not to be:** Shakespeare, W. (2007). *Hamlet.* (J. Dolven, Ed.). New York: Barnes & Noble. Act III, Scene I, Line LV.

30 **In 1930, Sigmund Freud, the most prominent figure in the history of psychology:** Freud, S. (1930). *Civilization and Its Discontents.* London: Hogarth Press.

31 **"What the English call 'comfort,'" Hegel wrote:** Quote emphasized in the intriguing writings of Daniel Bell, especially in Bell, D. (1996). *The Cultural Contradictions of Capitalism: 20th Anniversary Edition.* New York: Basic Books. x.

Hegel's leftist writings were influential in the creation of Marxism. For people who lived during the cold war, the common "us versus them" attitude will be familiar. In the United States, we felt that our system—democracy—was superior to the government of the Soviet Union in that ours provided for the ideals we value, such as freedom of speech and unrestricted travel. There was, however, a subtext. We felt that our economic system—capitalism—was also superior in that ours was able to provide for widespread comfort. By contrast, American children growing up in the 1960s, 1970s, and 1980s were exposed to images, often black- and-white, of long lines of Soviet citizens waiting for bread and other basic needs. The implication is clear: a society is successful, in part, to the extent it can provide comfort and convenience to its citizenry.

31 **In a study of pace of life, psychologist Robert Levine:** Levine, R. V., West, L. J., & Reis, H. T. (1980). "Perceptions of time and punctuality in the United States and Brazil." *Journal of Personality and Social Psychology*, 38(4), 541–550.

32 **Researchers measure *disgust sensitivity* in all sorts of creative:** Rozin, P., Millman, L., & Nemeroff, C. (1986). "Operation of the laws of sympathetic magic in disgust and other domains." *Journal of Personality and Social Psychology*, 50(4), 703–712.

One of the major contributions of Paul Rozin and his colleagues to the field of emotion in general, and disgust in particular, is in their exploration of magical thinking. Not only can disgust be biological—rotting food for instance—but it can also be moral. People are often afraid of moral contamination by coming into contact with "bad people" as in the case of likely unwillingness to wear Hitler's sweater for a day.

33 **Researchers Robert Bixler and Myron Floyd were curious to explore:** Bixler, R. D., & Floyd, M. F. (1997). "Nature is scary, disgusting, and uncomfortable." *Environment and Behavior*, 29(4), 443–467.

34 **In fact, researcher Shigehiro Oishi—of the Jesus study mentioned earlier—and his colleagues used Google to track:** Oishi, S., Graham, J., Kesebir, S., & Galinha, I. C. (2013). "Concepts of happiness across time and cultures." *Personality and Social Psychology Bulletin*, 39(5), 559–577.

35 **The year 1996 was the first time in history that students at college health clinics began complaining of anxiety:** Benton, S. A., Robertson, J. M., Tseng, W. C., Newton, F. B., & Benton, S. L. (2003). "Changes in counseling center client problems across 13 years." *Professional Psychology: Research and Practice*, 34(1), 66–72.

35 **In statistics gathered for the AAA Foundation for Traffic Safety, the number of aggressive incidents:** AAA Foundation for Traffic Safety. (1996). *"Road rage" on the rise: AAA foundation reports reported aggressive driving incidents.*

36 **the term *experiential avoidance* entered the psychological lexicon:** Hayes, S. C., Wilson, K. G., Gifford, E. V., Follette, V. M., & Strosahl, K. (1996). "Experiential avoidance and behavioral disorders: A functional dimensional approach to diagnosis and treatment." *Journal of Consulting and Clinical Psychology*, 64(6), 1,152–1,168.

This article was part of a special series,"Theoretically Coherent Alternatives to the DSM-IV." It would be absurd to think that the more than three hundred psychological and psychiatric disorders in the fifth edition of the *Diagnostic and Statistical Manual of Mental Disorders* (2014) is an accurate reflection of human functioning. Many of these so-called disorders are arbitrary in their distinctiveness. Research continues to emerge showing that there is often a continuum from healthy to severe distress and impairment (as opposed to two categories of either healthy or psychologically disordered). For this reason, researchers have been exploring an alternative approach that tackles dysfunctional processes that cut across multiple disorders such as experiential avoidance, rumination, sleep disturbances, and anhedonia (or deficits in positive experiences and the ability to derive rewards from seemingly positive events). Experiential avoidance, in particular, has been strongly linked to anxiety, stress, depression, substance abuse, deliberate self-harm and suicidality, intolerance of chronic pain, problem gambling, compulsive pornography use, borderline personality disorder, homophobia and racism, and less frequent positive emotions, life satisfaction, meaning in life, and inauthenticity, among other undesirable outcomes. It is because of the impressive ability of experiential avoidance to explain a large amount of variance in a wide variety of psychopathology and behavioral problems that we spend substantial time on this construct. If you want to make room for unwanted emotions and thoughts so that behavior can be directed toward what matters most, then there is great merit in learning about, attending to, and reducing experiential avoidance. Our research lab has published several articles that build on the seminal work by Steven Hayes, Kelly Wilson, and Kirk Strosahl:

Hayes, S. C., Strosahl, K. D., & Wilson, K. G. (2003). *Acceptance and Commitment Therapy: An Experiential Approach to Behavior Change.* New York: Guilford Press.

Kashdan, T. B., Barrios, V., Forsyth, J. P., & Steger, M. F. (2006). "Experiential avoidance as a generalized psychological vulnerability: Comparisons with coping and emotion regulation strategies." *Behaviour Research and Therapy,* 9, 1,301–1,320.

Kashdan, T. B., & Breen, W. E. (2007). "Materialism and diminished well-being: Experiential avoidance as a mediating mechanism." *Journal of Social and Clinical Psychology,* 26, 521–539.

Kashdan, T. B., Farmer, A. S., Adams, L. Ferssizidis, P., McKnight, P. E., & Nezlek, J. B. (2013). "Distinguishing healthy adults from people with social anxiety disorder: Evidence for the value of experiential avoidance and positive emotions in everyday social interactions." *Journal of Abnormal Psychology,* 122, 645–655.

Kashdan, T. B., Goodman, F. R., Machell, K. A., Kleiman, E. M., Monfort, S. S., Ciarrochi, J., & Nezlek, J. B. (in press). A contextual approach to experiential avoidance and social anxiety: Evidence from an experimental interaction and daily interactions of people with social anxiety disorder. *Emotion.*

Machell, K. A., Goodman, F. R., & Kashdan, T. B. (in press). "Experiential avoidance and well-being: A daily diary analysis." *Cognition and Emotion.*

36 **Between the 1950s and the 1970s, the average number of hours of household television viewing:** Committee on Physical Activity, Health,

Transportation, and Land Use. (2005). *"Does the Built Environment Influence Physical Activity? Examining the Evidence."* Transportation Research Board Special Report No. 282. Washington, DC: National Academy of Sciences.

37 **With good reason, leaders of the American Psychological Association named Dr. Albert Ellis:** Smith, D. (1982). "Trends in counseling and psychotherapy." *American Psychologist*, 37(7), 802. See table 3.

38 **Rebranded in 1990 as *learned optimism*:** Seligman, M. E. P. (1991). *Learned Optimism: How to Change Your Mind and Your Life.* New York: Knopf.

38 **Then some of the hippies exposed to the human potential movement and Eastern philosophy in the 1960s grew up:** Hayes, S. C., Luoma, J. B., Bond, F. W., Masuda, A., & Lillis, J. (2006). "Acceptance and commitment therapy: Model, processes and outcomes." *Behavior Research and Therapy,* 44(1), 1–25.

This is their first book together, cited more than three thousand times and influencing thousands of researchers and practitioners around the world to revise their approach to health and disorder and how to intervene:

Hayes, S. C., Strosahl, K. D., & Wilson, K. G. (1999). *Acceptance and Commitment Therapy: An Experiential Approach to Behavior Change.* New York: Guilford Press.

40 **It might be fair to say that, when anxiety is concerned, there is really:** Building off the prior references to work by Dr. Steven Hayes and his colleagues exploring acceptance and commitment therapy and other mindfulness and acceptance approaches: Kashdan, T. B., Farmer, A. S., Adams, L. Ferssizidis, P., McKnight, P. E., & Nezlek, J. B. (2013). "Distinguishing healthy adults from people with social anxiety disorder: Evidence for the value of experiential avoidance and positive emotions in everyday social interactions." *Journal of Abnormal Psychology*, 122, 645–655.

41 **Australian researchers Trine Fotel and Thyra Thomsen were curious to see:** Fotel, T., & Thomsen, T. U. (2003). "The surveillance of children's mobility." *Surveillance & Society*, 1(4), 535–554.

41 **Despite statistics showing that accidents involving bicycling children are declining:** National Highway Traffic Safety Admin-

istration. (2013). "Traffic safety facts: Children." Retrieved from: http://www-nrd.nhtsa.dot.gov/pubs/811767.pdf

This phenomenon is not limited to sending children out into potentially dangerous traffic. Modern parents are equally wary of their children's taking Halloween candy from strangers, speaking with strangers, and even going to the shopping mall with friends. The push for safety can especially be seen in the trend of modern American schools to practice lockdown drills.

41 **After complaining about dangerous traffic conditions, one mother concluded:** Fotel, T., & Thomsen, T. U. (2003). "The surveillance of children's mobility." *Surveillance & Society*, 1(4), 535–554.

42 **In a recent study on playground safety, Anita Bundy and her colleagues:** Bundy, A. C., Luckett, T., Tranter, P. J., Naughton, G. A., Wyver, S. R., Ragen, J., & Spies, G. (2009). "The risk is that there is 'no risk': A simple, innovative intervention to increase children's activity levels." *International Journal of Early Years Education*, 17(1), 33–45.

42 **This is what sociologist Catharine Warner calls *emotional safeguarding*:** Warner, C. H. (2010). "Emotional safeguarding: Exploring the nature of middle-class parents' school involvement." *Sociological Forum* 25(4), 703–724.

In early 2014, one of us (RBD) gave a TEDx talk on comfort addiction in which he emphasized emotional safeguarding. Of everything contained in chapter 2 of this book (and in the TEDx talk), this point appears to specially capture the public's attention. We have subsequently received dozens of pieces of written gratitude from parents who champion intellectual challenge and emotional safety without ever realizing the potential downsides.

44 **People from Asian cultures are often referred to as collectivists:** Triandis, H. C. (1995). *Individualism & Collectivism*. Boulder, CO: Westview Press.

45 **Legendary social psychologist Robert Wyer once summed it up this way:** R. S. Wyer, personal communication, 1990.

45 **However, when the same question is posed to a South Korean woman:** Suh, E., Diener, E., Oishi, S., & Triandis, H. C. (1998). "The shifting basis of life satisfaction judgments across cultures: Emotions versus norms." *Journal of Personality and Social Psychology*, 74(2), 482–493.

45 **Researchers have discovered interesting cultural differences:** Tsai, J. L. (2007). "Ideal affect: Cultural causes and behavioral consequences." *Perspectives on Psychological Science*, 2(3), 242–259.

45 **In one study we conducted, we examined the emotional experiences of people from various cultures:** Napa Scollon, C. N., Diener, E., Oishi, S., & Biswas-Diener, R. (2005). "An experience sampling and cross-cultural investigation of the relation between pleasant and unpleasant affect." *Cognition and Emotion*, 19(1), 27–52. Also, Napa Scollon, C. N., Diener, E., Oishi, S., & Biswas-Diener, R. (2004). "Emotions across cultures and methods." *Journal of Cross-Cultural Psychology*, 35(3), 304–326.

47 **In one study, researchers showed a funny clip to both European Americans:** Chentsova-Dutton, Y. E., Chu, J. P., Tsai, J. L., Rottenberg, J., Gross, J. J., & Gotlib, I. H. (2007). "Depression and emotional reactivity: Variation among Asian Americans of East Asian descent and European Americans." *Journal of Abnormal Psychology*, 116(4), 776–785. Also: Chentsova-Dutton, Y. E., Tsai, J. L., & Gotlib, I. H. (2010). "Further evidence for the cultural norm hypothesis: Positive emotion in depressed and control European American and Asian American women." *Cultural Diversity and Ethnic Minority Psychology*, 16(2), 284–295.

47 **This point has been brilliantly illustrated in a series of studies by Jeanne Tsai:** Tsai, J. L., Louie, J., Chen, E. E., & Uchida, Y. (2007). "Learning what feelings to desire: Socialization of ideal affect through children's storybooks." *Personality and Social Psychology Bulletin*, 33(1), 17–30.

48 **In fact, a wide range of research suggests that Asians also have a tendency to avoid savoring positive emotional experiences:** Tsai, J. (2013). "Culture and emotion." In R. Biswas-Diener and E. Diener (Eds.), *Noba: Psychology*. Champaign, IL: DEF Publisher. http://www.nobaproject.com

Tsai discusses a wide range of interesting research on the ways that culture influences how people deal with both positive and negative life events. Although it might seem strange to Westerners that East Asians could feel worried after a big win, Tsai points to the fact that East Asians have more dialectical thinking about emotions and are more likely to see emotions as being mixed between positive and negative rather than simply being one or the other.

50 **He was able, for example, to compute the speed:** Hunt, M. (1993). *The Story of Psychology.* New York: Doubleday. Anyone wanting a fascinating and in-depth look at the history of psychology should read this book. Of particular interest is the section on Mesmer, one of the fathers of hypnotism. He knew Mozart, Benjamin Franklin, and other notables.

Chapter 3: What's So Good About Feeling Bad?

54 **Roy Baumeister and his colleagues:** Baumeister, R. F., Bratslavsky, E., Finkenauer, C., & Vohs, K. D. (2001). "Bad is stronger than good." *Review of General Psychology*, 5(4), 323.

54 **When sex works well in a marriage:** McCarthy, B. W. (1999). "Marital style and its effects on sexual desire and functioning." *Journal of Family Psychotherapy*, 10, 1–12.

55 **Schoolchildren were asked whether anybody in their class:** French, D. C, Waas, G. A., Tarver-Behring, S. A. (1986). "Nomination and rating scale sociometrics: Convergent validity and clinical utility." *Behavioral Assessment*, 8, 331–340.

55 **People react more strongly to unpleasant smells:** Gilbert, A. N., Fridlund, A. J., & Sabini, J. (1987). "Hedonic and social determinants of facial displays to odors." *Chemical Senses*, 12, 355–363.

55 **negativity is our evolutionary birthright:** Cacioppo, J. T., Gardner, W. L., & Berntson, G. G. (1999). "The affect system has parallel and integrative processing components: Form follows function." *Journal of Personality and Social Psychology*, 76(5), 839–855. Also see: Rozin, P., & Royzman, E. B. (2001). "Negativity bias, negativity dominance, and contagion." *Personality and Social Psychology Review*, 5(4), 296–320.

56 **This may be because negative words carry more specific meaning:** A wide range of research has been conducted on how people evaluate, learn, and remember positive and negative language. Taken together these studies tend to point to the greater power of negative words. See for instance: Garcia, D., Garas, A., & Schweitzer, F. (2012). "Positive words carry less information than negative words." *EPJ DataScience*, 1(3), *1–12. doi: 10.1140/epjds3.*

56 **In another study, researchers interested in how people remember the emotional events of their lives:** Thomas, D., & Diener, E. (1990).

"Memory accuracy in the recall of emotions." *Journal of Personality and Social Psychology*, 59, 291–297. This article is part of a larger interesting body of research examining the relationship between memory and feelings.

57 **Research by Kate Harkness from Queen's University shows:** Harkness, K., Sabbagh, M., Jacobson, J., Chowdrey, N., & Chen, T. (2005). "Enhanced accuracy of mental state decoding in dysphoric college students." *Cognition & Emotion*, 19(7), 999–1,025. Additional studies can be found here:

Harkness, K. L., Jacobson, J. A., Sinclair, B., Chan, E., & Sabbagh, M. A. (2012). "For love or money? What motivates people to know the minds of others?" *Cognition & Emotion*, 26(3), 541–549.

Harkness, K. L., Washburn, D., Theriault, J. E., Lee, L., & Sabbagh, M. A. (2011). "Maternal history of depression is associated with enhanced theory of mind in depressed and nondepressed adult women." *Psychiatry Research*, 189(1), 91–96.

57 **We wouldn't either:** It is important to acknowledge that in this chapter we are talking about people with mild dysphoria as opposed to people with a psychiatric disorder such as major depressive disorder. In a 2013 article in the *Journal of the American Medical Association* (Murray et al., 2013), researchers examined 291 diseases and injuries in 187 countries from 1990 to 2010. By calculating the years of life lost to diseases and premature death, you end up with a metric referred to as disability adjusted life years. The years of life lost to disability due to depression ranked number 5 on the global burden list, ahead of every other health condition with the exception of heart disease, pulmonary disease, low back pain, and cancer. These are sobering numbers and in turn, the presence of major depressive disorder should not be considered a benefit or strength. The distinction between the shallow (dysphoria) and deep depths of depression are detailed beautifully in Jonathan Rottenberg's 2014 book, *The Depths: The Evolutionary Origins of the Depression Epidemic.* And see: Murray, C. J., Abraham, J., Ali, M. K., Alvarado, M., Atkinson, C., Baddour, L. M., . . . & Gutierrez, H. R. (2013). "The state of US health, 1990-2010: Burden of diseases, injuries, and risk factors." *JAMA*, 310(6), 591–606.

60 **Dr. Hi Po Bobo Lau from the University of Hong Kong and his team:** Lau, H. P. B., White, M. P., & Schnall, S. (2013). "Quantifying the value of emotions using a willingness to pay approach." *Journal of Happiness Studies*, 14(5), 1,543–1,561.

63 **Up to 60 percent of adults:** Wakefield, J. C., Schmitz, M. F., & Baer, J. C. (2010). "Does the DSM-IV clinical significance criterion for major depression reduce false positives? Evidence from the National Comorbidity Survey replication." *American Journal of Psychiatry*, 167(3), 298–304.

64 **Researchers were interested in the term *hotheaded*:** Wilkowski, B. M., Meier, B. P., Robinson, M. D., Carter, M. S., & Feltman, R. (2009). "'Hot-headed'" is more than an expression: The embodied representation of anger in terms of heat." *Emotion*, 9(4), 464–477.

68 **In our data, we coded 3,679 days when people reported feeling angry in everyday life:** Kashdan, T. B., Goodman, F. R., Mallard, T. T., & Nguyen, L. (2014). "What triggers anger in everyday life?" Unpublished manuscript, George Mason University.

69 **In one study, participants were asked to turn over as many of thirty-two cards:** Baumann, J., & DeSteno, D. (2012). "Context explains divergent effects of anger on risk taking." *Emotion*, 12(6), 1,196–1,199.

69 **This finding was also supported by a research team interested in how people make risk assessments:** Lerner, J. S., & Keltner, D. (2001). "Fear, anger, and risk." *Journal of Personality and Social Psychology*, 81(1), 146–159.

70 **In one study, researchers gave people either angry or neutral feedback on a different assignment and then had them complete the uses-for-a-brick task:** Van Kleef, G. A., Anastasopoulou, C., & Nijstad, B. A. (2010). "Can expressions of anger enhance creativity? A test of the emotions as social information (EASI) model." *Journal of Experimental Social Psychology*, 46(6), 1,042–1,048.

71 **In a study of construction managers in the United Kingdom:** Lindebaum, D., & Fielden, S. (2011). "'It's good to be angry': Enacting anger in construction project management to achieve perceived leader effectiveness." *Human Relations*, 64(3), 437–458.

72 **In one series of studies, participants were given the task of negotiating for the highest price possible for a batch of mobile phones:** Van Kleef, G. A., De Dreu, C. K., & Manstead, A. S. (2004). "The interpersonal effects of anger and happiness in negotiations." *Journal of Personality and Social Psychology*, 86(1), 57–76.

72 **In one study, the researchers found that when a trained actor faked surface anger, as opposed to expressing deep anger:** Côté, S.,

Hideg, I., & Van Kleef, G. A. (2013). "The consequences of faking anger in negotiations." *Journal of Experimental Social Psychology*, 49(3), 453–463.

73 **"At the very time when my studies were most successful . . .":** Du Bois, W. E. B. (2007). "Dusk of Dawn: An essay toward an autobiography of a race concept." In H. L. Gates (Ed), *The Oxford W. E. B. Du Bois Reader*: Oxford (p. 44). Oxford: Oxford University Press.

74 **The deep prejudice against anger is largely unjustified:** For a recent review of evidence on the virtuousness of anger in predictable contexts, read the following article:
Van Doorn, J., Zeelenberg, M., & Breugelmans, S. M. (in press). "Anger and prosocial behavior." *Emotion Review*.

Abstract

Anger is often primarily portrayed as a negative emotion that motivates antagonistic, aggressive, punitive, or hostile behavior. We propose that this portrayal is too one-sided. A review of the literature on behavioral consequences of anger reveals evidence for the positive and even prosocial behavioral consequences of this emotion. We outline a more inclusive view of anger and its role in upholding cooperative and moral behavior, and suggest a possible role of equity concerns. We also suggest new predictions and lines of research derived from our perspective.

It is not enough to give lip service to negative emotions by stating the obvious: one cannot be happy all the time, and over time, everyone wants to have positive emotions more frequently than negative emotions. As alluded to by Van Doom, Zeelenberg, and Breugelmans, it is time for a more inclusive, honest, and promising view of distinct types of negative emotions. In 2005, scientist Cecilia Cheng observed that "the predominant use of any type of coping strategy can be debilitating" and "people need to be flexible in the deployment of coping strategies for effective coping with diverse types of situations" (p. 860). Echoing this sentiment, in our review of the available scientific evidence, we are confident that the adaptive value of flexibility is superior to building a limited number of positive emotions, positive thoughts, and positive personality traits.

Cheng, C., & Cheung, M. W. (2005). "Cognitive processes underlying coping flexibility: Differentiation and integration." *Journal of Personality*, 73(4), 859–886.

For recent literature reviews

Kashdan, T. B., & Rottenberg, J. (2010). "Psychological flexibility as a fundamental aspect of health." *Clinical Psychology Review*, 30(7), 865–878. Bonanno, G. A. (2013). "Meaning making, adversity, and regulatory flexibility." *Memory*, 21(1), 150–156.

Bonanno, G. A., & Burton, C. L. (2013). "Regulatory flexibility: An individual differences perspective on coping and emotion regulation." *Perspectives on Psychological Science*, 8(6), 591–612.

75 **Dr. Ernest Harburg and his research team at the University of Michigan School of Public Health:** Harburg, E., Julius, M., Kaciroti, N., Gleiberman, L., & Schork, M. A. (2003). "Expressive/suppressive anger-coping responses, gender, and types of mortality: A 17-year follow-up (Tecumseh, Michigan, 1971–1988)." *Psychosomatic Medicine*, 65(4), 588–597.

76 **Psychologist and editor of *Anger Disorders*, Dr. Howard Kassinove, mentions:** https://www.apa.org/helpcenter/recognize-anger.aspx.

77 **techniques for slowing down the speed of threatening events:** Riskind, J. H., Rector, N. A., & Taylor, S. (2012). "Looming cognitive vulnerability to anxiety and its reduction in psychotherapy." *Journal of Psychotherapy Integration*, 22(2), 137–162.

For additional research on this topic, see other studies by John Riskind's research team, such as: Riskind, J. H., Calvete, E., Gonzalez, Z., Orue, I., Kleiman, E. M., & Shahar, G. (2013). "Direct and indirect effects of looming cognitive style via social cognitions on social anxiety, depression, and hostility." *International Journal of Cognitive Therapy*, 6(1), 73–85.

78 **this speedometer example:** We modified ideas that were generated in Kassinove, H., & Tafrate, R. C. (2002). *Anger Management: The Complete Treatment Guidebook for Practitioners*. Atascadero, CA: Impact Publishers.

81 **According to the National Recidivism Study of Released Prisoners conducted by the US Bureau of Justice:** http://www.bjs.gov/index.cfm?ty=dcdetail&iid=270

82 **In recent research, Dr. Tangney found that inmates who were prone to feeling guilty about past wrongs suffered more:** Tangney, J. P., Stuewig, J., & Martinez, A. G. (in press). "Two faces of shame: Understanding shame and guilt in the prediction of jail inmates' recidivism." *Psychological Science.*

82 **For instance, researchers have found that adults prone to feeling guilty were less likely to drive drunk:** Tibbetts, S. G. (2003). "Self-conscious emotions and criminal offending." *Psychological Reports*, 93, 101–126.

84 **The interviewer was either Dr. Jessica Tracy:** Randles, D., & Tracy, J. L. (2013). "Nonverbal displays of shame predict relapse and declining health in recovering alcoholics." *Clinical Psychological Science*, 1(2), 149–155.

87–88 **When we experience too much anxiety too often, we age prematurely:** Epel, E. S., Lin, J., Wilhelm, F. H., Wolkowitz, O. M., Cawthon, R., Adler, N. E., . . . & Blackburn, E. H. (2006). "Cell aging in relation to stress arousal and cardiovascular disease risk factors." *Psychoneuroendocrinology*, 31(3), 277–287.

88 **So authors, performance experts, and business leaders aim for people to experience the "just right" amount of anxiety:** This is an idea that has been around for decades and received greater attention with the following best-selling book: Csikszentmihalyi, M. (1990). *Flow: The Psychology of Optimal Experience*. New York: Harper and Row. An idea that continues to be discussed anew in both books and popular magazines such as:

Rosen, R. H. (2008). "Just enough anxiety: The hidden driver of business success." Portfolio; Retrieved from: http://www.forbes.com/sites/travisbradberry/2014/02/06/how-successful-people-stay-calm/.

89 **To take an example from evolutionary psychologists John Tooby and Leda Cosmides:** Tooby, J., & Cosmides, L. (2005). "Conceptual foundations of evolutionary psychology." In D. M. Buss (Ed.), *The Handbook of Evolutionary Psychology* (pp. 5–67). Hoboken, NJ: Wiley.

91 **In one fascinating research study, group members were led to believe that they had accidentally activated a computer virus:** Ein-Dor, T. (in press). "Social defense theory: How a mixture of personality traits in group contexts may promote our survival." In M. Mikulincer & P. R. Shaver (Eds.), *Nature and Development of Social Connections: From Brain to Group*. Washington, DC: American Psychological Association. Also see: Ein-Dor, T., & Perry, A. (2014). "Full house of fears: Evidence that people high in attachment anxiety are more accurate in detecting deceit." *Journal of Personality*, 82,

83–92; Ein-Dor, T., Mikulincer, M., Doron, G., & Shaver, P. R. (2010). "The attachment paradox: How can so many of us (the insecure ones) have no adaptive advantages?" *Perspectives on Psychological Science*, 5, 123–141; Ein-Dor, T., & Perry, A. (2012). "Diversity is bliss: How a mixture of personality traits in group contexts may promote our survival." In B. O. Hunter & T. J. Romero (Eds.), *Psychology of Threat* (pp. 55–74). Hauppauge, NY: Nova Science.

91–92 **Researchers found that being extraverted, sociable, and dominant were unrelated to the single-minded, gritty determination of anxious people:** An important scientific discovery is that although we might think that being extraverted implies being an emotionally stable person, these separate dimensions of personality are only slighted related and, in some cases, unrelated. What this means is that knowing that someone is extraverted does not provide any useful information about whether that same person experiences frequent, intense, intolerable negative emotions. In a similar vein, how sensitive a person is to rewards (that is, the intensity and duration of positive emotions when a desirable reward is obtained) is unrelated to how sensitive the individual is to punishment or the inability to obtain rewards (that is, the intensity and duration of distress in a stressful situation). See:

Elliot, A. J., & Thrash, T. M. (2002). "Approach-avoidance motivation in personality: Approach and avoidance temperaments and goals." *Journal of Personality and Social Psychology*, 82(5), 804–818.

Gable, S. L., Reis, H. T., & Elliot, A. J. (2003). "Evidence for bivariate systems: An empirical test of appetition and aversion across domains." *Journal of Research in Personality*, 37(5), 349–372.

Watson, D., & Clark, L. A. (1997). "Extraversion and its positive emotional core." In R. Hogan, J. A. Johnson, & S. R. Briggs (Eds.), *Handbook of Personality Psychology* (pp. 767–793). San Diego, CA: Academic Press.

Chapter 4: How Positive Emotion Can Lead to Your Downfall

95 **If you observe a really happy man:** Wolfe, W. Béran (1932). *How to Be Happy Though Human*, reprinted in 1999, 2001. London: Routledge.

96 **In 1965, Dr. Hadley Cantril, a pioneer in happiness studies:** Cantril, H. (1965). *The Pattern of Human Concerns*. New Brunswick, NJ: Rutgers University Press.

97 **Happiness is a state of mind and, as such, can be measured, studied, and enhanced:** This is echoed by two of the leading happiness researchers (Sonja Lyubomirsky and Ken Sheldon) who on page 115 of their widely cited 2005 article on the nature of happiness state, "Here we define happiness as it is most often defined in the literature, that is, in terms of frequent positive affect, high life satisfaction, and infrequent negative affect." Lyubomirsky, S., Sheldon, K. M., & Schkade, D. (2005). "Pursuing happiness: The architecture of sustainable change." *Review of General Psychology*, 9, 111–131. Also see: David, S., Boniwell, I., & Ayers, A. C. (Eds.). (2013). *Oxford Handbook of Happiness*. Oxford: Oxford University Press; Diener, E., Suh, E. M., Lucas, R. E., & Smith, H. L. (1999). "Subjective well-being: Three decades of progress." *Psychological Bulletin*, 125(2), 276–302.

97 **In a review of 225 academic papers on happiness, for instance, psychologist Sonja Lyubomirsky and her colleagues found that feeling upbeat is linked to all sorts of real-life benefits:** Lyubomirsky, S., King, L. A., & Diener, E. (2005). "The benefits of frequent positive affect." *Psychological Bulletin*, 131, 803–855.

98–99 **Yukiko Uchida, a researcher at Kyoto University, asked a question that would likely get her kicked out of an American happiness club:** Uchida, Y., & Kitayama, S. (2009). "Happiness and unhappiness in east and west: Themes and variations." *Emotion*, 9(4), 441–456. Also see: Uchida, Y., & Ogihara, Y. (2012). "Personal or interpersonal construal of happiness: A cultural psychological perspective." *International Journal of Wellbeing*, 2(4), 354–369.

99 **One of the earliest published studies to identify a cost of positive emotion was published in 1991 by Ed Diener and his colleagues at the University of Illinois:** Diener, E., Colvin, C. R., Pavot, W. G., & Allman, A. (1991). "The psychic costs of intense positive affect." *Journal of Personality and Social Psychology*, 61(3), 492–503.

100 **Recognizing this happiness trap and taking advantage of it:** Harris, R. (2007). *The Happiness Trap: Stop Struggling, Start Living*. Auckland, New Zealand: Exisle Publishing.

101 **Psychologist Shigehiro Oishi and his international collaborators collected current dictionary definitions of happiness in thirty countries:** Oishi, S., Graham, J., Kesebir, S., & Galinha, I. C.

(2013). "Concepts of happiness across time and cultures." *Personality and Social Psychology Bulletin*, 39(5), 559–577.

102 **Happy people, by contrast, are more likely to overlook details in favor of the big picture:** Forgas, J. P., & Koch, A. (2013). "Mood effects on cognition." In M. D. Robinson, E. Harmon-Jones, E. R. Watkins (Eds.), *Handbook of Emotion and Cognition* (pp. 231–252). New York: Guilford Press. Also see: Forgas, J. P. (2013). "Don't worry, be sad! On the cognitive, motivational, and interpersonal benefits of negative mood." *Current Directions in Psychological Science*, 22(3), 225–232.

102 **In three studies, judges rated the quality of unhappy people's arguments as approximately 25 percent more impressive and 20 percent more concrete than those made by happy folks:** Forgas, J. P. (2007). "When sad is better than happy: Negative affect can improve the quality and effectiveness of persuasive messages and social influence strategies." *Journal of Experimental Social Psychology*, 43, 513–528.

103 **Dr. Joseph Forgas and his fellow Australian researchers wanted to determine how good happy people—with their more superficial processing style (paying greater attention to the gist, not the details)—are at detecting deceit:** Forgas, J. P., & East, R. (2008). "On being happy and gullible: Mood effects on skepticism and the detection of deception." *Journal of Experimental Social Psychology*, 44, 1,362–1,367.

104 **the emotion called sadness (which, by the way, is not the same thing as depression):** Rottenberg, J. (2014). *The Depths: The Evolutionary Origins of the Depression Epidemic.* New York: Perseus Books; Rottenberg, J. (2005). "Mood and emotion in major depression." *Current Directions in Psychological Science*, 14(3), 167–170. Also see: Rottenberg, J. (2014). *The Depths: The Evolutionary Origins of the Depression Epidemic.* New York: Basic Books.

104 **If happy people rely on cursory, superficial strategies to collect information from the outside world, then they are going to bemore prone to using stereotypes:** Storbeck, J., & Clore, G. L. (2005). "With sadness comes accuracy; with happiness, false memory: Mood and the false memory effect." *Psychological Science*, 16(10), 785–791.

104–105 **In another experiment, students sitting in a classroom watched a nervous woman walk up to the instructor and physically assault him:** Forgas, J. P., Vargas, P., & Laham, S. (2005). "Mood effects on eyewitness memory: Affective influences on susceptibility to misinformation." *Journal of Experimental Social Psychology*, 41, 574–588.

105 **Soon after the terrorist attacks of September 11, 2001, participants played a first-person shooter game in which they were told to kill any screen character carrying a gun:** Unkelbach, C., Forgas, J. P., & Denson, T. F. (2008). "The turban effect: The influence of Muslim headgear and induced affect on aggressive responses in the shooter bias paradigm." *Journal of Experimental Social Psychology*, 44, 1,409–1,413.

105 **On average, happy people tend to be kind, feel grateful, and put a priority on being a good community citizen:** Oishi, S., Diener, E., & Lucas, R. E. (2007). "The optimum level of well-being: Can people be too happy?" *Perspectives on Psychological Science*, 2(4), 346–360. Also see: Diener, E., Suh, E. M., Lucas, R. E., & Smith, H. L. (1999). "Subjective well-being: Three decades of progress." *Psychological Bulletin*, 125(2), 276–302.

107 **To test this, Jonathan Schooler, Dan Ariely, and George Loewenstein randomly gave participants one of four sets of instructions before listening to Stravinsky's *The Rite of Spring*:** Schooler, J., Ariely, D., & Loewenstein, G. (2003). "The pursuit and assessment of happiness can be self-defeating." In I. Brocas and J. Carrillo (Eds.), *Psychology and Economics*, Vol 1. (pp. 41–70). Oxford: Oxford University Press.

108 **In another example of the paradoxical effect of pursuing happiness, researchers Iris Mauss and Maya Tamir gave adults one of two doctored newspaper articles:** Mauss, I. B., Tamir, M., Anderson, C. L., & Savino, N. S. (2011). "Can seeking happiness make people unhappy? Paradoxical effects of valuing happiness." *Emotion*, 11, 807–815.

108 **In another study, these same researchers gave adults a questionnaire asking them how much importance they place on attaining happiness and about the amount of stress in their lives:** Mauss, I. B., Tamir, M., Anderson, C. L., & Savino, N. S.

(2011). "Can seeking happiness make people unhappy? Paradoxical effects of valuing happiness." *Emotion*, 11, 807–815. Also see: Gruber, J., Mauss, I. B., & Tamir, M. (2011). "A dark side of happiness? How, when, and why happiness is not always good." *Perspectives on Psychological Science*, 6(3), 222–233.

110 **High, off-kilter expectations for happiness compromise the experience of happiness and success another way:** Baron, R. A., Hmieleski, K. M., & Henry, R. A. (2012). "Entrepreneurs' dispositional positive affect: The potential benefits—and potential costs—of being 'up.'" *Journal of Business Venturing*, 27(3), 310–324.

112 **Building on the idea that anger promotes successful confrontations—to take a single example—researchers have shown that when given a choice of music to listen to before confronting a perpetrator:** Tamir, M., Mitchell, C., & Gross, J. J. (2008). "Hedonic and instrumental motives in anger regulation." *Psychological Science*, 19, 324–328. Also see: Tamir, M., & Ford, B. Q. (2012). "When feeling bad is expected to be good: Emotion regulation and outcome expectancies in social conflicts." *Emotion*, 12, 807–816.

113 **In one experiment, Maya Tamir and her colleagues instructed volunteers to collect donations in two scenarios that involved asking someone for help:** Hackenbracht, J., & Tamir, M. (2010). "Preferences for sadness when eliciting help: Instrumental motives in sadness regulation." *Motivation and Emotion*, 34(3), 306–315.

114 **Victoria Visser and her colleagues conducted two studies looking at how displaying happiness or unhappiness in a leadership position:** Visser, V. A., Van Knippenberg, D., Van Kleef, G. A., & Wisse, B. (2013). "How leader displays of happiness and sadness influence follower performance: Emotional contagion and creative versus analytical performance." *The Leadership Quarterly*, 24(1), 172–188.

115 **Psychologist Seth Kaplan asked a group of people to complete what can only be described as an incredibly boring simulation of what airtraffic controllers do:** Kaplan, S., Cortina, J., Mullin, H., Hu, X., Nicolaides, V., Weiss, E., Gilrane, V., & Vega, R. (2013). "*Investigation of leader emotion management processes.*" Technical Report,

Fort Leavenworth Research Unit. Fort Belvoir, VA: US Army Research Institute for the Behavioral and Social Sciences.

117 **The reason, of course, is that you did a poor job of predicting your future state, falling prey to what psychologists call *projection bias*:** Loewenstein, G., O'Donoghue, T., & Rabin, M. (2003). "Projection bias in predicting future utility." *Quarterly Journal of Economics*, 118(4), 1,209–1,248.

117 **A common one is known as *impact bias*:** Gilbert, D. T., Driver-Linn, E., & Wilson, T. D. (2002). "The trouble with Vronsky: Impact bias in the forecasting of future affective states." In L. F. Barrett & P. Salovey (Eds.), *The Wisdom in Feeling: Psychological Processes in Emotional Intelligence* (pp. 114–143). New York: Guilford Press.

117 **A third happiness bias—*distinction bias*—is beautifully illustrated by researcher Christopher Hsee:** Hsee, C. K., & Hastie, R. (2006). "Decision and experience: Why don't we choose what makes us happy?" *Trends in Cognitive Sciences*, 10(1), 31–37. Also see: Hsee, C. K., & Zhang, J. (2010). "General evaluability theory." *Perspectives on Psychological Science*, 5(4), 343–355.

118 **The single most toxic decision-making bias, where happiness is concerned, is the *wanting/liking bias*:** Berridge, K. C., & Robinson, T. E. (2003). "Parsing reward." *Trends in Neurosciences*, 26(9), 507–513; Berridge, K. C., Robinson, T. E., & Aldridge, J. W. (2009). "Dissecting components of reward: 'Liking', 'wanting', and learning." *Current Opinion in Pharmacology*, 9(1), 65–73; Gilbert, D. T., & Wilson, T. D. (2000). "Miswanting: Some problems in the forecasting of future affective states." In J. Forgas (Ed.), *Thinking and Feeling: The Role of Affect in Social Cognition* (pp. 178–197). Cambridge: Cambridge University Press.

120 **Here, and throughout the book, we are not talking about emotional problems and disorders as hidden gifts:** See chapter 3, page 56 note for "In another study, researchers interested . . ." about the distinction between sadness and clinical depression.

Chapter 5: Beyond the Obsession with Mindfulness

123 **"The critical difference between the thinking of humans and of lower animals":** Neisser, U. (1963). "The multiplicity of thought." *British Journal of Psychology*, 54(1), 10.

124 **If you want specific persuasive data, look no further than the two leading scientists who were both instrumental in popularizing mindfulness practices in the West:** Davidson, R. J., Kabat-Zinn, J., Schumacher, J., Rosenkranz, M., Muller, D., Santorelli, S. F., . . . & Sheridan, J. F. (2003). "Alterations in brain and immune function produced by mindfulness meditation." *Psychosomatic Medicine*, 65(4), 564–570.

124 **Researchers found a 400 percent increase in left-sided activation:** Ibid.

128 **"Conscious thought stays firmly under the searchlight":** Dijksterhuis, A., & Meurs, T. (2006). "Where creativity resides: The generative power of unconscious thought." *Consciousness and Cognition*, 15(1), 138.

128 **Research shows that people are able to make unconscious categorical judgments about others at amazing speeds:** Bar, M., Neta, M., & Linz, H. (2006). "Very first impressions." *Emotion*, 6(2), 269–278; Curhan, J., & Pentland, A. (2007). "Thin slices of negotiation: Predicting outcomes from conversational dynamics within the first five minutes." *Journal of Applied Psychology*, 92, 802–811; Willis, J., & Todorov, A. (2006). "First impressions making up your mind after a 100-Ms exposure to a face." *Psychological Science*, 17(7), 592–598.

129 **Across a wide range of studies, researchers have found that these "thin slice" observations are well above chance in accuracy:** Ambady, N., & Rosenthal, R. (1992). "Thin slices of expressive behavior as predictors of interpersonal consequences: A meta-analysis." *Psychological Bulletin*, 111, 256–274.

129 **Rick van Baaren and his colleagues at the Radbouds University of Nijmegen found that when servers repeated customer orders:** Van Baaren, R. B., Holland, R. W., Steenaert, B., & van Knippenberg,

A. (2003). "Mimicry for money: Behavioral consequences of imitation." *Journal of Experimental Social Psychology*, 39(4), 393–398.

130 **Psychologists at the University of Groningen, Duke University, and Yale University explored our reactions to "negatively tinged social cues":** Leander, N. P., Chartrand, T. L., & Bargh, J. A. (2012). "You give me the chills: Embodied reactions to inappropriate amounts of behavioral mimicry." *Psychological Science*, 23(7), 772–779.

132 **By strong situations, we mean those times when we feel intense emotions and are pushed to do something:** Cooper, W. H., & Withey, M. J. (2009). "The strong situation hypothesis." *Personality and Social Psychology Review*, 13, 62–72; Meyer, R. D., Dalal, R. S., & Hermida, R. (2010). "A review and synthesis of situational strength in the organizational sciences." *Journal of Management*, 36(1), 121–140.

133 **In two studies, Iris Mauss at the University of California, Berkeley and James Gross at Stanford University asked participants to unscramble sentences:** Mauss, I. B., Evers, C., Wilhelm, F. H., & Gross, J. J. (2006). "How to bite your tongue without blowing your top: Implicit evaluation of emotion regulation predicts affective responding to anger provocation." *Personality and Social Psychology Bulletin*, 32(5), 589–602. For additional research on this topic: Mauss, I. B., Cook, C. L., & Gross, J. J. (2007). "Automatic emotion regulation during anger provocation." *Journal of Experimental Social Psychology*, 43(5), 698–711.

133 **What are the takeaways from this research:** Mauss, I. B., Bunge, S. A., & Gross, J. J. (2007). "Automatic emotion regulation." *Social and Personality Psychology Compass*, 1(1), 146–167.

133 **Third, simple, brief, low-cost interventions can push and pull us toward healthier:** Sheeran, P., Gollwitzer, P. M., & Bargh, J. A. (2013). "Nonconscious processes and health." *Health Psychology*, 32, 460–473.

134 **In an article on constructive mindlessness, psychologist Scott Barry Kaufman:** McMillan, R. L., Kaufman, S. B., & Singer, J. L. (2013). "Ode to positive constructive daydreaming." *Frontiers in Psychology*, 4.

The following references provide scientific evidence behind this statement:

Baars, B. J. (2010). "Spontaneous repetitive thoughts can be adaptive: Postscript on 'mind wandering'." *Psychological Bulletin*, 136(2), 208–210.

Baird, B., Smallwood, J., Mrazek, M. D., Kam, J. W., Franklin, M. S., & Schooler, J. W. (2012). "Inspired by distraction mind wandering facilitates creative incubation." *Psychological Science*, 23(10), 1,117–1,122.

Baird, B., Smallwood, J., & Schooler, J. W. (2011). "Back to the future: Autobiographical planning and the functionality of mind-wandering." *Consciousness and Cognition*, 20(4), 1,604–1,611.

Immordino-Yang, M. H., Christodoulou, J. A., & Singh, V. (2012). "Rest is not idleness implications of the brain's default mode for human development and education." *Perspectives on Psychological Science*, 7(4), 352–364.

Kaufman, S. B. (2013). *Ungifted: Intelligence Redefined*. New York: Basic Books.

Singer, J. L. (1975). "Navigating the stream of consciousness: Research in daydreaming and related inner experience." *American Psychologist*, 30(7), 727–738.

Singer, J. L. (2009). "Researching imaginative play and adult consciousness: Implications for daily and literary creativity." *Psychology of Aesthetics, Creativity, and the Arts*, 3(4), 190–199.

Singer, J. L., & Schonbar, R. A. (1961). "Correlates of day dreaming: A dimension of self-awareness." *Journal of Consulting Psychology*, 25, 1–6.

Stawarczyk, D., Majerus, S., Maquet, P., & D'Argembeau, A. (2011). "Neural correlates of ongoing conscious experience: Both task-unrelatedness and stimulus-independence are related to default network activity." *PLoS One*, 6(2), e16997.

Wang, K., Yu, C., Xu, L., Qin, W., Li, K., Xu, L., & Jiang, T. (2009). "Offline memory reprocessing: Involvement of the brain's default network in spontaneous thought processes." *PloS One*, 4(3), e4867.

135 **From this personal perspective, it is much easier to understand why people are drawn to mind wandering and willing to invest nearly 50 percent of their waking hours engaged in it:** Killingsworth, M. A., & Gilbert, D. T. (2010). "A wandering mind is an unhappy mind." *Science*, 330, 932.

135 **This point echoed in an essay on sloth by author Thomas Pynchon:** "The deadly sins/sloth; Nearer, my couch, to thee" by Thomas Pynchon, *New York Times Book Review*, June 6, 1993.

136 **After all, creativity has long been associated with unconscious incubation, a point often underscored by Nobel laureates:** Ghiselin, B. (1952). *The Creative Process: A Symposium* (Vol. 717). Oakland: University of California Press.

136–137 **people who doodle show a nearly 25 percent bump in remembering what happened while they were doodling:** Andrade, J. (2010). "What does doodling do?" *Applied Cognitive Psychology,* 24(1), 100–106; Schott, G. D. (2011). "Doodling and the default network of the brain." *The Lancet,* 378 (9,797), 1,133–1,134.

137 **research shows that this can aid concentration and provide a platform for calm, focused, long-lasting activity:** Dziedziewicz, D., Oledzka, D., & Karwowski, M. (2012). "Developing 4- to 6-year-old children's figural creativity using a doodle-book program." *Thinking Skills and Creativity,* 9(August), 85–95. doi: 10.1016/j.bbr.2011.03.031.

137 **Imagine that long flight from London to Sydney:** Rosekind, M. R., Graeber, R. C., Dinges, D. F., et al. (1994). "Crew factors in flight operations IX: Effects of planned cockpit rest on crew performance and alertness in long haul operations." NASA Technical Memorandum 108839. Moffett Field, CA: NASA Ames Research Center.

137 **To find out more about why turning consciousness off is helpful, we turn to Andrei Medvedev:** Medvedev, A. V. (2012). "Does the resting state connectivity have hemispheric asymmetry? A near-infrared spectroscopy study." Presented at the Annual Meeting of the Society for Neuroscience, New Orleans, LA.

138 **When researchers inquired about the origins of the most creative ideas produced by 104 public relations specialists for organizations in the United Kingdom:** http://www.rainierpr.co.uk/home_pages/white_paper_018.html and http://www.pwkpr.com/downloads/The_Management_of_Creativity_in_the_PR_Process_PW&K.pdf.

139 **Researchers have found, for instance, that the most creative people, and those who are most invested in increasing their creative output, intuitively look to nonconscious states for inspiration:** Pagel, J. F., & Kwiatkowski, C. F. (2003). "Creativity and dreaming: Correlation of reported dream incorporation into

waking behavior with level and type of creative interest." *Creativity Research Journal*, 15(2–3), 199–205.

141 **Two well-meaning people end up creating a high-maintenance interaction:** Finkel, E. J., Campbell, W. K., Brunell, A. B., Dalton, A. N., Chartrand, T. L., & Scarbeck, S. J. (2006). "High-maintenance interaction: Inefficient social coordination impairs self-regulation." *Journal of Personality and Social Psychology*, 91, 456–475.

141 **But what if you drained a person's energy prior to the conversation so that they simply lacked the oomph to hide, escape, or water down what they were thinking:** Apfelbaum, E. P., & Sommers, S. R. (2009). "Liberating effects of losing executive control: When regulatory strategies turn maladaptive." *Psychological Science*, 20, 139–143.

141 **Additional support for the value of impulsive, or less regulated, action comes from an unlikely source: cognitive declines in old age:** Apfelbaum, E. P., Krendl, A. C., & Ambady, N. (2010). "Age-related decline in executive function predicts better advice-giving in uncomfortable social contexts." *Journal of Experimental Social Psychology*, 46(6), 1,074–1,077. And although we don't discuss it in this chapter, read this article for additional evidence for the benefits of being impulsive in social situations: Van Dillen, L. F., Papies, E. K., & Hofmann, W. (2013). "Turning a blind eye to temptation: How cognitive load can facilitate self-regulation." *Journal of Personality and Social Psychology*, 104(3), 427–443.

142 **In their article "The risk of polite misunderstandings," Jean-François Bonnefron and his colleagues conclude that:** Bonnefron, J. F., Feeney, A., & De Neys, W. (2011). "The risk of polite misunderstandings." *Current Directions in Psychological Science*, 20(5), 321–324.

144 **Take your time and let the unconscious deal with it:** Dijksterhuis, A. (2004). "Think different: The merits of unconscious thought in preference development, and decision making." *Journal of Personality and Social Psychology*, 87, 586–598.

144 **Nowhere is this rule more pronounced than in the research of Ap Dijksterhuis:** Ibid. Bos, M. W., Dijksterhuis, A., & Van Baaren, R. B. (2011). "The benefits of 'sleeping on things': Unconscious thought leads to automatic weighting." *Journal of Consumer Psychology*, 21(1), 4–8; Also see: Pessiglione, M., Schmidt, L., Draganski, B., Kalisch, R., Lau, H., Dolan, R.

J., & Frith, C. D. (2007). "How the brain translates money into force: A neuroimaging study of subliminal motivation." *Science,* 316(5,826), 904–906. Pessiglione et al. (2007) tested this idea using a novel reward priming paradigm. In an experiment, people were exposed to coins (of high versus low value), some of which they could earn by squeezing a handgrip: the harder they squeezed, the greater the proportion of the coins they received. It was not surprising that people squeezed harder when the coins were more valuable. Sometimes, however, coins were presented very briefly, so that they could not be consciously perceived (i.e., they were subliminally presented). Remarkably, even in this case, people worked harder when a more valuable coin was at stake, leading to the intriguing discovery that rewards do not need to be consciously perceived to trigger the recruitment of effort.

144 **In one compelling study, Dijksterhuis was interested in whether football fanatics:** Dijksterhuis, A., Bos, M. W., Van der Leij, A., & Van Baaren, R. B. (2009). "Predicting soccer matches after unconscious and conscious thought as a function of expertise." *Psychological Science*, 20(11), 1,381–1,387.

145 **In a similar study, adults with advanced training in psychology were asked to determine what, if any, psychological disorders a patient suffered from:** De Vries, M., Witteman, C. L., Holland, R. W., & Dijksterhuis, A. (2010). "The unconscious thought effect in clinical decision making: An example in diagnosis." *Medical Decision Making*, 30(5), 578–581.

145 **In fact, experts making the more mindless decisions were five times as accurate as those making carefully considered decisions:** Expertise makes a crucial difference here. Obviously an expert has lots of experience and training to unconsciously draw on. This is not an ideal strategy for you if you are making a decision about something that is foreign to you. And if you lack any formal or informal training in psychological disorders, you simply will not have the internal software for wise gut reactions.

146 **In 2011, Dijksterhuis and his colleagues conducted an experiment in which participants had to find one or two ideal choices out of twelve possible apartments:** Nordgren, L. F., Bos, M. W., & Dijksterhuis, A. (2011). "The best of both worlds: Integrating conscious and unconscious thought best solves complex decisions." *Journal of Experimental Social Psychology*, 47(2), 509–511.

148 **At a call center, Gary Latham and Ronald Piccolo tested out a low-cost intervention on employees by giving them a photograph to view before calling customers:** Latham, G. P., & Piccolo, R. F. (2012). "The effect of context specific versus nonspecific subconscious goals on employee performance." *Human Resource Management,* 51, 535–548.

149 **In a similar vein, when smokers view antismoking advertisements, they end up smoking more:** Harris, J. L., Pierce, M., & Bargh, J. A. (in press). "Priming effect of antismoking PSAs on smoking behaviour: A pilot study." *Tobacco Control.*

149 **When shown positive images and words about black Americans on a computer screen:** Kawakami, K., Phills, C. E., Steele, J. R., & Dovidio, J. F. (2007). "(Close) Distance makes the heart grow fonder: Improving implicit racial attitudes and interracial interactions through approach behaviors." *Journal of Personality and Social Psychology,* 92, 957–971; Phills, C. E., Santelli, A. G., Kawakami, K., Struthers, C. W., & Higgins, E. T. (2011). "Reducing implicit prejudice: Matching approach/avoidance strategies to contextual valence and regulatory focus." *Journal of Experimental Social Psychology,* 47(5), 968–973.

Chapter 6: The Teddy Effect

156 **Edwin Lawrence Godkin, editor in chief of the *Evening Post*, devoted many articles to Teddy's "bellicose temperament," claiming:** Morrs, E. (2000). *Theodore Rex (p. 546).* New York: Random House.

156 **Curious about the adaptive nature of seemingly bad social traits, psychologist Scott Lilienfeld and his colleagues examined the leadership provided by forty-two US presidents:** Lilienfeld, S. O., Waldman, I. D., Landfield, K., Watts, A. L., Rubenzer, S., & Faschingbauer, T. R. (2012). "Fearless dominance and the U.S. presidency: Implications of psychopathic personality traits for successful and unsuccessful political leadership." *Journal of Personality and Social Psychology,* 103(3), 489–505.

158 **The modern positivity movement has placed an emphasis on gentle tactics by leaders who, according to Tom Rath of Gallup:** Rath, T. (2004). "The impact of positive leadership." *Gallup Management Journal.* Retrieved from: http://businessjournal.gallup.com/content/11458/impact-positive-leadership.aspx. Also see:

Achor, S. (2010). *The Happiness Advantage: The Seven Principles of Positive Psychology That Fuel Success and Performance at Work.* New York: Crown Publishing.

Achor, S. (2013). *Before Happiness: The 5 Hidden Keys to Achieving Success, Spreading Happiness, and Sustaining Positive Change.* New York: Crown Publishing.

Buckingham, M., & Coffman, C. (1999). *First, Break All the Rules What the World's Greatest Managers Do Differently.* New York: Simon & Schuster.

Our thesis about psychological flexibility and the importance of wholeness can be viewed as an alternative to the need for positivity messages put forward by Tom Rath, Marcus Buckingham, and Shawn Achor, among others. These two camps are not mutually exclusive, for by no means do we discount the importance of positive emotions, attempts to up-regulate positive emotions, happiness, mindfulness, kindness, and other interpersonal strengths. Instead, like a growing group of social scientists, we believe it is time to reorient people to the underappreciated benefits of so-called negative emotions, thoughts, and social behaviors. From this, we argue that being psychologically flexible trumps an overreliance on any single type of emotion, emotion regulation strategy, or side of one's personality. See Bonanno, 2013; Bonanno & Burton, 2013 (p. 247).

160 **"He must stick to the good so long as he can":** Machiavelli, Niccoló (1988). *The Prince.* Translated by Harvey C. Mansfield. 2nd ed. Chicago: University of Chicago Press.

161 **Psychologist Roy Baumeister and his colleagues studied the potential upsides of narcissism and found that "people with a high sense of entitlement did not report stronger or weaker desires, but they reported less conflict about these desires than other people did":** Hofmann, W., Baumeister, R. F., Förster, G., & Vohs, K. D. (2012). "Everyday temptations: An experience sampling study of desire, conflict, and self-control." *Journal of Personality and Social Psychology,* 102(6), 1,318–1,335.

161 **In other words, grandiose people possess a willingness to pursue lofty aspirations that most people might dismiss as foolish, self-absorbed, or impossible:** You might be asking yourself, do grandiose people really pursue these aspirational goals? Entitlement often refers to the beliefs that you deserve something and don't believe it is necessary to do anything to get it. In the research reported in this section, people are

measured on narcissism and these scores are examined in relation to outcomes such as goal striving and creativity. The average person high in narcissism, who does not meet diagnostic criteria for narcissistic personality disorder, has greater courage to pursue ambitious goals. And they are less deterred by obstacles. Part of narcissism is vitality and a desire to do great things such that one's behavior comes close to the high ideals that they have for themselves. It is worth noting that narcissistic personality disorder is a psychiatric diagnosis that, by definition, leads to impairment in daily functioning. In the most recent edition (fifth) of the *Diagnostic and Statistical Manual of Mental Disorders* (DSM-V), the essential features of a personality disorder are impairments in personality (self and interpersonal) functioning and the presence of pathological personality traits. To diagnose narcissistic personality disorder, a person must exhibit a pervasive pattern of grandiosity (in fantasy or behavior), need for admiration, and lack of empathy, beginning by early adulthood and present in a variety of contexts, as indicated by characteristics such as:

- a grandiose sense that one is better than others (e.g., exaggerating achievements and talents)
- fantasizing about profound success, power, brilliance, or attractiveness
- believing that one is special and acting accordingly (e.g., only associating with other special/powerful/high-status people)
- expecting constant praise and admiration
- expecting others to give favorable treatment or immediately comply with one's plans or desires
- takes advantage or exploits other people to satisfy one's needs
- expressing disdain for those believed to be inferior
- failing to acknowledge other people's feelings or needs
- being envious of others
- believing others are envious or jealous of one's attractive qualities, accomplishments, and/or possessions
- possessing a fragile self-esteem, where one is easily hurt and rejected
- appearing arrogant and unemotional

In addition, the impairments in personality functioning and the individual's personality trait expression must be relatively stable across time and consistent across situations. The impairments in personality functioning and the individual's personality trait expression are not better understood as normative for the individual's developmental stage or sociocultural environment. The impairments in personality functioning and the individual's personality trait expression cannot be due to the direct physiological effects of a substance (e.g., a drug of abuse, medication) or a general medical condition (e.g., severe head trauma). People who meet all of these criteria must experience significant impairment in their life from this condition, and people with narcissistic personality disorder are often unaware of these impairments because of a lack of self-insight.

Being narcissistic is different than meeting the diagnostic criteria for a psychiatric disorder. Recent research suggests that narcissism is more nuanced than previously thought. There is a healthy side to narcissism that can be referred to as narcissistic admiration, and there is an unhealthy side that can be referred to as narcissistic rivalry. Narcissists can accomplish their goal to maintain a grandiose self by promoting themselves, striving for uniqueness (putting their personal stamp on the world), and acting in a charming manner toward other people. All of these behaviors can lead to desirable social outcomes such as being viewed as attractive (intelligent, interesting, powerful, etc.), an increase in social status, success, receiving praise and affection and deference, and being chosen to lead others. This is the healthy element of narcissism we refer to in this chapter. We are not suggesting that people act on the unhealthy or maladaptive element of narcissism, in which one is in defense mode, preventing negative self-views and social failure. This defensive style is characterized by a hostile and socially insensitive mindset—other people are devalued and attacked with the aim of crushing perceived social rivals in the pursuit of supremacy over them.

In sum, narcissism is erroneously viewed as a single, bad quality. An unhealthy dimension called narcissistic rivalry is a barrier to success, particularly in social interactions and relationships. But do not oversimplify narcissism, because narcissistic admiration is an often neglected path to attaining great achievements as well as largely positive social outcomes.

Back, M. D., Küfner, A. C., Dufner, M., Gerlach, T. M., Rauthmann, J. F., & Denissen, J. J. (2013). "Narcissistic admiration and rivalry: Disentangling the bright and dark sides of narcissism." *Journal of Personality and Social Psychology*, 105(6), 1,013–1,037.

162 **The three elements of Machiavellianism, narcissism, and psychopathy (we call them the Dark Triad):** Research on the Dark Triad of personality is abundant, and much of this work points out that these nonpathological qualities are often annoying and offensive and, at

the same time, in the right situation, highly relevant to success and fulfillment. A few examples of related research on this topic follow:

Ames, D. R. (2008). "In search of the right touch interpersonal assertiveness in organizational life." *Current Directions in Psychological Science,* 17(6), 381–385.

Cheng, J. T., Tracy, J. L., Foulsham, T., Kingstone, A., & Henrich, J. (2013). "Two ways to the top: Evidence that dominance and prestige are distinct yet viable avenues to social rank and influence." *Journal of Personality and Social Psychology*, 104(1), 103–125.

Hirsh, J. B., Galinsky, A. D., & Zhong, C. B. (2011). "Drunk, powerful, and in the dark: How general processes of disinhibition produce both prosocial and antisocial behavior. *Perspectives on Psychological Science*, 6(5), 415–427.

Jonason, P. K., Li, N. P., & Teicher, E. A. (2010). "Who is James Bond?: The Dark Triad as an Agentic Social Style." *Individual Differences Research*, 8(2), 111–120.

Molinsky, A., & Margolis, J. (2005). "Necessary evils and interpersonal sensitivity in organizations." *Academy of Management Review*, 30(2), 245–268.

Paulhus, D. L., & Williams, K. M. (2002). "The dark triad of personality: Narcissism, Machiavellianism, and psychopathy." *Journal of Research in Personality*, 36(6), 556–563.

164 **Researchers Angela Evans and Kang Lee investigated the moral integrity of four-year-olds:** Evans, A. D., & Lee, K. (2013). "Emergence of lying in very young children." *Developmental Psychology*, 49(10), 1,958–1,963.

164 **This so-called better-than-average effect shows that most people believe that they are above average, which, of course, is a mathematical impossibility:** A review of all the studies in this section and more can be found in the following excellent review: Dunning, D., Heath, C., & Suls, J. M. (2004). "Flawed self-assessment implications for health, education, and the workplace." *Psychological Science in the Public Interest*, 5(3), 69–106.

164 **In fact, research on the better-than-average effect is mirrored in other studies that suggest that narcissism—a heavy dose of me-focus—is on the rise:** Twenge, J. M., Campbell, W. K., & Gentile, B. (2013). "Changes in pronoun use in American books and the rise of individualism, 1960–2008." *Journal of Cross-Cultural Psychology*,

44(3), 406–415; Twenge, J. M., Campbell, W. K., & Gentile, B. (2012). "Increases in individualistic words and phrases in American books, 1960–2008." *PloS One,* 7(7); DeWall, C. N., Pond Jr., R. S., Campbell, W. K., & Twenge, J. M. (2011). "Tuning in to psychological change: Linguistic markers of psychological traits and emotions over time in popular US song lyrics." *Psychology of Aesthetics, Creativity, and the Arts,* 5(3), 200–207; Twenge, J. M. (2013). "Overwhelming evidence for generation me: A reply to Arnett." *Emerging Adulthood,* 1(1), 21–26; Twenge, J. M., & Foster, J. D. (2010). "Birth cohort increases in narcissistic personality traits among American college students, 1982–2009." *Social Psychological and Personality Science,* 1(1), 99–106; Twenge, J. M., Konrath, S., Foster, J. D., Keith Campbell, W., & Bushman, B. J. (2008). "Egos inflating over time: A cross-temporal meta-analysis of the Narcissistic Personality Inventory." *Journal of Personality,* 76(4), 875–902.

164 **Such antagonistic rivalries and zero-sum games stress out all involved and are harmful to our mental health:** Aggression is one of many by-products of narcissism. When narcissistic people are insulted, they produce aggression at a much greater rate than people who dislike or even hate themselves. Bushman, B. J., & Baumeister, R. F. (1998). "Threatened egotism, narcissism, self-esteem, and direct and displaced aggression: Does self-love or self-hate lead to violence?" *Journal of Personality and Social Psychology,* 75(1), 219–229; Baumeister, R. F., Bushman, B. J., & Campbell, W. K. (2000). "Self-esteem, narcissism, and aggression: Does violence result from low self-esteem or from threatened egotism?" *Current Directions in Psychological Science,* 9(1), 26–29; Twenge, J. M., & Campbell, W. K. (2003). "'Isn't it fun to get the respect that we're going to deserve?' Narcissism, social rejection, and aggression." *Personality and Social Psychology Bulletin,* 29(2), 261–272.

166 **But as Twenge, Campbell, and others bemoan the imminent apocalypse, forgotten is that a healthy side of narcissism, what has been called *the striving for supremacy*, is also on the rise:** See chapter 6, page 161 note ("Psychologist Roy Baumeister . . .") for details on this neglected, healthy aspect of narcissism; Back, M. D., Küfner, A. C., Dufner, M., Gerlach, T. M., Rauthmann, J. F., & Denissen, J. J. (2013). "Narcissistic admiration and rivalry: Disentangling the bright and dark sides of narcissism." *Journal of Personality and Social Psychology,* 105(6), 1,013–1,037.

167 **To find out, psychologist Mehmet Mahmut used trained actors to determine what it takes for a bystander to intervene:** These researchers uncovered a range of factors that influence when psychopathy leads to an increased likelihood of helping or prosocial behavior. Factors included whether the problem being faced by a stranger was clear or unclear, whether the problem being witnessed was in public, the proximity to the person in need, and the sex of the person helping and the person in need. For example, when the person in need did not solicit help after dropping a bunch of papers in a public setting, men and women high in psychopathy helped just as often as people lacking in psychopathy. This research adds to our point that Dark Triad personality traits are not universally problematic: it depends on the situation. We deny ourselves psychological strengths that come in handy in predictable ways when we reflexively label certain qualities such as psychopathy as universally bad or evil; Mahmut, M., & Cridland, L. (2011). "Exploring the relationship between psychopathy and helping behaviours." Presented at the Annual Conference of the Society for the Scientific Study of Psychopathy, Montreal, Canada.

167 **When there was potential for heroism, when a display of virtue would look good to outsiders, when anxiety about what do is high, psychopathic characters stepped up, whereas more compassionate folks tended to walk by:** For simplicity, we are making it appear as if there were a competition between compassionate and psychopathic people. This research actually had people complete a questionnaire, and those scoring higher in psychopathy were more likely to stop and help. We focused on why psychopathy would make you more likely to stop. We could flip this around and ask why do kinder, more compassionate people keep walking? We can only speculate, but one reason is that courage requires a willingness to experience pain and failure. Compassionate people might have a strong desire to help, but this is not enough to get them past the anxiety, self-consciousness, and assertiveness to approach someone in need who fails to solicit help. How compassionate you are is relatively independent from how courageous and neurotic you tend to be. Knowledge about how compassionate someone is tells us nothing about what they will do in a situation requiring heroics.

167 **Narcissistic people want to be admired, and this motivates them to take action in situations that will appeal to the outside world:** This gets into a debate into whether any gestures are truly altruistic or whether everything can be boiled down to some degree of self-interest.

We both believe these debates are less important than whether people are helpful or hurtful toward other people. We are interested in what people do rather than in dissecting the motives behind every person's movements. From this perspective, it would be wrong to say that someone who is viewed as kind who engages in generous behavior is better or worse than someone who is a less agreeable and more psychopathic. We argue for a better metric: the helpfulness footprint that a person leaves as they navigate the social world.

172–173 **In thinking about hard approaches, it's important to look beyond a long history of con men using shady dealings to fleece public trust and money:** Take the egregious example of social psychologist Diederik Stapel. Although you probably haven't heard of Stapel, he's a well-known psychologist in the Netherlands. His main claim to fame is the sheer cleverness of his research. In one study, for example, he and his colleagues examined the effects of environmental disorder on racial attitudes. To do this, they parked a car with two wheels on the curb, left an "abandoned" bicycle on the ground, and removed tiles from the sidewalk. They found that that people who filled out surveys in this location, but not control participants from another location, showed higher scores on measures of racial stereotyping.

The only problem is that Stapel never actually conducted this—or almost any—of his studies. Instead, he took the easier route of simply fabricating data. (Don't worry, we don't use any of his research to substantiate points in this book.) Stapel used an elaborate scheme to fool students and colleagues. He would lead research meetings with a team of graduate students and fellow scientists. Ideas would be debated until they arrived at an exciting research question and then, together, they designed every detail of an experiment. Next, the coercion began. Stapel would suggest a school where they could collect data. Although students were interested in obtaining firsthand knowledge on entering into schools, running experiments, and understanding the day-to-day skills of a gifted, prolific researcher, Stapel insisted that he had to go into the schools alone because they knew and trusted him. We now know that Stapel pretended to visit these schools, made up imaginary research assistants who helped, and created fake data sets. This was also true for experiments he conducted in trains, courtrooms, and other settings. This make-believe data was handed over to students—to be used as their PhD dissertations. According to the investigative report, Stapel intimidated those who questioned him: "When a young researcher asked for access to raw data, Stapel accused the researcher of 'calling his capacities and experience as a renowned professor into question.'" Bragging about his brilliance, he would tell a lucky collaborator, "Be aware that you have gold in your hands!" Unlike other scientists who failed to find evidence to support their hypotheses, Stapel found that his experiments worked out exactly as he planned, and thus, any student of his looked brilliant.

By the time he had published dozens of influential publications, Stapel's tactics had raised considerable suspicion and three young researchers presented a report to his university. As of today, fifty-four of his papers have been retracted from academic journals, exposed as fraudulent lies. He was dismissed from his university, and he issued apologies in all the right places.

Information derived from: *Stapel Investigation.* (2012, November). "Flawed science: The fraudulent research practices of social psychologist Diederik Stapel." Tilburg, Groningen, Amsterdam: Levelt Committee, Noort Committee, and Drenth Committee. https://www.commissielevelt.nl/; Tom Bartlett, (2011, November 3). "The fraud who fooled (almost) everyone." *Chronicle of Higher Education.* Retrieved from: http://chronicle.com/blogs/percolator/the-fraud-who-fooled-almost-everyone/27917

175 **You simply cannot have a genuine conversation with another person and influence them without temporarily switching your perspective to theirs in order to understand what they want and what motivates them to take action:** Scientists have started to seriously study perspective-taking and created strategies for improving this skill. McHugh, L., & Stewart, I. (2012). *The Self and Perspective Taking: Contributions and Applications from Modern Behavioral Science.* Oakland, CA: New Harbinger; Stewart, I., & McHugh, L. (2013). "Perspective taking." In T. B. Kashdan & J. Ciarrochi (Eds.), *Mindfulness, Acceptance, and Positive Psychology: The Seven Foundations of Well-Being.* Oakland, CA: New Harbinger.

179 **Some folks have a black or white attitude about lying:** For instance, author and neuroscientist Sam Harris claims he has lied to his child only, once (once!) his child's entire life. If so, he's is cut from a different cloth than the rest of us flawed parents. "The high cost of tiny lies." *Sam Harris* Retrieved from: http://www.samharris.org/blog/item/the-high-cost-of-tiny-lies.

182 **Interested in the effects of narcissism in a group setting, Jack Goncalo and his research team at Cornell University created teams of four people:** Goncalo, J. A., Flynn, F. J., & Kim, S. H. (2010). "Are two narcissists better than one? The link between narcissism, perceived creativity, and creative performance." *Personality and Social Psychology Bulletin,* 36(11), 1,484–1,495.

183 **"Throughout history, narcissists have always emerged to inspire people and to shape the future . . .":** Maccoby, M. (2000). "Narcissistic leaders: The incredible pros, the inevitable cons." *Harvard Business Review,* 78(1), 68–78.

184 **Thankfully, we can turn to more than a decade of creativity research by Jennifer Mueller and her colleagues at the Wharton School of Business:** Mueller, J. S., Melwani, S., & Goncalo, J. A. (2012). "The bias against creativity: Why people desire but reject creative ideas." *Psychological Science,* 23(1), 13–17.

Chapter 7: The Whole Enchilada

188 **"There is no coming to consciousness without pain . . .":** Jung. C. G. (1928). *Contributions to Analytical Psychology.* London: Kegan Paul, 193.

190 **In a story arc called "The Trench," Aquaman demonstrates:** Johns, G., Reis, I., & Prado, J. (2013). *Aquaman Vol. 1: The Trench* (The New 52). DC Comics.

192 **This *positivity bias*, as psychologists call it, is the tendency:** Over the last decade, University of Chicago researcher John Cacioppo and his colleagues have investigated the phenomenon of positivity offset as both a natural human tendency and as a phenomenon that varies from person to person:

Cacioppo, J. T., Gardner, W. L., & Berntson, G. G. (1997). "Beyond bipolar conceptualizations and measures: The case of attitudes and evaluative space." *Personality and Social Psychology Review,* 1(1), 3–25.

Ito, T. A., & Cacioppo, J. T. (2005). "Variations on a human universal: Individual differences in positivity offset and negativity bias." *Cognition and Emotion,* 19(1), 1–26.

Norris, C. J., Larsen, J. T., Crawford, L. E., & Cacioppo, J. T. (2011). "Better (or worse) for some than others: Individual differences in positivity offset and negativity bias." *Journal of Research in Personality*, 45(1), 100–111.

192 **For instance, when asked by researchers to rate their satisfaction:** Diener, E., Napa Scollon, C. K., Oishi, S., Dzokoto, V., & Suh, E. M. (2000). "Positivity and the construction of life satisfaction judgments: Global happiness is not the sum of its parts." *Journal of Happiness Studies: An Interdisciplinary Periodical on Subjective Well-Being*, 1(2), 159–176.

192 **Researchers at the University of Michigan led by Dr. Edward Chang found:** Edward Chang and his colleagues have long investigated the way that culture and socialization can affect a person's outlook:

Chang, E. C., Asakawa, K., & Sanna, L. J. (2001). "Cultural variations in optimistic and pessimistic bias: Do Easterners really expect the worst and Westerners really expect the best when predicting future life events?" *Journal of Personality and Social Psychology*, 81(3), 476.

Chang, E. C., & Asakawa, K. (2003). "Cultural variations in optimistic and pessimistic bias for self versus a sibling: Is there evidence for self-enhancement in the West and self-criticism in the East when the referent group is specified?" *Journal of Personality and Social Psychology*, 84(3), 569–581.

193 **Defensive pessimists, according to Dr. Julie Norem at Wellesley College:** There is a large research literature on defensive pessimism including but not limited to:

Norem, J. K. (2001). "Defensive pessimism, optimism, and pessimism." In E. C. Chang (Ed.), *Optimism and Pessimism: Implications for Theory, Research, and Practice* (pp. 77–100). Washington, DC: APA Press.

Norem, J. K., & Cantor, N. (1986). "Anticipatory and post hoc cushioning strategies: Optimism and defensive pessimism in 'risky' situations." *Cognitive Therapy and Research*, 10(3), 347–362.

Norem, J. K., & Cantor, N. (1986). "Defensive pessimism: Harnessing anxiety motivation." *Journal of Personality and Social Psychology*, 51(6), 1,208–1,217.

Norem, J. K., & Chang. E. C. (2001). "A very full glass: Adding complexity to our thinking about the implications and applications of optimism and pessimism research." In E. C. Chang (Ed.). *Optimism and Pessimism: Implications for Theory, Research and Practice* (pp. 347–367). Washington, DC: APA Press.

Norem, J. K., & Illingworth, K. S. (2004). "Mood and performance among defensive pessimists and strategic optimists." *Journal of Research in Personality,* 38(4), 351–366.

Spencer, S. M., & Norem, J. K. (1996). "Reflection and distraction: Defensive pessimism, strategic optimism, and performance." *Personality and Social Psychology Bulletin,* 22(4), 354–365.

Showers, C, & Ruben, C. (1990). "Distinguishing defensive pessimism from depression: Negative expectations and positive coping mechanisms." *Cognitive Therapy and Research,* 14(4), 385–399.

194 **By imagining worst-case scenarios, defensive pessimists transform:** See references in previous note.

194 **What's more, initial research evidence indicates that these types:** Researcher Shigehiro Oishi and his colleagues have been leaders in investigating cross-cultural differences in the architecture of emotion. One of the Oishi team's most intriguing findings relates to the number of positive events it takes to psychologically "undo" the sting of negative events. For European Americans, almost two positive events are needed to restore positive feelings. Japanese people by contrast, feel good again after experiencing only a single positive event: Oishi, S., Diener, E., Choi, D. W., Kim-Prieto, C., & Choi, I. (2007). "The dynamics of daily events and well-being across cultures: When less is more." *Journal of Personality and Social Psychology,* 93, 685–698.

195 **We see much the same scenario when we look at negative stereotypes about the intellectual ability:** Brower, A. M., & Ketterhagen, A. (2004). "Is there an inherent mismatch between how black and white students expect to succeed in college and what their college expects from them?" *Journal of Social Issues,* 60, 95–116.

195 **Even optimists strategically use pessimism; they just don't know it:** Sanna, L. J., & Chang, E. C. (2003). "The past is not what it used to be: Optimists' use of retroactive pessimism to diminish the sting of failure." *Journal of Research in Personality,* 37(5), 388–404.

197 **Roy Baumeister, a trailblazing psychologist at Florida State University, deviates from his peers:** Storr, W. (2014) "The man who destroyed America's ego: How a rebel psychologist challenged one of the 20th century's biggest—and most dangerous—ideas." Retrieved from: https://medium.com/matter/94d214257b5

197 **Take, for instance, a new study by Alison Wood Brooks:** Brooks, A. W. (in press). "Get excited: Reappraising pre-performance anxiety as excitement." *Journal of Experimental Psychology: General*. Advance online Publication. doi: 10.1037/a0035325. For additional support for this phenomena, see this more recent study: Beltzer, M. L., Nock, M. K., Peters, B. J., & Jamieson, J. P. (in press). "Rethinking butterflies: The affective, physiological, and performance effects of reappraising arousal during social evaluation." *Emotion*.

200 **As we've seen, wholeness is predicated on a series of skills:** Kashdan, T. B., & Rottenberg, J. (2010). "Psychological flexibility as a fundamental aspect of health." *Clinical Psychology Review*, 30(7), 865–878. For more details, see a recent review by one of the researchers who inspired us to switch from the current obsession with positivity to emotional, cognitive, and social agility:

Bonanno & Burton (2013) (p. 247).

In both review articles, you will find references to seminal studies conducted by George Bonanno, Lisa Feldman Barrett, James Gross, Charles Carver, Cecilia Chang, Jack Block, and other researchers who deserve greater attention for their willingness to test the importance of psychological flexibility over any limited set of emotions, regulatory strategies, or interpersonal behaviors. We are extremely grateful for these scientists and their bold research designs and risky predictions.

201 **On the one hand is a long tradition of researchers who have studied what is known as *hedonia*:** Kraut, R. (1979). "Two conceptions of happiness. *Philosophical Review*, 87, 167–196.As quoted in: Waterman, A. S. (2008). Reconsidering happiness: A eudaimonist's perspective." *Journal of Positive Psychology*, 3(4), 234–252.

201 **On the other hand are those scientists who have fixated on *eudaimonia*:** Waterman, A. S. (2007). "On the importance of distinguishing hedonia and eudaimonia when contemplating the hedonic treadmill." *American Psychologist*, 62(6), 612–613. And see: Waterman, A. S. (1990). "The relevance of Aristotle's conception of eudaimonia for the psychological study of happiness." *Theoretical & Philosophical Psychology*, 10(1), 39–44.

202 **Eudaimonic activity is volunteering time to help somebody:** Steger, M. F., Kashdan, T. B., & Oishi, S. (2008). "Being good by doing

good: Daily eudaimonic activity and well-being." *Journal of Research in Personality*, 42(1), 22–42.

For details on the difficulties of defining and understanding what eudaimonia is, read: Huta, V., & Waterman, A. S. (in press). "Eudaimonia and its distinction from hedonia: Developing a classification and terminology for understanding conceptual and operational definitions." *Journal of Happiness Studies*.

By viewing table 2 in Huta and Waterman (in press), one striking thing is that some positive emotions such as interest are included in definitions of eudaimonia, which is supposed to be distinct from the type of happiness called hedonia, defined by the presence of positive emotions. This is one of many reasons we have suggested that people reconsider the idea that eudaimonia and hedonia are two distinct types of happiness. If interested, you can read our target article and the commentaries that followed in this intellectual debate:

Target Article

Kashdan, T. B., Biswas-Diener, R., & King, L.A. (2008). "Reconsidering happiness: The costs of distinguishing between hedonics and eudaimonia." *Journal of Positive Psychology*, 3, 219–233.

Commentaries

Delle Fave, A., & Bassi, M. (2009). "The contribution of diversity to happiness research." *Journal of Positive Psychology*, 4(3), 205–207.

Keyes, C. L., & Annas, J. (2009). "Feeling good and functioning well: Distinctive concepts in ancient philosophy and contemporary science." *Journal of Positive Psychology*, 4(3), 197–201.

Ryan, R. M., & Huta, V. (2009). "Wellness as healthy functioning or wellness as happiness: The importance of eudaimonic thinking (response to the Kashdan et al. and Waterman discussion)." *Journal of Positive Psychology*, 4(3), 202–204.

Waterman, A. S. (2008). "Reconsidering happiness: A eudaimonist's perspective." *Journal of Positive Psychology*, 3(4), 234–252.

Response to Commentaries

Biswas-Diener, R., Kashdan, T. B., & King, L.A. (2009). "Two traditions of happiness research, not two distinct types of happiness." *Journal of Positive Psychology*, 4, 208–211.

202 **For these folks, fun is superficial, whereas being authentic and pursuing goals that are bigger than the self:** Seligman, M. E. (2002). *Authentic Happiness: Using the New Positive Psychology to Realize Your Potential for Lasting Fulfillment.* New York: Free Press.

204 **This is exactly what psychologist Jinhyung Kim and her colleagues:** Kim, K., Kang, P., & Choi, I. (in press). "Pleasure now, meaning later: Temporal dynamics between pleasure and meaning." *Journal of Experimental Social Psychology.*

204 **This research dovetails with a recent publication by Roy Baumeister and his colleagues:** Baumeister, R. F., Vohs, K. D., Aaker, J. L., & Garbinsky, E. N. (2013). "Some key differences between a happy life and a meaningful life." *Journal of Positive Psychology,* 8(6), 505–516.

206 **When researchers asked people exactly these questions, they found a predictable trend:** See study 2 in Kim, K., Kang, P., & Choi, I. (in press) (above).

206 **On the other hand, a life fully given over to the pursuit of pleasure may miss out on the benefits:** Frankl, V. (1946). *Man's Search for Meaning.* New York: Washington Square Press. Modern research on meaning and purpose in life can be found in the following article and academic volumes:

Markman, K. D., Proulx, T., & Lindberg, M. J. (2013). *The Psychology of Meaning.* Washington, DC: American Psychological Association.

McKnight, P. E., & Kashdan, T. B. (2009). "Purpose in life as a system that creates and sustains health and well-being: An integrative, testable theory." *Review of General Psychology,* 13, 242–251.

Wong, P. T. P. (2012). *The Human Quest for Meaning: Theories, Research, and Applications.* New York: Routledge.

206 **As a formula, that dynamic would look like this:** To reveal how people manage the seesaw between pleasure and meaning, psychologist Michael Steger has proposed that meaning in life can be divided into *comprehension,* or when we detect significance in our lives, and *purpose.* One of the reasons people arbitrarily pick between a life of pleasure and meaning is that they often lack a firm grasp on this thing called purpose in life. Here we rely on a definition from our prior work.

Purpose is defined as a central, self-organizing life aim. It is central in that if present, purpose is a predominant theme of a person's identity. If we envision a person positioning descriptors of their personality on a dartboard, purpose would be near the innermost, concentric circle. Purpose is self-organizing in that it provides a framework for systematic behavior patterns in everyday life. Self-organization should be evident in the goals people create, the effort devoted to these goals, and decision making when confronted with competing options of how to allocate finite resources such as time and energy. A purpose motivates a person to dedicate resources in particular directions and toward particular goals and not others. That is, terminal goals and projects are an outgrowth of a purpose. As a life aim, a purpose cannot be achieved. Instead continual targets for efforts to be devoted. Taken together, meaning in life is the degree to which an individual makes sense of and sees significance in their life and believes their life to have an overarching purpose.

Kashdan, T. B., & McKnight, P. E. (2009). "Origins of purpose in life: Refining our understanding of a life well lived." *Psychological Topics,* 18, 303–316.

Kashdan, T. B., & McKnight, P. E. (2013). "Commitment to a purpose in life: An antidote to the suffering by individuals with social anxiety disorder." *Emotion,* 13(6), 1,150–1,159.

207 **Researcher Shigehiro Oishi and his colleagues asked retirees and nonretirees to rate the importance:** Oishi, S., Miao, F. F., Koo, M., Kisling, J., & Ratliff, K. A. (2012). "Residential mobility breeds familiarity seeking." *Journal of Personality and Social Psychology,* 102(1), 149–162.

208 **But too much stability and you begin to feel like a caged animal:** Fahlman, S. A., Mercer-Lynn, K. B., Flora, D. B., & Eastwood, J. D. (2013). "Development and validation of the multidimensional state boredom scale." *Assessment,* 20(1), 68–85.

208 **"if you're bored, then you're boring":** From the song lyrics of Harvey Danger singing "Flagpole Sitta."

208 **In fact, a recent study by Brigid Carroll and her colleagues found that dozens of CEOs:** Carroll, B., Parker, P., & Inkson, K. (2010). "Evasion of boredom: An unexpected spur to leadership?" *Human Relations*, 63, 1,031–1,049.

209 **The American Academy of Pediatrics released a 2007 consensus statement on how child-directed, exploratory play is far superior:**

Ginsburg, K. R. (2007). "The importance of play in promoting healthy child development and maintaining strong parent-child bonds." *Pediatrics,* 119(1), 182–191.

209 **Edward O. Wilson describes the value of boredom:** Wilson, E. O. (1994). *Naturalist (pp. 86–87).* Washington, DC: Island Press.

211 **You can't always be happy, but you can almost always be profoundly aware and curious:** Kashdan, T. B. (2009). *Curious? Discover the Missing Ingredient to a Fulfilling Life.* New York: William Morrow.

213 **In the days that followed, two interviewees responded very differently:** from PBS NewsHour: Campus Reactions. Terrence Smith, Journalist (September 16, 2001).

215 **In fact, several research teams, including our own, have found that using this approach:** A variety of researchers have investigated this phenomenon:

Kashdan, T. B., Adams, L., Read, J., & Hawk, L. W., Jr. (2012). "Can a one-hour session of exposure treatment modulate startle response and reduce spider fears?" *Psychiatry Research,* 196, 79–82.

Öst, L. G., Alm, T., Brandberg, M., & Breitholtz, E. (2001). "One vs five sessions of exposure and five sessions of cognitive therapy in the treatment of claustrophobia." *Behaviour Research and Therapy,* 39(2), 167–183.

Öst, L. G., Svensson, L., Hellström, K., & Lindwall, R. (2001). "One-session treatment of specific phobias in youths: A randomized clinical trial." *Journal of Consulting and Clinical Psychology,* 69(5), 814–824.

Zlomke, K., & Davis, T. E., III (2008). "One-session treatment of specific phobias: A detailed description and review of treatment efficacy." *Behavior Therapy,* 39(3), 207–223.

215 **Here's what three psychologists from UCLA did:** Kircanski, K., Lieberman, M. D., & Craske, M. G. (2012). "Feelings into words: Contributions of language to exposure therapy." *Psychological Science,* 23(10), 1,086–1,091.

217 **Here are some specific supportive findings from our research laboratory:** Boden, M. T., Bonn-Miller, M. O., Kashdan, T. B., Alvarez, J., & Gross, J. J. (2012). "The interactive effects of emotional clarity and cognitive reappraisal in posttraumatic stress disorder." *Journal of Anxiety Disorders,* 26, 233–238.

Kashdan, T. B., DeWall, C. N., Masten, C. L., Pond, R. S., Jr., Powell, C., Combs, D., Schurtz, D. R., & Farmer, A. S. (2014). "Who is most vulnerable to social rejection? The toxic combination of low self-esteem and lack of emotion differentiation on neural responses to rejection." *PLoS One,* 9(3).

This line of work was initiated by Lisa Feldman Barrett. Here are a few relevant examples of her profound contributions to understanding the psychological construction of emotions and their impact on well-being:

Kashdan, T. B., & Farmer, A. S. (in press). "Differentiating emotions across contexts: Comparing adults with and without social anxiety disorder using random, social interaction, and daily experience sampling." *Emotion.*

Kashdan, T. B., Feldman-Barrett, L., & McKnight, P. E. (2014). *Emotion Differentiation as Transdiagnostic Skill: Transforming Unpleasant Experience by Perceiving Distinctions in Negativity.* Unpublished manuscript.

Kashdan, T. B., Ferssizidis, P., Collins, R. L., & Muraven, M. (2010). "Emotion differentiation as resilience against excessive alcohol use: An ecological momentary assessment in underage social drinkers." *Psychological Science,* 21, 1,341–1,347.

Pond, R. S., Kashdan, T. B., Dewall, C. N., Savostyanova, A. A., Lambert, N. M., & Fincham, F. D. (2012). "Emotion differentiation buffers aggressive behavior in angered people: A daily diary analysis." *Emotion,* 12, 326–337.

Barrett, L. F. (in press). "Construction as an integrative framework for the science of emotion." To appear in L. F. Barrett and J. A. Russell (Eds.), *The Psychological Construction of Emotion.* New York: Guilford Press.

Barrett, L. F., Gross, J., Conner, T., & Benvenuto, M. (2001). "Knowing what you're feeling and knowing what to do about it: Mapping the relation between emotion differentiation and emotion regulation." *Cognition and Emotion,* 15, 713–724.

218 **One reason people do not naturally engage in emotion differentiation tactics, even those that would be helpful, is the natural tendency:** For an interesting read on the psychology of categorization, see Murphy, G. (2013). "Categories and concepts." In R. Biswas-Diener and E. Diener (Eds.), *Noba Psychology Textbook.* Champaign, IL: DEF Publisher. Retrieved from: www.nobaproject.com

INDEX